SONS OF THE CONQUEROR

SONS OF
THE CONQUEROR

*Robert Curthose, William Rufus, Henry Beauclerc
and the grandson, Stephen*

GEORGE SLOCOMBE

HUTCHINSON OF LONDON

HUTCHINSON & CO. *(Publishers)* LTD
178-202 Great Portland Street, London, W.1

London Melbourne Sydney
Auckland Bombay Toronto
Johannesburg New York

First published 1960

*This book has been set in Fournier type face. It has
been printed in Great Britain by The Anchor Press,
Ltd., in Tiptree, Essex, on Antique Wove paper
and bound by Taylor Garnett Evans & Co., Ltd.,
in Watford, Herts*

For
DOUGLAS SLOCOMBE

CONTENTS

CONTENTS

ILLUSTRATIONS

PLATES

BETWEEN PAGES 112 AND 113

GENEALOGICAL TABLE

MAPS

I

THE DEATH OF WILLIAM THE CONQUEROR

A REARING WAR-HORSE, maddened at the touch of hot ashes from a burning church in Mantes, had abruptly terminated William the Conqueror's last campaign. Nearly sixty years old and corpulent, William had been thrown heavily against the iron peak of his saddle and had suffered grave internal injuries. In the hot summer of 1087 he lingered for six weeks, conscious to the last, in the priory of St. Gervais in the western hills outside the walls of Rouen, to which he had been carried in a litter drawn by slow oxen. There he calmly surveyed his life, and made dispensation of his lands and his treasures. He ordered payment to be made to the priests of Mantes for the rebuilding of their devastated churches, and he disposed of his kingdom of England, his duchy of Normandy and his county of Maine, between his two elder surviving sons.

Defying feudal tradition almost for the first time in his life, William had declared war on his suzerain, Philip I of France, a man of gross and licentious appetites. It was the same Philip to whom twenty-one years earlier William had offered the overlordship of England if he would aid in its conquest. Philip was then an adolescent youth and had but lately succeeded to the throne. He or his ministers refused aid to William, either not believing him capable of conquering England or fearing the consequences of so greatly enlarging the power of Normandy. The French King then ruled over an exiguous kingdom bounded by the five cities of Paris, Melun, Etampes, Sens and Orléans and the counties appertaining to them, but he received or claimed homage as overlord from many neighbouring lands, including Normandy, Flanders, Aquitaine and Auvergne. During William's minority Philip's predecessor Henry I had occupied the border territory known as the French Vexin, which included the three castles of Mantes, Pontoise and Chaumont-sur-Oise, and which was claimed by the Normans as part of the original grant to Rolf, the first Duke of Normandy. The immediate cause of William's campaign against Philip was the provocation offered by the French captains in the castle of Mantes, who frequently sallied out to burn and plunder the lands of the Norman barons. Short of temper with the approach of age, but vigorous in spite of his stoutness, William decided that the time had come to reconquer the French Vexin. In 1087 he sent his envoys from Rouen to King Philip in Paris protesting against the aggressions committed by his captains, and making a formal demand for the return of that part of the Vexin held by the French. Then he submitted himself to his physicians, who had prescribed for the Conqueror a severe regimen of dieting and bleeding to reduce his corpulence.

Philip's reply to the Conqueror's envoys was electrifying in its insolence and in its effects. It brought William from his bed swearing one of his magnificent and picturesque oaths. Philip had jested to the envoys about William's pretended lying-in, had referred with gross humour to the Conqueror's swollen figure, and had refused in outrageous terms to surrender the lands and castles demanded of him. 'By the Splendour of God,' swore King William, 'I will go for my churching to Nôtre-Dame of Paris, and will have 10,000 lances for my candles.'

Then had come the rapid march along the valley of the Seine from Rouen to Mantes, where the towers of the churches and the great castle were mirrored in the water of the river. The French had been taken by surprise. It was harvest-time, and the soldiers of the garrison, themselves the sons of peasants, had joined the harvesters in the fields outside the city walls. At the first charge of the English and Norman cavalry, the men in the fields, closely pressed by the Conqueror's advance guard, crowded back through the open gates of the city. Before the last of the garrison had regained the castle, and before the gates could be closed, the Anglo-Normans were inside the walls and throwing their flaming torches and aiming their burning arrows at the thatched roofs and half-timbered walls of the houses. It was through a terrified and burning town that the Conqueror now grimly rode. The flames still leapt from roof-top to rooftop, the clouds of smoke darkened the sky above the burning churches and abbeys, the invaders went from building to building, looting its contents and setting fire to the pillaged houses.

Then the blow fell, which brought this hasty and violent Anglo-Norman march on Paris, with all its incalculable consequences for history, to an abrupt halt. The Conqueror's horse stumbled on a hot ember from a burning church. The charger reared and plunged. William

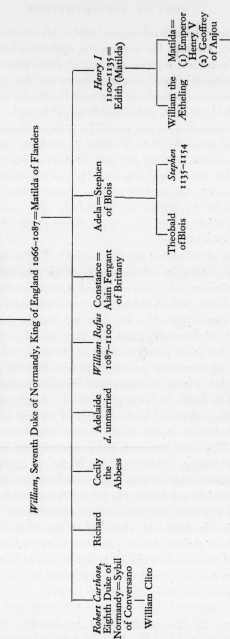

THE FAMILY OF WILLIAM THE CONQUEROR

Robert the Magnificent, Sixth Duke of Normandy — Arlette of Falaise

William, Seventh Duke of Normandy, King of England 1066–1087 = Matilda of Flanders

- *Robert Curthose*, Eighth Duke of Normandy = Sybil of Conversano
  - William Clito
- Richard
- Cecily the Abbess
- Adelaide *d.* unmarried
- *William Rufus* 1087–1100
- Constance = Alain Fergant of Brittany
- Adela = Stephen of Blois
  - Theobald of Blois
  - *Stephen* 1135–1154
- *Henry I* 1100–1135 = Edith (Matilda)
  - William the Ætheling
  - Matilda = (1) Emperor Henry V (2) Geoffrey of Anjou
    - *Henry II*

was thrown violently forward on the horn of his saddle, which ended in a peak of iron. He kept his seat on the maddened horse, but he had received grave internal injuries and was in great pain. He was helped down from the saddle, placed on a litter and carried slowly back to Rouen.

The peasants in the fields, as he passed the border of the Normandy in which he had been born, and to which he had brought such distinction, crossed themselves in awe and fear. The cortège of the fatally stricken warrior wound through the river valley to the King's palace in Rouen, but the noise of that bustling city and the cries of the street traders fell painfully on the ears of the dying man. He was removed to the priory of St. Gervais in the western hills outside Rouen. There was no further conquest in sight for William of Normandy. The candles, when they were lighted for him at last, were not in Nôtre-Dame of Paris but in his own abbey church in Caen.

During the six weeks of his death-agony William had the stoicism and the clarity of mind to reflect, in spite of his pain, on his strange life and its achievements. The bastard son of Robert the Magnificent, sixth Duke of Normandy, and of Arlette, the tanner's daughter of Falaise, had overcome the opposition of his kinsmen and become the greatest Duke in the history of Normandy and the successful invader of England. He was now the most powerful ruler in Western, and perhaps in all, Europe. He had conquered a land far greater than his own, and to its conquest had led a host of experienced warriors recruited from many other lands. The battle of Hastings, which he fought and won, was to become the most celebrated in the history of his new kingdom. Besides Normandy, his birthright, and England, his conquest, he had made himself feared in Wales and Scotland, and it was said that Ireland, if he had lived two years longer, would have been his for the taking.

The Conqueror had now to make provision for his succession in England, Normandy and Maine. He knew full well, with that marvellous sense of reality which had always been his, that the succession was difficult. 'After my death,' he predicted to one of his intimates, 'there will be a great revolution.' It was a rich but a stormy heritage that he left to his sons, and many men would die before the last of them possessed it in peace. William's eldest son Robert, nicknamed by his father Curthose (*Courte-heuse*) for his short sturdy legs, was in exile when his father died. He had committed many acts of rebellion against the Conqueror, had defied him to his face and had finally abandoned his father's court and kingdom in anger and had lived in the lands of his father's enemies. Destined to inherit, to place in pawn and finally to lose the duchy of

Normandy, Robert fought brilliantly in the first Crusade and was said to have been offered, and to have refused, the crown of Jerusalem. The last twenty-eight years of his long life he spent as the prisoner of his youngest brother in a succession of English castles. Robert was his mother's favourite; gallant, witty and generous, but vain and unstable, the most attractive, if the least effectual, of the Conqueror's sons.

The King's second son Richard died in adolescence, before he reached an age to bear the arms of knighthood. He was fatally injured while hunting in the New Forest which William had created in Hampshire for his pleasure. He was the first of several members of the Conqueror's house who were to die there. Of all William's sons Richard most nearly re-sembled the Conqueror in looks, and perhaps in spirit.

The third son William, known in his lifetime and since as Rufus or the Red King because of his ruddy complexion, was the favourite son of the Conqueror. He was the strangest of all the progeny of William I. Courageous and warlike and a brilliant military leader like his father, Rufus owed nevertheless most of his victories not to fighting, which he avoided when it was possible, but to bribery and persuasion. He had inherited neither his father's piety nor his respect for the Church. Profane and ungodly, a blasphemer and a professed unbeliever, he was also addicted to homosexual practices. During his reign flourished the only equivalent in English history of the sixteenth-century court of the Valois King Henry III and his minions. Rufus neither married a wife nor main-tained mistresses, and in an age of royal bastards none was attributed to him. The English chroniclers, and notably Eadmer the friend and bio-grapher of St. Anselm, who was Archbishop of Canterbury under Rufus, leave no doubt of the nature of his sexual preferences, to which they refer in scarcely veiled terms of abhorrence, blaming the Norman invasion for the introduction of vices which they profess to believe unknown in Saxon England.

Early in his reign William Rufus boldly faced and resolutely crushed a revolt of the Norman barons led by his two uncles Bishop Odo, Earl of Kent, and Robert of Mortain. After nearly thirteen years of firm govern-ment which the churches and the barons alike found harsh and exacting, Rufus was killed, like his elder brother Richard, in the New Forest, in one of the most mysterious episodes in English history.

The field was finally clear for the Conqueror's youngest son Henry, who profited by his brother Robert's absence on the Crusade to seize the vacant throne, to which Robert had been promised the succession. All three brothers had quarrelled over the undivided possession of their father's dominions, but Robert had been easily defeated in the contest. After his return from Jerusalem, before he had even made sure of his Norman duchy, Robert made one more ineffectual attempt to gain the Crown of England. After his capture in the battle of Tinchebray, to his death in Cardiff castle twenty-eight years later, he played no further role in either Norman or English history.

The most intelligent and capable of the sons of the Conqueror was Henry I. Born in England after the Conquest, he spoke English, and was praised, with some exaggeration, for his learning. He married the English or half-English Edith (afterwards called Matilda), daughter of Malcolm of Scotland and Margaret, the sister of the Ætheling Edgar and a grand-daughter of Edmund Ironside. By this marriage, and for the first time since the union of Ethelred the Unready and Emma of Normandy, Henry reunited the Norman dynasty with the line of the old English kings. He was to reign wisely and on the whole justly. He eventually brought England and Normandy under a single crown as they had been in the life-time of the Conqueror, and shortly before his death was to bring the lost county of Maine, and even the duchy of Anjou, under English influence. Like his father, Henry I died in Normandy, the presumed cause of his death, a surfeit of lampreys, being destined to impress and mystify succes-sive generations of English schoolboys.

We have left the sire of this unpredictable brood at death-grips with his last enemy in a bare cell in the priory of St. Gervais. During his last conscious moments the great King surveyed his past achievements and the future of his possessions with an unprejudiced eye. He had already promised Normandy and Maine to the exiled Robert, and although he knew the weaknesses of his eldest son, and viewed the prospects of his return to the duchy with misgiving, he would not gainsay his promise. The rule of primogeniture was respected by the Norman barons, and in their eyes the duchy, rightly or wrongly, belonged to Robert. He would not deprive his eldest son of his birthright. But England, which he had conquered by the sword, was not his to bestow. At this ultimate crisis in his life William no longer claimed that he was the lawful heir of Edward the Confessor. There was no law or tradition of primogeniture in England. The kingship was elective. But he could claim, as it had ever been the privilege of English kings, to recommend his successor to the people of England, and he now recommended to them his son William.

In a letter to Archbishop Lanfranc, who ruled England in his absence, the Conqueror requested him to crown William if he thought it wise, and he bade his son depart instantly for England. William the Red had always shown a dutiful affection for his father, and respect for his father's memory was one quality in his strange nature to which he never proved unfaithful. Armed with the Conqueror's letter he rode from Rouen to Wissant, and at the port from which Julius Caesar was said to have sailed to England he embarked in his turn. Rufus was crowned King at Westminster on 26 September 1087. He was about thirty years old.

Alone of the three sons of the Conqueror Henry remained at his deathbed. He had seen his father's dominions distributed between his brothers, and he is said to have complained that he had been ill-used. William then told him that he would give him 5,000 pounds of silver from his treasure-chest. When he objected that the treasure was useless to him without land in which to guard it, Henry heard his father console him, with prophetic wisdom, that one day he would possess all the lands the Conqueror held. Whereupon Henry prudently asked that the 5,000 pounds of silver should be weighed out to him then and there, and he saw that it was placed in security.

Henry was present at his father's strange funeral in the abbey church of St. Stephen which the Conqueror had built in Caen in penance for his marriage with his distant kinswoman Matilda of Flanders. The funeral ceremony was violently interrupted by the protest of a Norman named Ascelin, who shouted that the ground on which the abbey stood, and in which it was proposed to bury the King, had belonged to his father, who had never been recompensed by William. Henry promised the son that he should be paid the value of the land, gave him an earnest of his intention, and saw that the rest of the money was paid.

William the Conqueror had died on Thursday, 9 September 1087. Forty-eight years afterwards the three sons who survived him had all perished, and with them his sons' sons. The male line of the Norman kings was extinct on the death of Henry I. But the son of the Conqueror's daughter Adela, Stephen of Blois, who succeeded Henry, ruled for nineteen confused and tumultuous years.

Under the period of anarchy associated with the reign of the half-Norman Stephen, England experienced for the first time the unrestrained brigandage of lawless barons which had reigned in many lands across the Channel, and especially in Normandy in the childhood of William the Conqueror and under the rule of his son Robert. The imprudent concessions of Stephen, weak and generous, released the long pent-up tide of baronial appetites and ambitions. The Normans of the Conquest had been tamed by William. Their sons and their sons' sons, the second and third generation of the Normans in England, were restive under the royal

B

yoke. They dreamed of gold and conquest. Their elders had found both in southern Italy and in England. A number of their descendants embarked on the first Crusade and many of them never returned. But the others fought among themselves, burning and plundering castles and hamlets, abbeys and churches, to the ruin and despair of the victims.

During the struggle between Stephen and his cousin the Empress Matilda, there were men in England who regretted the absence of the firm Norman hand from the reins of power. Even the English looked back admiringly at the strong and even harsh rule of the Conqueror and his sons.

II

ROBERT CURTHOSE

THE rebellious Robert, eldest son of William the Conqueror and
Matilda of Flanders, was born in Normandy in or about 1054. His
father nicknamed him Curthose for his short legs and brief leggings. He
was, however, sturdy and powerfully built in spite of his modest stature.
Although indolent and slothful in his middle years he was active and
vigorous enough in his youth. That he was, like all his race, a magnificent
horseman is evident from the tale that during the first Crusade, which
attracted so many accomplished knights from Western Europe, no other
rider, Christian or infidel, could unseat him in battle or tournament.
Robert had the charm and spontaneous gaiety of his grandfather Robert
the Magnificent, who had died on a pilgrimage to Jerusalem. He was
lively and mirthful in manner, in spite of occasional fits of melancholy,
witty and eloquent in speech, with an excited, high-pitched voice. From
his early years onwards he was surrounded by a host of boon companions, the sons of the great Norman barons. He was the favourite child
of his mother, but his father preferred to him his three other sons, Richard,
William and Henry.

Before his invasion of England William of Normandy had called his
barons together and summoned them to swear an oath of allegiance to
Robert, as their future Duke. Robert was then twelve years old, almost
twice the age at which his father had inherited the troubled dukedom. If
some of the Norman nobles had misgivings at the choice of William's
successor, they concealed them. Robert was thus invested as the heir to
the ducal crown, and soon after the conquest of England he made the first
of a long series of demands to be given the duchy without waiting for
his father's death. When he reached the age of eighteen the Conqueror
gave him the privilege of assisting his mother Matilda in the government
of Normandy during the Conqueror's frequent absences in England. But

Robert was still dissatisfied. One day he boldly demanded that the King surrender to him his Norman inheritance immediately. The Conqueror looked at him grimly and retorted: 'It is not my habit to undress until I go to bed.'

From the beginning the struggle for authority between the father and the son had taken a violent turn. After Robert reached his majority his protests against the delay in granting him the duchy became more and more aggressive. The gay and generous temperament of the heir had encouraged a host of friends and sycophants to flock around him. They were mainly drawn from the irresponsible and irreverent youth of the country whose elders had won lands and wealth in England and Italy. They now waited impatiently for the fruits of their sires' conquests to fall into their own laps. The arrogant pretensions of Robert and his youthful followers irritated the Conqueror, and drew disparaging comments from his other sons. Robert's first armed rebellion against his father sprang from a quarrel with William Rufus and the young Henry.

The dispute occurred during one of William's disciplinary expeditions in Normandy. The Conqueror, accompanied by his sons, had set out to punish an insubordinate baron in the frontier regions of Corbonais. The King had taken up his headquarters in the town of Richer, called L'Aigle because of the large eagle's nest found in a tree as the castle was being built. William and his sons were lodged in the house of one Roger Chaussiègne. One day as Rufus and Henry were gambling with dice on a terrace of the house they saw Robert and some of his companions in the courtyard below. In a foolish mood of provocation they threw water over their brother.

Furious at the slight, and urged on by his friends, Robert drew his sword and rushed up the stairs to avenge the insult. But the Conqueror overheard the tumult and stood between his sons, cowing Robert and rebuking his brothers. That same night Robert and his friends secretly left the army of the King and rode to Rouen. There they attempted to seize the tower, but the castellan, Roger of Ivry, suspected that Robert was in rebellion against his father. He closed and barred the gates of the castle and sent a messenger to William informing him of Robert's attempt.

The Conqueror angrily denounced his son and his son's friends as rebels and ordered their arrest. Some of them, among whom were sons of powerful barons, were taken prisoner. Others, including Robert, succeeded in escaping from the King's wrath. They rode to the borders of Normandy and took refuge in the region of La Perche. There one of the dissident Norman magnates, Hugh the nephew of Albert the Ribald, placed at the disposal of the fugitives three of his castles, those of Châteauneuf-en-Thumerais, Sorel and Rémalard. In these Robert and his followers installed themselves and prepared to withstand the siege which the Conqueror promptly laid.

There is no record of the end of this rebellion, but it is probable that William succeeded in bringing the young rebels to reason, for a little later he was reconciled with Robert. Queen Matilda acted as a zealous and patient intermediary between the father and the son, and William seems to have shown great forbearance. He did not, however, retract an inch from his refusal to surrender Normandy, and the truce with Robert did not long endure. Robert had pressing reasons which made him eager to enter upon his heritage. His boundless generosity had emptied his treasury, and he owed great sums to usurers. Not even the grants in aid received from his mother, supplementing the sums more grudgingly doled out by the Conqueror, were sufficient to appease the appetites of his friends and his creditors. During one of his visits to England Robert made once again his claim to be invested as Duke of Normandy. William listened to him calmly, but steadfastly refused to grant his request. Without any sign of anger or impatience, he urged his son to choose for himself wiser counsellors, to abandon the advice of headstrong companions, and to put his trust in the wisdom of mature men like Archbishop Lanfranc.

This provoked Robert to another explosion of indignation. 'My Lord King,' he exclaimed petulantly, 'I came here to assert my rights, not to listen to sermons. Answer me therefore clearly, so that I know what I must do, for I am resolved not to live on the bread of others.'

This time the Conqueror replied with equal heat. He would not, he declared, give up Normandy. It belonged to him by hereditary right. Nor, as Robert had suggested, would he surrender to his son a part of England, which he had conquered with so much difficulty.

Robert answered defiantly. 'Very well,' he said, 'I will not fight in Normandy as a subordinate. I will go and serve strangers, and obtain from them what I am denied in my own country.'

Then, with a small company of followers, landless knights, rebellious younger sons and impecunious soldiers of fortune, Robert left the English court of the Conqueror and crossed the Channel. The Count of Flanders, his cousin Robert the Frisian, who had recently quarrelled with King William, gave the exiles hospitality for a time. Later Robert visited the courts of Philip I of France and the Duke of Aquitaine, calling on the great lords of the lands through which he travelled and pleading his cause with all the eloquence and charm which this attractive young man could display when he wished.

He was welcomed at foreign courts, and received hospitality and grants of money, partly for his own sake, and partly for political reasons. The French King and the Flemish Count were both eager to encourage and even to assist a claimant against the powerful King of England and Duke of Normandy. But Robert spent the money they gave him lavishly on his friends and his mistresses. As a political asset to the enemies of William the Conqueror he proved of little value. He was fickle and capricious, self-indulgent and lazy, inept at pursuing a consistent policy, incapable of lasting loves or enduring hates. He was always in severe financial straits. When he had squandered the gifts or the loans offered him, he borrowed money at high rates of interest from usurers.

His mother Matilda was for a long time his only unfailing source of aid. But when the Conqueror discovered her clandestine assistance to her erring and errant son he reproached her bitterly, and their first serious quarrel ensued. William then solemnly forbade her to send money to Robert from the treasury which he had placed under her care, rebuking her for supporting his enemies with his gold and silver. Matilda disobeyed the command, and William flew into one of his rare but memorable rages. The Queen employed a Breton named Samson as her messenger to carry money to Robert. The King sent soldiers to waylay Samson and swore to Matilda that he would have his eyes put out. But Matilda secretly despatched another messenger to warn Samson of his danger. The loyal Breton fled for protection to the Norman monastery of St. Evroul, where he remained unharmed until long after the death of the Conqueror.

Robert Curthose remained in exile for five years, wandering now gaily, now forlorn, in the lands on the borders of Normandy. He was accompanied by a numerous and even distinguished band of young men, who found amusement and occupation in the knightly tournaments then beginning at the castles of their French and Flemish hosts. They rejoiced in their freedom from the exacting military servitudes of the Conqueror's campaigns. They were normally not lacking in military ardour, but William's long wars in the savage north of England and the forests of rebellious Maine had wearied and discouraged them. But when Robert was invited by King Philip to install himself and his supporters in his great castle at Gerberoy, on the Norman border in the region of Beauvais, the young rebels accepted the invitation with delight. At Gerberoy Philip customarily gave hospitality to many exiles, enforced or voluntary, from the lands of his neighbours. Its situation on the frontier of Normandy was a constant challenge to the Norman dukes. Thither Robert now repaired with several hundred knights, recruited with promises of a rich reward in lands and money when he came into possession of his inheritance.

The Conqueror was then at Rouen holding his Christmas feast, and surrounded by the great prelates and barons of England and Normandy. When he heard of Robert's presence in Gerberoy, and of his threat to invade the duchy, he summoned his forces in haste, strengthened the garrisons on his western and southern borders against an eventual attack from Brittany or from France, and in the depth of winter set out for Gerberoy. There William besieged his rebellious son for three weeks.

Under the walls of Gerberoy castle William with his English and Norman soldiers did battle every day with the knights of Robert as they sallied from the gates. On one occasion, each unrecognized by the other, the father and the son are said to have come face to face, and even to have exchanged blows. The Conqueror and the rebel engaged in single combat, both clad in mail, with a helmet and nosepiece which partially concealed the face, although they did not, like the later helmet with visor, cover it entirely. Robert is reported to have wounded his father in the arm with the point of his lance, and the blow unseated the Conqueror and threw him from his horse.

Then the wounded man spoke, and Robert recognized his father's voice. He dismounted hastily and aided the fallen King into his saddle.

Another chronicler says that the dismounted Conqueror was defended from the onslaught of his furious son by an English knight, Tokig of Wallingford, a son of that Wiggod of Wallingford who was the kinsman and cup-bearer of Edward the Confessor.

The siege of Gerberoy was finally ended by William's withdrawal. The Conqueror persuaded King Philip, probably by the usual method of a handsome gift in lands or gold, to abandon the cause of Robert. William nevertheless returned to Rouen without having been reconciled to his son, and the unsuccessful siege was undoubtedly a blow to his pride. It was the first defeat he had ever sustained in battle, and the superstitious among the English saw in it a sign of Divine wrath at William's execution of Waltheof, the last English earl.

William was now more embittered than ever against Robert, whom he had succeeded neither in mastering nor in reconciling. In this quarrel with his eldest son he stood almost alone, except for the sympathy and counsel of his friend Archbishop Lanfranc. Many of William's companions of the Conquest almost openly sympathized with Robert, and their sons, either from friendship or from ambition, were his defiant partisans. A number of barons came one after another to William and pleaded with the King to pardon Robert. But William refused obstinately. 'My son is disloyal,' he said angrily. 'He has done his utmost to take Normandy from me, and with it the county of Maine. He has provoked a civil war against me. He has seduced from their loyalty young men whom I have indulged since their infancy, whom I have invested with the arms of knighthood. He has raised foreigners against me in arms. Have any of my ancestors since Rolf had to suffer such an attack from their own sons? Robert deserves to die!'

At last, however, the King relented. He listened to the pleading of Queen Matilda and the diplomatic arguments of the envoys of Philip of France. Eventually he agreed to become reconciled to his son. The King signed a fresh treaty reaffirming his recognition of Robert as his successor in the duchy of Normandy, and Robert thereupon abandoned his refuge in the castle of Gerberoy and returned to England. But this reconciliation lasted no longer than its predecessors. It enabled Robert, however, to show his military qualities as a leader in the field. In 1080, when King Malcolm of Scotland was threatening to raid Northumbria, King William sent Robert to Scotland in command of a large force to repel the advancing Scots. Robert marched as far north as Falkirk and then Malcolm was glad to make peace. Robert returned to England full of satisfaction at this exploit. He halted on the Tyne to build a great fortress which became known to after generations, like the town which grew up around it, as Newcastle, and returned to London to receive the felicitations of his father and the court.

But William's admiration was soon transformed into displeasure. Robert became more than ever prodigal in his extravagance and his promises. His recent success in Scotland had gone to his head, and he behaved with arrogance to his father's intimates and even to his father himself. When the Conqueror reproached him with his dissipation Robert retorted insolently. With one exception, that of the rebellious Roger of Breteuil, Earl of Hereford, now a prisoner in the tower of Rouen, no other man had ever dared to defy William of Normandy to his face. Robert now once again announced his decision to leave his father's kingdom and seek his fortune in other lands. With a band of his faithful companions, and with his father's solemn curse ringing in his ears, Robert rode lightheartedly to the coast and took ship for France.

He never saw William again. Two years later, on 2 November 1083, his mother Matilda died in Caen and was buried in the church of the Holy Trinity which the Conqueror had built for her. There is no record of any meeting between Robert and his mother after his final estrangement with

William, but in view of Matilda's profound affection for him, it is possible that they met clandestinely in Normandy.

The movements of Robert during the last years of the Conqueror's life are obscure. While his father lived he remained in exile in the court of France or Flanders. He was still an exile when William died in 1087. Then the prodigal could come at last into his stormy inheritance.

III

THE REBELLION OF BISHOP ODO

SEVENTEEN days after the Conqueror died his son William Rufus was
crowned by Archbishop Lanfranc at Westminster, on 26 September
1087. His coronation was unopposed, a tribute to the great authority of
Lanfranc and also to his popularity with the English. The rebellion which
broke out against Rufus a few months later was the work of Normans,
and was inspired and directed by his uncle, Bishop Odo, Earl of Kent,
only recently released from his imprisonment in the tower of Rouen.

Rufus has left an evil reputation. He extorted money from his subjects,
and particularly from the churches. He maintained an army of well-paid
mercenaries. He was impious and blasphemous, a scoffer and an atheist,
and he practised unnatural vice. No greater justification was needed for
the severe condemnation registered by the ecclesiastics who wrote the
historical records of the day. The strange thing is that all his English and
many of his Norman subjects rallied to Rufus with enthusiasm when he
needed their support to crush the rebellion of Odo.

Of all the prisoners in Rouen whom the Conqueror released before
his death, none inspired William with more profound misgiving than his
half-brother Odo. William well knew Odo's overweening ambition. He
was on his way to Rome with an escort of Norman knights to prepare his
election to the Papacy when William arrested him in the Isle of Wight,
personally arraigned him on charges of treason and abuse of power, and
condemned him to the tower of Rouen.

'I am a priest,' said Odo in protesting against his trial.

'It is not the Bishop that I seize,' had replied William, 'but the Earl, my
vassal, who has cruelly mistreated my subjects and laid waste churches
and monasteries.'

The 'Tamer of the English', as Odo had boasted of himself after his
ruthlessness in the North, had been liberated from the Tower of Rouen at

England, Wales and Southern Scotland: eleventh and twelfth centuries

the first = de la Pommeraie came with came in 1066 as one of the companions of Wm the Conqueror

the pleading of the Conqueror's other half-brother, Robert, Count of Mortain. At Christmas 1087 he had been restored to his earldom of Kent. Among the other prisoners released with Odo were the English Earl Morcar, former Earl of Northumberland, Wulfnoth the youngest brother of King Harold, Ulf, his son by Edith of the Swan-Neck, and Duncan, the son of King Malcolm of Scotland, who had been kept by the Conqueror as a hostage for his father's good faith after Malcolm's aggression in 1080. William Rufus brought Morcar and Wulfnoth to England and placed them in Winchester castle. Morcar was kept a prisoner and died in captivity in England, but the brother of Harold was at last released and entered a monastery. Ulf, the son of Harold and Edith of the Swan-Neck, and Duncan of Scotland fell into the hands of Robert Curthose who treated them with characteristic generosity. He set them at liberty and knighted them.

Almost immediately after his liberation, Bishop Odo justified the reluctance felt by the Conqueror to set him free. He began to conspire against his nephew Rufus. As one of the chief participants in the conquest of England, and for long his brother's deputy in the administration of the conquered land, Odo naturally counted on playing a similar role in the England of Rufus. But William II had taken as his most intimate counsellor William of St. Calais, Bishop of Durham, and Archbishop Lanfranc, although in the last years of his life (he died in 1089), still held unchallenged authority in England. He had crowned Rufus, and in the words of Eadmer, the biographer of Anselm, 'no one without his consent could acquire the kingdom'. Lanfranc had been the instigator of the arrest of Odo, and would certainly oppose his return to power. Odo was left, therefore, without a dominant role to fill. But as Earl of Kent he commanded an important strategic position on the frontiers of England. He governed Dover and Rochester, both strongly fortified places. His brother and fellow-conspirator Robert of Mortain held the castle of Pevensey. Between them they could protect the passage of the rebels in the cause of Duke Robert from Normandy to England.

Odo was a typical fighting bishop of the Middle Ages. His seal shows him in both his aspects: as a mitred bishop and as a mounted warrior. He held great authority over his nephew Duke Robert and over the majority of the barons of Normandy. He could also appeal to the interests of the Norman magnates in England, who resented the separation of Normandy, their ancestral home, from their acquired possessions in England. They foresaw the inevitable conflict between their feudal obligations to the King and to his brother the Duke.

Odo's rebellion against Rufus had therefore considerable chances of success. He was supported by, in addition to his brother Robert of Mortain, a large number of barons in England. Among them were the great marcher earl Roger of Montgomery, Earl of Shrewsbury, and his son Robert of Bellême, of whom more will be heard in this story, Hugh of Grandmesnil, Roger of Lacy, William of Eu, the elderly Geoffrey, Bishop of Coutances, who had been a valorous fighter at Hastings, and his nephew Robert of Mowbray, Earl of Northumberland. The rebels sent messages to Duke Robert in Normandy inviting him to take the leadership of the rebellion and assume the crown of England, which was rightfully his as eldest son of the Conqueror. They were influenced in this step as much by the indulgent character of Robert and their hopes of greater independence under his rule as by genuine dislike of the separation of England and Normandy under two rulers.

But not all the powerful barons rallied to the rebellious Odo. Rufus had supporters of wealth and consequence. The Earl of Chester, another marcher earl, called Hugh the Wolf from the wolf's head painted on his shield, William of Warenne, whom Rufus afterwards made Earl of Surrey and who married Gundrada, said to be a daughter of Queen Matilda, and Robert FitzHamon remained faithful to the Red King. Bishop William of Durham, although at one time the most trusted counsellor of Rufus, and one of the causes of Odo's revolt, seems to have betrayed the King and joined the rebels, although at his trial afterwards he vigorously denied the charges preferred against him.

In its early stages the revolt seemed likely to lead to a disastrous civil war. It spread from Bristol in the West to Norwich in the East, from the Welsh border to the Channel coast. Each local leader of the conspiracy marched from his castle and harried the widely dispersed possessions of the King and of Archbishop Lanfranc in the West of England. From Bristol William of Eu, a kinsman of the Conqueror, rode at the head of his supporters through Gloucestershire and looted the King's manor of Berkeley. On the Welsh border Earl Roger of Montgomery and the powerful baron Roger of Lacy advanced into Worcestershire, but they were met and defeated by a force of militia raised and led by the valiant old English Bishop Wulfstan of Worcester, the friend of King Harold, who had already helped to suppress an earlier rebellion of the Norman barons in the reign of the Conqueror. Geoffrey, Bishop of Coutances, who had once repressed an English revolt against William I in Somerset and Wiltshire, now led a Norman rebellion in the same region. He and his nephew Robert of Mowbray, Earl of Northumberland, sacked and burned the town of Bath and advanced on Ilchester, where they were halted.

Odo and his brother Robert of Mortain, the principal leaders of the rebellion, commanded operations in south-eastern England, where because of the proximity of Normandy the danger to the Red King was greatest. The Earl-Bishop fortified and garrisoned his castles at Tonbridge and Rochester and defied the King from these and other strongholds in his earldom. His brother Robert seized the castle of Pevensey, where the conquest of England had begun twenty-two years earlier.

William Rufus reacted to this first challenge of his reign with all the speed and ruthlessness of his father. He issued a striking proclamation to the English in which he declared worthy of the shameful name of *Nithing* (without honour) all men who should refuse to take up arms in defence of the realm at his summons. And the English rallied to his appeal with astonishing enthusiasm. The English leaders echoed the King's phrase. 'Let each man that is not a *nithing*, whether in the town or in the country, leave his house and come.' Thirty thousand men of all conditions assembled in the places appointed, and were given arms. Rufus had promised them good government, good law and justice, relief from their taxes and the relaxation of the forest laws against hunting in the King's reserves.

With the alacrity which the English subjects of William I had shown in repressing the revolt of his vassals in Maine, the English subjects of William II now attacked their Norman conquerors. At Worcester, under their fighting Bishop Wulfstan, they defeated the lords of the Welsh marches, Roger of Lacy, Bernard of Newmarket and Ralph of Mortimer. At Rochester and at Pevensey they besieged the castles of Bishop Odo and Robert of Mortain with a fury which astonished the half-brothers of the Conqueror.

Rufus captured first the castle of Tonbridge and then marched on Pevensey, which withstood a siege of six weeks. When it fell at last it surrendered into the King's hands the two chiefs of the rebellion, Odo and Robert. Taking his captive uncles with him, Rufus then advanced on Rochester, the strongest of the rebel castles and the centre of the revolt. It was commanded by Robert of Bellême and Eustace of Boulogne. Before the siege began Odo persuaded his nephew to allow him to negotiate with the conspirators, who sallied forth to meet him. But the wily Bishop, instead of returning with the rebels to Rufus, pretended to have been captured by them, and entered the castle in their company.

Rochester defied the King for some weeks, in spite of an Egyptian plague of flies which added to the trials of the besieged. But the English and Norman army of Rufus prevailed in the end, and Odo was compelled a second time to surrender, with the other barons, under the eyes of jeering English archers. Odo had requested that the King's trumpets should not celebrate his victory as the rebel garrison marched out of the castle. But Rufus refused angrily, saying that he would not concede this for a thousand gold marks. The Normans then left the castle with their banners lowered in sign of submission.

With bitter memories of the excesses committed in the North of England by Odo, in the Conqueror's reign, and his self-attributed title of Tamer of the English, the men of Rufus now clamoured for ropes with which to hang the rebellious leader. 'Bring us halters,' they cried, 'and we will hang this traitor bishop, with all his fellow-conspirators. O King, why dost thou let him go free? He is not worthy to live, the traitor, the perjured murderer of so many thousand men.'

But Rufus, like his father in the early years of his reign, pardoned easily. Odo was allowed to go free, but he was stripped of his English dignities, his earldom of Kent and his innumerable manors in many English shires, and was banished from England for ever. During the nine years which followed he was chiefly occupied with affairs in Normandy, and then he accompanied his other nephew Duke Robert to the first Crusade. But he never lived to take part in it. He was taken ill in Palermo and died there in February 1097.

The rebellion of Odo had collapsed in part because of the vigorous support given by the English to their crowned King. But it was also defeated by the characteristic failure of Duke Robert of Normandy to support his uncles in their enterprise on his behalf. He did not come to lead the revolt in person and did not stir from Normandy. He sent indeed a number of soldiers to aid Eustace of Boulogne and Robert of Bellême in the defence of Rochester. He also sent a small expedition to reinforce his uncles at Pevensey, but the men and ships never reached the English coast and were almost all destroyed in the Channel. Moreover the English clergy, under the powerful instigation of Archbishop Lanfranc and Bishop Wulfstan, had all, with the single exception of the Bishop of Durham, remained loyal to the King.

William of St. Calais, Bishop of Durham, was tried for treason before the King's court, and the case made history. The Bishop claimed ecclesiastical privilege and the right to be tried according to canon law. He refused to recognize the authority of 'the King sitting in judgment with his bishops and barons, his sheriffs and reeves, his huntsmen and other officers'. But Lanfranc, who took the leading part in the trial, pointed out to the accused that he was not being tried as a bishop but as lord of a fief and a secular officer of the King. He reminded the Bishop, moreover, of the famous arrest of Bishop Odo by the Conqueror in person, who had tried and sentenced his brother not as Bishop of Bayeux but as Earl of Kent.

The Bishop of Durham made a spirited defence. He demanded that his temporalities, which had been stripped from him, should be restored until he had been found guilty. He also claimed the right to clear his name by the ancient English rite of compurgation, which involved the swearing to his innocence by a number of his peers. This privilege was denied him, and the Bishop then announced that he would appeal to the Pope. Rufus refused to allow him to leave the country until he had surrendered the keys of Durham Castle. On 11 November 1088 the castle was surrendered, and William of St. Calais was permitted to leave the kingdom. He crossed to Normandy and went to the court of Duke Robert in Rouen. But he travelled no farther than Rouen, and abandoned his threat to appeal to Rome.

Three years later William of St. Calais sought a reconciliation with the King, and Rufus restored him to his see. In 1093, probably at the Christmas court at Gloucester, when Rufus sat at his feast, like the Conqueror before him, crowned with the crown of England, and sur- rounded by his great barons and prelates, the once rebellious and certainly equivocally acting Bishop of Durham won a concession on the point on which he had resisted so strenuously at his trial for treason. The King permitted him to hold his lands no longer in fee, but by a grant in free alms. He was no longer regarded as a lay baron and could not be brought for trial before a feudal court. Nevertheless, the Bishop showed little fidelity to his principles. In the subsequent council at Rockingham, when the dispute between Rufus and Lanfranc's successor Archbishop Anselm had reached a crisis, the now reconciled William of St. Calais firmly sup- ported the King against the reasonable demands of Anselm.

The great Lanfranc had died in May 1089, a year after the defeat of Odo's rebellion. With him disappeared the most powerful check on the King whom he had educated and crowned. Rufus had already refused to fulfil the pledge he had made to the people when he summoned them to his aid at the outbreak of the rebellion. When Lanfranc sternly admon- ished him on his breach of faith, the King flew into a rage and is said to have retorted: 'Who can be expected to keep all his promises?' He cer- tainly made no attempt to relieve the financial burden on the people, or to lighten the severity of the forest laws. And it may be surmised that with the death of the stern reproving Lanfranc Rufus indulged more openly in the homosexual habits which he had probably tried to conceal from the Conqueror and his Archbishop.

From the standpoint of conventional morality William Rufus was probably the worst King who ever occupied the English throne, but he was not disliked by the people. On his accession he had even been greeted with sympathy. During the rebellion of 1088 he had reached the height of his popularity, a level never thereafter attained. Among the more brilliant facets of his curious and many-sided personality was a passion for the then new cult of chivalry. He displayed a concern for knightly principles and practices to a degree hitherto unknown among the Norman rulers. His hand might be harsh against offenders against his laws, but to a prisoner taken in warfare or a garrison which surrendered he readily granted safety of life and limb. He dealt in characteristic leniency with the authors of the first rebellion against his rule, and the barons all escaped with their lives and liberty, and even, with the single exception of Bishop Odo, they were allowed to retain their possessions in England.

In this rebellion the younger brother of Rufus, Henry Beauclerc, seems to have taken no part. But in the following phases of the struggle for undivided possession of England and Normandy, Henry now sided with Rufus, now with Robert, and sometimes conspired against both brothers at the same time. After the capitulation of the Norman rebels in Rochester Henry went to England. He then boldly asked the King to cede to him the lands left by their mother Matilda, and this request Rufus granted.

Henry was now engaged in creating for himself a modest dominion in the duchy of his brother Robert. With 3,000 pounds of silver out of the 5,000 bequeathed to him by the Conqueror, he purchased from the ever-needy Robert the Cotentin peninsula in Normandy. This gave him possession of the towns of Avranches and Coutances, the famous rock of Mont St. Michel with its monastery, and the land that Hugh the Wolf, Earl of Chester, had once possessed in the region. Some years later he would acquire the powerful fortress town of Domfront, which had been built on the western border of Normandy by an early enemy of the Conqueror, and the citizens of which, weary of the cruelties and exactions of their lord Robert of Bellême, now freely placed themselves under the rule of Henry. The youngest of the three brothers, left landless by his father, was now launched upon his long and patient pursuit of wealth and power.

C

While Henry was consolidating himself in western Normandy, William Rufus began a more aggressive encroachment on its eastern borders. It is probable that in his first operations in Robert's duchy Rufus was greatly encouraged by the appeals he had received from the Norman churches. They were frequently despoiled in the disputes between rival barons and were the greatest victims, with the long-suffering peasantry, of the brigandage which had become general since the death of the Conqueror. Hardly was William I buried in his too-narrow tomb in the abbey at Caen before the barons expelled the loyal garrisons from the ducal castles and pillaged each other's lands without heed to the meagre authority of their new Duke. However harshly the hand of Rufus was to bear upon the churches of England, the bishops and abbots of Normandy preferred even his stern rule and ruthless exactions to the anarchy which prevailed in his brother Robert's territory. For quite other reasons the more violent of the Norman freebooters preferred the lazy and indulgent Duke to the martial King.

The attitude of Philip I, Robert's overlord, was for once unequivocal. Normandy under Robert presented no challenge to the French King, who resembled Robert in his self-indulgence and his habits of procrastination. He loved the pleasures of the table and the alcove more than the trimphs of war. He preferred Robert to Rufus, as he had taken the part of Robert against the Conqueror.

He did not desire a Duke of Normandy who was also King of England. His own kingdom, despite the power and importance of his vassals, was smaller and less wealthy than the prosperous duchy. But he was open, like most of his contemporaries, to financial persuasion. When William Rufus set out in 1089 to establish order in his brother's duchy, Robert appealed for aid to his suzerain, and Philip seemed to grant it. In the scornful and vivid phrase of William of Malmesbury, Philip 'belching from daily excess came hiccuping to the war'. But Rufus offered him a bribe, and Philip returned to his feasting.

In spite of his military talents and his love of action, in his partial conquest of Normandy Rufus resorted to the use of gold rather than to the power of arms. He had begun in England, with the aid of his agent Ranulf Flambard, the systematic exploitation of the churches and abbeys, which at the end of his father's reign were rich and prosperous. He used the proceeds to bribe and seduce the governors and garrisons of castle after castle in Normandy. Scarcely two years after the death of William I he obtained possession of the port of St. Valéry at the mouth of the Somme, from which the Conqueror had sailed to England. St. Valéry lay in the fief of Ponthieu, the land of that Count Guy who had captured the English Earl Harold and held him to ransom. The port provided a useful base for operations against Normandy, as it had already served for the invasion of England. Using agents and intermediaries from St. Valéry, and without himself appearing on the scene, Rufus secured one after another the frontier castles of Eu, Aumale and Gournay, and almost all of the other strongholds on the right bank of the Seine. The only vassal of Robert in eastern Normandy who remained faithful to the Duke was Helias of St. Saen's, who had married a daughter of Robert by one of his mistresses. Helias defended against Rufus the castle of Arques. All his life he was to prove loyal and devoted to Robert and his son William Clito.

Rufus gave money to the barons of eastern Normandy to restore and strengthen their castles. His cousin Stephen of Aumale, Count of Champagne, fortified his castle and reinforced its garrison. Girard of Gournay swore allegiance to Rufus for the towns and castles of Gournay, La Ferté and Gaille-Fontaine, as also did Robert of Eu, Walter Giffard, Count of Longueville, and Ralph of Mortimer. On the left bank of the Seine the fortress of Conches, in the lordship of Ralph of Tosny, passed also under allegiance to Rufus.

In the meantime Rufus had called the Anglo-Norman barons in England to a Council at Winchester, and had revealed to them his intention of restoring the peace and order of the Conqueror in the duchy of Normandy. He proposed to punish his brother Robert for his complicity in the rebellion of Odo. In 1090 the King's agents succeeded in fomenting the most serious rising against Robert which had yet occurred. It broke out in his own capital city of Rouen. It was organized by a wealthy burgher called Conan, whose name suggests his Breton origin. Conan, like many other traders in the city, valued the close commercial connection between Rouen and England and feared to lose it in the separation of England and Normandy. He raised the banner of insurrection in the name of King William II and attacked the garrison in the tower of Rouen. There was bloody fighting in the streets, and the revolt was only quelled after the joint intervention of the Duke's youngest brother Henry and of the powerful Robert of Bellême. Where the Duke himself was at the time and what he was doing is not known, but it is characteristic of the idle and negligent, but by no means cowardly, prince that he entrusted to an envious brother and an insolent vassal the task of subduing a serious rising against his own authority. The most striking action during the revolt is attributed to Henry. He is said to have killed the burgher Conan with his own hands, by hurling him to his death from a high window in the Tower of Rouen.

Two years after this abortive rising the plans of Rufus for a serious intervention in Normandy were complete. Towards the end of January 1091 he crossed the Channel with a considerable fleet and installed his court in the castle of Eu, on the eastern border of the duchy, where the young Duke William of Normandy had met his affianced bride Matilda of Flanders more than forty years earlier. Robert's first impulse, on learning of his brother's arrival at Eu, was to appeal to King Philip I. But the desertion of a number of his barons to the court of Rufus made any French intervention ineffectual, even if it had been forthcoming. Rufus now offered Robert terms of compromise, and Robert was glad to accept them. The treaty was drafted by the English King's supporters in Rouen, and its execution was guaranteed by twelve barons for the King and twelve for the Duke. According to one chronicler it was agreed between the two brothers that the King, if he survived the Duke, should inherit the duchy of Normandy and that the Duke, if he survived the King, should become King of England.

Robert moreover conceded to his brother the title to the lands on the east of the Seine which Rufus in fact already occupied—the countries of Eu and Aumale, the lordship of Gournay—and on the west bank of the river the lordship of Conches. He also ceded to Rufus the great abbey of Fécamp, which had been the favourite monastery of William the Conqueror and of all the other Dukes of Normandy since its founder Richard I. The treaty even granted to the King places like Cherbourg and Mont St. Michel which no longer belonged to Robert, since he had already sold them to his brother Henry. But such inconsistencies were frequent in the discordant relations between the three brothers. Rufus, for his part in this very one-sided treaty, promised to aid Robert to recover the county of Maine, which owed allegiance to William the Conqueror, but since his death had rebelled against the Norman overlord.

The treaty between Rufus and Robert was inevitably challenged by Henry, furious at being dispossessed even of the meagre lands which he had purchased with a large part of his inheritance. He was further outraged by the desertion of his one important vassal, Hugh the Wolf, Earl of Chester. Earl Hugh already owed allegiance to Rufus for his English earldom. He now surrendered to the King his county of Avranches. Having been driven out of Avranches and probably also Coutances, Henry was forced to take refuge on Mont St. Michel where rose the first of a series of fortress-like monasteries. The natural strength of the position, defended by a tidal river and the dangerous quicksands, from which Earl Harold had rescued two Norman soldiers under the eyes of the future

Conqueror, made it possible for Henry's small following to withstand a siege for several weeks. His brothers Robert and William appeared before the rock with their armies and waited for their brother to surrender under the double pressure of hunger and thirst. There were inadequate supplies of water in the besieged citadel, and Henry's men, and above all their horses, suffered greatly. Henry is said to have appealed to his brothers to allow water to be brought to the rock. Rufus refused the request, but the more generous Robert protested. 'What?' he cried. 'Our brother is athirst and we deny him water?'

Whatever may be the truth of this tale, the two brothers granted Henry and his knights an honourable departure from the monastic fortress with all their arms, their banners flying and lances raised. Henry rode over the nearby border into Brittany (there were Bretons among his followers) and from Brittany rode into France. He spent two years in exile, mostly dependent on the meagre hospitality of King Philip. He is said to have lived in extremely modest fashion in the French Vexin, south of the Norman border. The youngest son of the Conqueror, the future Henry I of England, was reduced to a household consisting of a single knight, a priest and three squires.

The suddenly achieved harmony between William Rufus and Robert Curthose was still maintained in the summer of the same year, 1091. With Henry temporarily out of the way and the disorder in Normandy increasing, Robert and Rufus solemnly ordered an inquiry into the rights and privileges of the Norman dukes. This inquiry resulted in a pretentious document entitled *Consuetidines et Justicia*, signed at Caen on 18 July 1091, which had as its purpose the restoration of ducal authority in the country. But events in England, and particularly on the Welsh and Scottish borders, required urgently the presence of Rufus. King Malcolm of Scotland, in the company of his wife Margaret's brother Edgar the Ætheling, was then making one of his periodic incursions into England. King William, taking Robert with him, and even summoning from his exile the dispossessed Henry, returned to England.

The three brothers, thus briefly reunited, took part in the campaign against Scotland. Rufus and Robert marched as far north as the Firth of Forth, and Malcolm crossed the estuary to meet them in Lothian, for which the Scottish King had been required in the reign of the Conqueror to do homage. Malcolm offered to do homage to Robert, as the Conqueror's eldest son, but at first refused it to Rufus. But Robert diplomatically persuaded Malcolm to renew to Rufus the submission he had made to the Conqueror in the treaty of Abernethy, and Rufus confirmed

Malcolm in possession of his English lands. Even Edgar the Ætheling, who was suspected of having instigated Malcolm's aggression, was now reconciled to William Rufus, and was permitted by him to accompany Duke Robert back to Normandy.

During the following year, 1092, the Red King extended the frontiers of England northwards to include the site of Carlisle, which had been destroyed by the Danes, and the modern county of Cumberland, which had been held by a Northumbrian lord called Dolfin as the man of the Scottish Kings. Rufus marched into this desolate Scottish appanage, drove out Dolfin, rebuilt the city of Carlisle and fortified it with walls and a castle. The restored city became, in the reign of Rufus's brother Henry I, the seat of a new bishopric, and English and Flemish colonists were sent northwards to till the long-neglected land around it.

The reconciliation between Malcolm of Scotland and William Rufus did not last long, and both kings soon had reason to complain of breaches of the new treaty of Abernethy. The Scots King was summoned, or invited, to meet Rufus at his Council at Gloucester on 24 August 1093. Malcolm went to the meeting-place and found there the Ætheling Edgar, his habitual counsellor and now his mediator. But Rufus was in one of his periodical moods of stubborn anger and refused to see him. Malcolm went away equally angry. He did not long survive this fresh quarrel with Rufus. Either during his homeward journey, or during a new raid over the English border, he was waylaid at Alnwick, near his own frontier, on 14 November 1093 and killed by Robert of Mowbray, Earl of Northumberland, and his nephew Morel. Malcolm's eldest son and heir Edward was also killed. The assailants were two of the worst ruffians among the Normans in England, and a few years later they provoked a sanguinary revolt against Rufus himself. Malcolm's wife Margaret, the granddaughter of Edmund Ironside, who was afterwards beatified by the Church for her pious restoration of Columba's ruined monastery on Iona, died not long after the murder of Malcolm, after having sent her two daughters Edith and Mary to the protection of her sister Christina, the Abbess of Romsey. Edith, under the name of Matilda, later became the wife of Henry I.

Notwithstanding his aid to Rufus in settling the question of the unfortunate Malcolm's oath of allegiance, Duke Robert received no help from his brother in subduing his own malcontents in Maine. He had returned to Normandy before Christmas 1091 and struggled alone against his subjects in both Maine and Normandy. In the following year his brother Henry came to Normandy to respond to the appeal of the burghers of Domfront, one of the many towns which groaned under the tyranny of Robert of Bellême. From Domfront, which remained a favourite city for Henry even after he had become King of England, he set out to reconquer the region of the Cotentin of which he had been deprived by his brothers both by treaty and by force of arms. This time, with the encouragement of Rufus, who now had more pressing matters on his hands, Henry met with a large measure of success.

A second great rebellion of the barons in England now menaced the throne of Rufus. It was led by Robert of Mowbray, Earl of Northumberland, the assassin of King Malcolm of Scotland. Robert was a typically violent and unruly baron of the period, but he surpassed all the Normans, save only Robert of Bellême, in his cruelty and arrogance. He was the son of the Conqueror's vassal Roger of Mowbray and the nephew of the warlike Geoffrey, Bishop of Coutances, one of the Norman paladins of the battle of Hastings. In addition to his earldom he possessed no fewer than 280 manors in England with which the Conqueror had rewarded the Bishop, who was more apt in ranging men in order of battle and wielding the lance than in instructing his priests in the chanting of the psalms. Robert, the nephew, was a tall and powerful man, dark and hairy, bold and cunning, with a sombre and brooding countenance. He spoke little and rarely laughed. Barely three months before his rebellion he had married Matilda, the daughter of that Richer of L'Aigle who had once been the host of the Conqueror and his quarrelling sons.

The profound causes of Mowbray's rising lay doubtless in the severity of the forest laws imposed by the Conqueror and now confirmed by his son Rufus, in spite of his pledge at the rebellion of Odo. The object of the conspirators was said to be to kill the King and offer his crown to his cousin Count Stephen of Aumale, the son of the Conqueror's sister Adelaide by her third husband Odo, Count of Champagne. But the incident which provided the immediate cause of the revolt was sufficiently curious in itself. Four large trading vessels from Norway had landed on the coast of Northumberland and, with their cargoes, had been seized by Earl Robert and his nephew Morel, his associate in the waylaying and killing of King Malcolm of Scotland. The Norwegian merchants, despoiled of their goods, went to Rufus and complained of their loss. The King immediately ordered Earl Robert to disgorge, but the Earl disdainfully refused. Whereupon the King reimbursed the traders with the value of their merchandise and summoned Robert of Mowbray to appear before his council. Upon the Earl's further refusal, except on the condition that the King furnish him with hostages and a safe-conduct, Rufus reacted with a grim determination and rapidity of movement worthy of his father. He got together an army and marched northwards to the Tyne, where the lawless Earl and his supporters were preparing to defend themselves in the castles of Tynemouth and Bamborough.

As Rufus approached the Earl's lands one of the conspirators, Gilbert of Tonbridge, came to the King and warned him not to proceed farther in the direction he was taking because an ambush had been prepared by the Earl in a forest that the King was about to enter. The same Gilbert, who had repented of his clandestine role in the rebellion, revealed the names of the other conspirators. 'Your enemies lie in wait for you,' he told Rufus, 'and will do their utmost to kill you. We have plotted against you and have sworn your death.'

Thus warned, Rufus took another road through the forest unharmed and laid siege to the two castles. After a resistance which lasted two months Tynemouth surrendered. The castle of Bamborough, in which Earl Robert and his young wife were besieged, was considered practically impregnable because of its strong natural position on a great rock almost completely surrounded by water and marshlands. Imitating the favourite tactics of the Conqueror, Rufus ordered another castle to be built facing the fortress of Bamborough, to the dismay of the Earl and his accomplices, some of whom with their retainers now deserted to the King's camp. The proud Earl had the mortification of recognizing from his battlements familiar figures among his fellow-conspirators join the King's men as they laboured to build the rival fortress, and he even rebuked them by name, thus denouncing them to the King. But Rufus laughed at the Earl's discomfiture, and leaving his men to complete the new castle, went off to deal with other more pressing dangers, among them an incursion by the Welsh.

During the King's absence Earl Robert made a nocturnal sortie from Bamborough Castle, provoked, according to one account, by a ruse of the enemy. He fell into the hands of the King's men, but his valiant young wife, Matilda of L'Aigle, continued the resistance on the formidable rock until she was threatened that her husband would be blinded under her own eyes if she did not surrender. Matilda then capitulated, and the rebellion was over.

Rufus had too easily pardoned the leaders of the insurrection of 1088. These, with the exception of Bishop Odo, Robert of Mortain and Eustace of Boulogne, were nearly all implicated in the revolt of 1084. On this occasion the King dealt severely with the rebel chiefs, and more leniently with the minor associates. Robert of Mowbray was deprived of his earldom and condemned to perpetual captivity. He spent nearly thirty years in fetters, and then, it is said, he was released from prison to become a monk of St. Alban's. The courageous Matilda, wife of a man condemned to lifelong imprisonment, eventually and successfully petitioned Pope Paschal II to be permitted to marry again. Her second husband, Nigel of Aubigny, treated her less gallantly than she deserved. After the death of her solitary surviving male relative, her brother Gilbert of L'Aigle, he repudiated her on the ground of her previous marriage to a distant kinsman of his own. He then married Gundrada, the sister of Hugh of Gournay. Such repudiations and remarriages, as often inspired by political or pecuniary reasons as by sentimental, were frequent enough in feudal times. The repudiated marriages were often followed by violent reprisals by the families of the victim and were often sanguinarily avenged.

Of the other rebels of 1094, Roger of Lacy was banished and his possessions in England were given to his brother Hugh, who had remained loyal to the King. Hugh of Salisbury, after a private conversation with Rufus, was pardoned on payment of a fine of three thousand pounds. Other rebels, particularly those with powerful family connections in Normandy, were received back into the King's favour on similar terms. And Rufus had the adroitness not to submit these repentant conspirators to judicial examination and trial. By refraining from exposing them to public humiliation, he sometimes gained their gratitude and at least avoided their lasting resentment. The negotiations, the penalty and the pardon were alike kept secret.

As to Morel, the nephew of Robert of Mowbray, and his aid and accomplice in all his murderous exploits, he succeeded in escaping from England, and after wandering in many countries, finished his life in exile.

Nearly two years after the abortive revolt, in Janaury 1096, William of Eu, a powerful descendant of the ancient line of Norman dukes, and a close kinsman of Rufus, was charged with conspiracy. He had been implicated in the two earlier rebellions, and he was now formally appealed of treason by Geoffrey of Baynard before the King's Council assembled at Salisbury. William's treason was too notorious to be concealed, and Rufus decided to punish him severely. He gave him the opportunity to clear himself in the judicial combat, or ordeal by battle, one of the tests of innocence established by the Conqueror, but William was defeated in the test. Rufus thereupon condemned him to have his eyes put out and to be emasculated. According to Orderic Vital, the last-named punishment was added at the instigation of William's brother-in-law Hugh, Earl of Chester, whose sister William had married. Since then he had engendered three children by a mistress, and Earl Hugh demanded that this affront to his family should be avenged.

A kinsman of William of Eu, William of Alderi, was also convicted of treason and was hanged, protesting his innocence to the last. Among those less severely punished, and merely imprisoned, was Odo, Count of Champagne and lord of Holderness, which suggests that there was some truth in the suggestion that his son Stephen of Aumale was to have had the succession of Rufus if the conspiracy had succeeded.

Rufus himself, until his mysterious death four years later, had no further revolt in England to put down. He ruled over a realm at peace.

IV

ROBERT OF BELLÊME

IF THE rule of Rufus was harsh, it was not more oppressive to the
English than to the Normans, and it was natural that the King's
English subjects took a sombre delight in the repression of the revolts of
the Norman barons. While Rufus was thus engaged in England, in
Normandy his brother Robert had been less successful in dealing with
his own unruly vassals. During the whole of the reign of Rufus and during
the early years of the reign of his successor Henry I, the arrogance and
lawlessness of Robert of Bellême, his insolent independence of King and
Duke, his cruelty and rapacity, laid waste the duchy and mocked at the
futile efforts of Duke Robert to govern.

Robert of Bellême was one of the most curious personalities of the
Middle Ages. He descended on his mother's side from a notorious race
of ruffians. He was the great-grandson of William Talvas I, Lord of
Bellême, a cruel and savage baron of the western borderlands of Normandy who had cursed the infant William of Normandy in his cradle,
and had brought death and devastation to the rival clan of Giroye. His
son William Talvas II, no less ferocious than his father, but called 'the
Hare' for his timidity in battle, was none the less detested for his cruelty
and treachery. He had ordered his wife Hildeburge, a meek and pious
woman, to be strangled on her return from Mass. And during the festivi-
ties of his second marriage he had attacked and atrociously mutilated one
of the guests, William Giroye of Montreuil, who had imprudently
accepted an invitation to the feast.

The daughter of William Talvas II, Mabel of Bellême, was fully
worthy of her sires. She had married Roger of Montgomery, one of the
Conqueror's companions in the invasion of England and afterwards a
great lord of the Welsh marches. Mabel was one of the cruellest and most
vindictive women of her time. Short and garrulous, she had a terrible

reputation as a poisoner, and she had enlarged her possessions in Normandy at the expense of her victims. All her life she continued her family's long feud against the house of Giroye. Five years before the death of William the Conqueror Mabel had met with a savage but not unmerited retribution for her many crimes. Among the innumerable victims of her rapacity and cunning was a man called Hugh of Saugei, a tenant of the dispossessed Giroye clan who had himself been driven by Mabel from his lands. On a winter day, after bathing in the river Dives which flowed at the foot of her castle at Bures, the hardy Mabel retired to her chamber. She was lying naked on her bed when Hugh of Saugei with his three brothers forced their way into the castle with drawn swords, in spite of the presence of Mabel's son, Hugh of Montgomery, and of sixteen knights. The fearless intruders entered Mabel's room, and one of them, seizing her by the hair, cut off her head. They carried it from the room and made good their escape. Mabel was buried headless.

The sequel is an interesting example of the crude judicial methods of the time. Hugh of Saugei and his brothers were never captured. They took refuge among the Normans in Italy, and one of them at least made his way to Syria, as will appear later in this work. Suspicion had fallen, however, upon another of Mabel's victims, one William Pantol, whom she had also deprived of some of his lands. Mabel's widower Roger of Montgomery and his sons seized the suspect's remaining possessions, and Pantol, with his wife and children, fled for sanctuary to the famous Norman monastery of St. Evroul. They lived there for some time until one day William Pantol boldly went to the ducal court at Rouen and claimed the right to prove his innocence by the ordeal of hot iron. His request was granted, and Pantol submitted to the test, with the men of the house of Mongtomery, armed to the teeth, watching to see that he did not deceive the court. William Pantol is said to have borne the white-hot bar of iron without showing any marks of burning, and to have been acquitted. Afterwards, as a sign of gratitude to the abbey which had granted him protection, he presented the monks of St. Evroul with a handsome chasuble.

Mabel's son Robert of Bellême had inherited the treachery and vindictiveness of his maternal ancestors. Of all the bloodthirsty, dark and cruel men of his clan he was the most justifiably feared and hated. The barbarity of his actions revolted his friends and vassals and even the members of his own family. He is said to have regarded it as a sport to put out the eyes and to cut off the hands and feet of his prisoners, and to delight in inventing even more fiendish cruelties for his victims, laughing

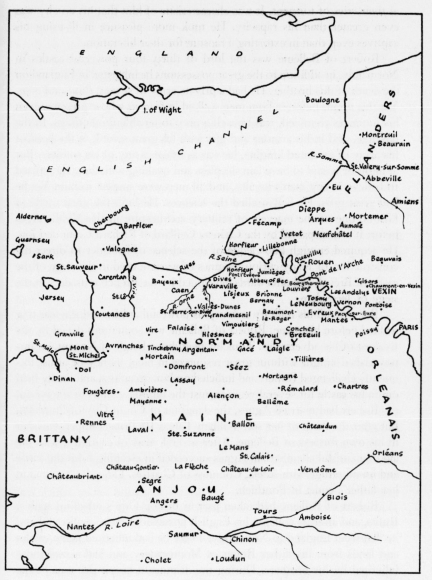

Normandy and her neighbours: eleventh and twelfth centuries.

at their cries of torment. It was characteristic of him that his cruelty was even greater than his rapacity. He took more pleasure in ill-using his captives even than in extorting a ransom for their liberation.

Robert of Bellême was the lord of thirty-four powerful castles in Normandy, in addition to the great possessions he inherited in England on the death of this brother. He had a private army of several thousand men. Yet this tyrant before whom men walked in fear, in whose presence even his intimates trembled, was himself a prey to terrible forebodings. In the daytime, clad in his armour and girt with his great sword, at the head of his array of mounted knights, he was as brave as any of his soldiers. But at night he is said to have lain sleepless and quaking with fear. He refused to believe in any man's loyalty, and all men were suspect to him. Yet he had great gifts. He had studied the sciences. He built the great castle of Gisors, one of the marvels of military architecture in the Middle Ages before it was surpassed by the Château Gaillard of Richard Cœur de Lion. He acquired enough knowledge of the science of ballistics to direct the construction of many curious engines of warfare used in the siege of the castle of Bréval, and afterwards developed by the French crusaders in the siege of Jerusalem.

But with all his military ardour, his powerful armies and the fear that walked before his name, Robert of Bellême was sometimes defied by the weakest of his adversaries. Thus his neighbour Hugh of Nonant, an impoverished knight without great resources in men, money or arms, frequently challenged Robert and inflicted on him great loss, and finally held out in his castle for several years against the furious assaults of the tyrant.

Robert had married Agnes, the daughter of Count Guy of Ponthieu, but after the birth of her son William Talvas III Robert imprisoned her in his own fortress of Bellême. After several years of captivity, with the aid of a faithful chamberlain Agnes succeeded in escaping from the castle and found refuge with Adela, Countess of Chartres. Later she returned to her father's court in Ponthieu.

Robert of Bellême had taken part in Bishop Odo's rebellion against Rufus, and after its collapse his English possessions were confiscated and he fled from England to Normandy. There he had inherited many castles and lands from his father Roger of Montgomery and had seized those inherited by his brothers. During the disputes between the sons of the Conqueror he sided now with Duke Robert, now with his brother Henry, in their respective quarrels with Rufus. Later in the reign of Rufus he became, at least outwardly, reconciled with the King and aided him in his campaigns in Maine.

The siege of Bréval, in which Robert displayed his knowledge of ballistics, was the sequel to a curious and typically feudal dispute between William of Breteuil, one of the sons of the Conqueror's intimate friend William FitzOsbern, and his vassal Ascelin Goel. A brother of Goel had been punished by William of Breteuil, as lord of the region, for having outraged a woman near Pacy on the Eure. The seducer had been summoned to appear before the baron's court of justice and publicly humiliated. His brother Goel avenged him by entering and seizing by ruse the lord's castle at Ivry. The captured castle was then handed over to ever-needy Duke Robert, who permitted William of Breteuil to purchase it back for a large sum of money. But Goel's vengeance was not yet complete. With the aid of Richard of Montfort and with troops furnished by King Philip of France, the bold vassal again attacked his lord, dispersed his supporters, captured William of Breteuil in person, with other members of his family, and held them prisoners in his castle at Bréval. Goel kept his captives almost naked in the middle of winter, exposed to a north wind entering their dungeon by an open window. After three months of captivity the unhappy William purchased his liberty by giving his daughter Isabella in marriage to Goel, and with her the sum of 3,000 pounds, and a present of horses and arms.

In the following year the marriage-truce between these two Norman adversaries was broken. Indignantly, William of Breteuil marched on Ivry, where his dangerous son-in-law again occupied the castle, laid siege to it and fortified the abbey of Ivry as a base for his besieging knights. But Goel set fire to the abbey buildings, took a number of William's knights prisoner and almost captured William himself. The Count of Breteuil now appealed for aid to Duke Robert and to the French King, who in return for the gold offered was not loath to change sides in the quarrel. Both King and Duke sent aid, and for two months William of Breteuil now besieged his son-in-law in the castle of Bréval.

Since his destruction of the monastery of Ivry Ascelin Goel was held in such horror by the Church that monks and priests came in procession with their sacred banners to swell the army of besiegers below the walls of Bréval. Robert of Bellême, who had no more love for Goel than any other Norman, had old grievances to avenge. He therefore joined King Philip and the Duke in their siege and brought to Bréval his own engineer, who afterwards lent his skill to the siege of Jerusalem. This man built a number of complicated machines which were pushed on rollers against the castle walls. They projected enormous stones and rocks over the walls which smashed the roofs of the houses inside and crushed the defenders under the débris.

The castle of Bréval had been built in a wild and desolate region, behind the heights overlooking the Seine on the left bank above Vernon, and represented years of labour. It was surrendered by Ascelin Goel, who saw no shame in submitting to far superior forces, after a siege of two months. He also surrendered the fortress of Ivry, which had been built by Albareda, the wife of Count Ralph of Bayeux. It is said of Albareda that after its construction she cut off the head of its architect Lanfred to ensure that he never built another. Later Albareda attempted to drive her own husband from the castle, and was killed by him in reprisal.

After the surrender of Bréval, Robert of Bellême made a sudden attack on the castle of his adversary Robert Giroye at St. Cénéri. The garrison, believing its arch-enemy to be still preoccupied with the siege of Bréval, and ignorant of its fall, had gone outside the castle walls to work in the fields. But Robert Giroye learned of his enemy's intentions in time to forestall him, and rushed to place his castle in a state of defence. In consequence the Count of Bellême arrived too late to seize the fortress. He had perforce to be content with harrying and pillaging in the region. He killed one knight and did a great deal of destruction, and then departed in a fury at his failure.

Among Robert's other enemies at this time was Henry of England, who as we have seen had occupied the Bellême fief of Domfront at the request of the inhabitants. Robert also entertained a feud with Geoffrey of Mayenne and William of Sillé. These two barons, with the aid of Robert Giroye, pillaged the country around Alençon, in the very home territory of the Bellême clan, for a period of three months. But now a second time Robert Giroye rode out of his castle of St. Cénéri, and on this occasion to his misfortune. During his absence a rumour spread through the garrison that the baron had been killed, and the soldiers were in a panic at the news. Radegonde, the wife of Robert Giroye and a woman of great courage, resolved to defend the castle against all attack, but many of her soldiers deserted.

When Robert of Bellême appeared a second time at the gates of the castle he found it almost abandoned. He entered without difficulty and saw a strange spectacle. In the empty kitchens the fires were lit and great platters of meat roasted on them. In the great hall of the castle the long tables were laid for dinner. Loaves of bread and flagons of wine awaited the absent company. The raiding baron and his men helped themselves freely to all they found, and feasted royally. Then they set fire to the castle and all its contents. Robert Giroye returned to discover the destruction of all his possessions, including the gifts he had received from Duke Robert of Normandy on his return from Italy. His wife Radegonde died in the same year, and soon afterwards his young son William Giroye, who had been seized by Robert of Bellême as a hostage, died of poisoning.

Bent on revenge, and aided by his friends and kinsmen, Robert Giroye built another castle at Montaigne from which he harried the lands of his enemy. Duke Robert of Normandy, under pressure from his powerful vassal of Bellême, weakly consented to send his own army against the new castle. But Geoffrey of Mayenne and other lords of Maine who were kinsmen to Robert Giroye, interceded with the Duke on Robert's behalf and persuaded the Duke to withdraw his troops from the quarrel. A temporary truce was declared under the terms of which the lord of Giroye agreed to the destruction of his newly built castle at Montaigne and Robert of Bellême consented to restore the other possessions he had seized. The existence of this powerful castle of Montaigne threatened the security of the Count of Bellême, and he was anxious for its destruction, but Robert Giroye showed no eagerness to begin the task. Accordingly Robert of Bellême himself requisitioned hundreds of labourers from the region, among them the tenants of the Abbot of St. Evroul. The Abbot Roger went to England to protest to King William Rufus against the exactions of his brother's powerful vassal. And this and other complaints from the churches and abbeys of Normandy furnished Rufus with the pretext he desired. He now decided to intervene against the inept rule of his brother Robert.

But other events were shortly to place all Normandy under the power of Rufus. In 1096 Robert Curthose, like many other princes and nobles in Western Europe, good or bad, cruel or indulgent, heard the appeal of Pope Urban to liberate the Holy Places from the dominion of the Turk. Robert shared the extraordinary enthusiasm aroused by the Papal eloquence and the fire and zeal of Peter the Hermit. In September of this year Robert was reconciled to Rufus by the efforts of Gerunto, Abbot of the monastery of St. Benignus at Dijon, who was sent by the Pope as an envoy to England. Robert needed a large sum of money to equip himself and his followers to the Holy Land. Through the Abbot he offered to pledge Normandy to his brother for three years. Rufus agreed to pay a sum of ten thousand marks of silver, and his agent Ranulf Flambard was immediately set to work to raise the money in England. Many marriageable English maids, many heirs to great estates, treated as wards of the King, contributed towards the geld imposed by Rufus for the payment of

D

the Crusader Robert. The pledge-money was paid over. Rufus was ever generous with bribes and subsidies when the fulfilment of his territorial ambitions was involved. Robert set out bravely on the first Crusade, leaving his tormented duchy in the hands of a more resolute ruler.

The Duke was followed by a great company of eminent Norman barons of all ages. Among them were his uncle Bishop Odo of Bayeux, Philip the Clerk, son of the famous Count Roger of Beaumont, Rotrou, son of Geoffrey, Count of Mortagne, Walter, Count of St. Valéry on the Somme, and a grandson of Duke Richard II of Normandy, Girard of Gournay, Ralph of Guader, formerly Earl of Norfolk, who had raised a rebellion against William the Conqueror and had escaped from England in time to avoid the Conqueror's wrath, Hugh of St. Paul, Yves and Alberic, sons of the Hugh of Grandmesnil of the Conquest, and many other nobles and knights.

In Rome Duke Robert and Bishop Odo were welcomed by Pope Urban. They spent the autumn and winter of 1096 in Calabria and Sicily, where Odo died. He was buried in Palermo and his funeral sermon was preached by Gilbert, Bishop of Evreux. About the same time another group of rulers and vassals set out from Flanders and the countries east of the Rhine, led by Godfrey of Bouillon, Duke of Lower Lorraine. He was accompanied by Baldwin and Eustace, the two sons of that Count Eustace of Boulogne who played a curious role in English history preceding and following the Norman Conquest. With him also went Baldwin, Count of Mons, Robert, Count of Flanders, a nephew of the Conqueror's Queen Matilda, and Raymond the German. They left the shores of the North Sea at the head of several thousand crusaders. Yet another group of enthusiasts, several thousands strong, marched from southern France under the leadership of Naymar Bishop of Le Puy and Raymond, Count of Toulouse.

V

RUFUS AND HELIAS OF MAINE

T HE ocean-raiding exploit of a Norwegian King was now to affect the changing fortunes of Robert of Bellême. Since the invasion threat of the last Cnut of Denmark had been abandoned in the later years of the Conqueror, no other Scandinavian ruler had endangered the peace of England. But now in the eleventh year of the reign of Rufus appeared off the shores of Britain another Northern fleet, commanded by King Magnus Barefoot of Norway. In the heroic Norse tradition Magnus had fought in the first Crusade and had taken part in the attack on Tyre. Returning to Scandinavia by way of Russia he had taken to wife Malfrida, the daughter of the King of Muscovy, and on his arrival in Norway had inherited the throne. Now came a dispute between Magnus and the King, or one of the kings, of Ireland, whose daughter Magnus had at one time married. The King of Norway had also at least one mistress, a captive English noble-woman, and by her he had a son named Sigurd who afterwards succeeded his half-brother as King.

The father of Magnus's Irish bride had not furnished the dowry promised on his daughter's marriage, and in accordance with custom Magnus, either before or after his journey to the Holy Land, sent the Irish princess back to her father. This was the origin of a bitter quarrel which sent Magnus with a fleet of sixty ships and an army of Vikings on a voyage of plunder and conquest around the northern shores of Britain. He had with him in the fleet a young Englishman, the son of King Harold and Edith of the Swan-Neck, the last historic reminder of an unforgotten epic of English history.

Magnus landed in the Orkneys, where as in the Shetland islands a colony of Norsemen had long been settled. He then sailed past the almost deserted Isle of Man to Anglesey. From Anglesey he planned to raid the coast of Ireland, but the Irish King had been warned of the coming invasion and had massed his warriors to withstand it. While Magnus waited at Anglesey in some uncertainty six of his ships, commanded by his leading warrior, made an appearance off the coast of Wales. The Norwegian captain had hung a red shield on his mast as a sign of peace, but the inhabitants of the region did not understand the signal, and seeing a fleet of unknown vessels approaching them with barbaric-looking warriors on board, they rushed in alarm to the nearest Norman garrison and appealed for aid.

The lords of the marches, Earl Hugh of Chester and Earl Hugh of Shrewsbury, fearing that the Welsh tribesmen might join forces with the invaders, hastily mobilized a force of Normans and English and marched to the coast. Hugh of Shrewsbury, who was the first to reach the scene of the supposed invasion, was the solitary victim of an aggression unintended by the Norse King. One of Magnus's warriors, acting on a sudden impulse, aimed an arrow at the Norman earl as he rode on his horse on the lonely shore. The arrow sped to its mark, and Hugh of Shrewsbury fell to the ground mortally wounded and his body was soon covered by the incoming tide. King Magnus offered his regrets to the surviving Earl of Chester and gave him assurances of his pacific intentions. 'I lead my army against the Irish,' he told him, 'not against the English, and I have no desire to invade any other land.'

The body of the dead Earl was recovered from the sea only after long search, and not buried at Shrewsbury until seventeen days had elapsed. Hugh was a son of Roger of Montgomery and Mabel of Bellême, and the only one among her many sons who did not inherit her harsh and cruel nature. On Hugh's death the earldom was sold by Rufus to his brother Robert of Bellême for the sum of 3,000 pounds. Once installed as lord of the Welsh marches, Robert divided his ruthless activities between the Welsh and the English. To contain the Welsh he built a powerful castle on the Severn at Bridgnorth, and for a great sum he bought the manor of Blithe from his cousin Roger of Butley. The English and the Welsh, who had hitherto treated as fabulous the tales of Robert's ferocity, now felt, in the words of one chronicler, the iron claws of their Earl, and realized that they had been told the truth.

Robert of Bellême had long practised his cruelties in Maine and there his most valiant opponent was Count Helias of La Fléche. Helias, who was to play a notable role in the reigns of both Rufus and Henry I, was a cousin of Hugh, Count of Maine and was a kinsman of a famous ruler of that ancient Roman settlement, Herbert Wake-Dog. He had acquired the county partly by inheritance, partly by purchase. Helias was an attractive personality in that age of ruthlessness and ruse. He is described as being tall, dark and slender, with his hair cut short contrary to the effeminate fashion of long hair which was then beginning. He was polite and affable in conversation, stern towards the arrogant and charitable to the meek. After the appeal of Pope Urban and the departure of Duke Robert of Normandy for the Crusade, Helias came to King Rufus in his court at Rouen, told him of his desire to take the Cross and asked him for permission to depart in peace.

Rufus said to him gruffly: 'Go where you will, but hand over to me the city of Le Mans and all the county of Maine, for I would have all that my father had.'

Helias replied firmly: 'I possess the county of my ancestors by hereditary right, and with God's help I will leave it to my children as free as it is now. If you wish to plead, I will willingly submit to judgment, and I will keep or lose my heritage according to the verdict.'

Rufus then retorted: 'I also will plead, but it will be with swords, lances and arrows without number.'

Count Helias then turned to the assembled barons in the presence of Rufus and said to them: 'I wished to fight in the name of the Redeemer against the infidel, but here is a new battlefield against Christ's enemies. Hear me, all you lords here present. I shall not give up the Cross which I have taken as a pilgrim, but I shall place it on my shield, on my helmet, on all my armour, and on the saddle and bridle of my horse. They who attack me will attack a soldier of Christ.'

But this exalted language was not likely to impress an unbeliever like Rufus. He replied sardonically: 'Go where you please and do what you will. I do not wish to fight Crusaders, but I will not give up the city which was in my father's possession on the day he died. Hasten then to repair the ruined ramparts of your strongholds and rebuild your walls, for I shall soon come to visit the citizens of Le Mans. I will show myself with a hundred thousand lances and my banners at their gates, and I will myself lead my troops and the gay drivers of my ox-waggons laden with arrows and javelins.'

After this stormy scene Helias retired to his castles in Maine. At that time Rufus had his hands already full with troubles on the other three borders of Normandy, the French, the Breton and the Flemish, and Helias took advantage of the fact to fortify his threatened heritage. He built a strong castle at Dangeul to contain the aggressions of his Norman neighbours.

Robert of Bellême easily persuaded the irritated Rufus to lead an army against Dangeul. He also induced him to pay for the construction of a series of castles ostensibly for the King's use but in reality for his own. In 1098 during a sortie from Dangeul, Helias was separated from the main body of his followers and fell into an ambush prepared by Robert of Bellême. Helias, his standard-bearer and almost all his small company were taken prisoner, and Robert of Bellême had the grim satisfaction of presenting his captives to Rufus in Rouen. The King, however, received Helias with all the honour and dignity due to his rank, for Rufus was always generous to his war captives. He treated them customarily with indulgence, gaiety and affability.

Rufus now exploited the opportunity offered by the seizure of Helias to extend his authority over the whole of Maine. In June 1098 he assembled an army of well-paid mercenaries, French and Burgundian, Flemish and Breton, marched to Alençon and then advanced on Le Mans. At Frenay, when he demanded the surrender of the castle, its lord, Viscount Ralph of Beaumont, suggested adroitly that he defer the question of his surrender until Rufus had reached Le Mans, and without receiving orders from his superiors, he would bring shame upon his house. A loyal vassal, he pleaded, should seek to obey the orders of his lord and not to give them.

Always sensitive in matters of feudal custom, Rufus praised the viscount for his loyalty and accepted his suggestion. Other great lords of Maine, among them Geoffrey of Mayenne and Rotrou of Montfort, made the same proposal to Rufus and equally secured his acquiescence. The English King seems to have had an impressive force at his command. Gilo of Sully, a Frenchman who had had much experience of large assemblies, surveyed the army of Rufus from the top of a hill and said afterwards that he had never seen so many soldiers north of the Alps. He estimated its numbers at 500,000, but making all allowances for the wild exaggeration common to mediaeval observers, it is scarcely possible that the army exceeded 50,000 and more probably one-tenth of that number.

On the third day of his march into Maine Rufus halted at Coulans on the banks of the Sarthe and about nine miles from Le Mans. The King pitched his tents in the meadows along the river and planted his bowmen and slingers among the vines on the road to Coulans, to guard the approaches.

The battle of Rufus for Le Mans recalled the incidents of the Conqueror's victories in Maine. Since the captivity of Count Helias, Le Mans, the capital, was defended by its overlord, Fulk Réchin (the Wry-Mouthed),

Count of Anjou. Fulk had been welcomed into the city by the burghers, and he garrisoned the ramparts with a strong body of archers and slingers. As soon as Rufus was sighted from the city walls, the knights of Maine made a vigorous sortie and fought valiantly all day against the English and Norman cavalry. There were gallant exploits on both sides, and the valour of the defenders was fully equal to that of the knights and mercenaries of Rufus. Rufus then had recourse to the tactics of his father. He destroyed the vines and the crops in the vicinity of the besieged city, but his own army suffered almost as cruelly from the pangs of hunger as the besieged. There was a terrible scarcity of oats, which were considered essential to maintain war-horses in vigour. The King finally decided to suspend the siege until the autumn, and meanwhile to dismiss his soldiers to their farms that they might harvest their crops.

The Red King found one submissive baron in Maine, Pains of Montdoubleau, Lord of Ballon, who had always proved a friend to the Normans. This welcome ally now opened to Rufus his castle at Ballon, and by its means the King hoped to subdue the whole county. He placed the castle under the command of Robert of Bellême and gave him 300 well-armed knights to defend it. Then he marched back to Normandy. This was an opportunity which the defenders of Maine did not neglect. Count Fulk of Anjou left his citadel at Le Mans to lay siege to Ballon, whose garrison sent an appeal to Rufus for aid. Meanwhile an unexpected hazard came to their aid. The beggars of the town of Ballon, wandering out towards the besieging force to appeal for alms, found Count Fulk and his knights in their tents at dinner. Having begged for charity and received it, the mendicants hastened back to the castle of Ballon to report what they had seen. Whereupon a number of Norman knights sallied forth from the castle and took the men of Count Fulk by surprise. A total of 140 knights and a great number of foot-soldiers were captured in this successful sortie. The rest of Fulk's force took to flight.

When finally in the third week of July Rufus arrived with reinforcements for Ballon he found the garrison in full celebration of their victory. He was escorted into the castle in triumph, with many signs of jubilation. Rufus now gave one of the few shining examples of magnanimity during his reign. The victims of the recent sortie were still lying in chains in the castle dungeon. Hearing the sounds of the King's arrival they cried out with one voice: 'Noble King William, give us our freedom.' Rufus heard the appeal and at once ordered the prisoners' fetters to be struck off. He further commanded that they be released from their dungeon and be given a generous meal. He invited them to walk freely in the courtyard of the castle. And after they had dined he set them free on their parole.

The Normans around the King expostulated at this leniency, but Rufus reprimanded them severely on their harshness. 'Far be it from me,' he cried, 'to believe that a brave knight would break his word. If he did so he would be as contemptible as a man without law.'

A passionate belief in the laws of chivalry had always been characteristic of Rufus, even when they ran contrary to his own immediate interests. It took the place of the religion which he rejected and the conventional morality to which he was indifferent.

After his mishap under the walls of Ballon Count Fulk of Anjou had retired to the tranquillity of a monastery in Le Mans in which he calmly awaited the course of events. His counsellors gave him no immediate prospect of a victory over William Rufus; his forces were not equal to the occasion. They recommended negotiations, and both Fulk and Rufus agreed. The terms of the peace which followed gave full satisfaction to the demands of the English King. Le Mans and the other two cities which had been in the possession of William the Conqueror on the day of his death were restored to his successor. Count Helias, the nominal ruler of Maine, was to be set free, together with the prisoners held by both armies.

After the signature of the treaty Rufus ordered his commander, Robert the son of Hugh of Montfort, to take possession of the forts of Le Mans with 700 knights in armour. When the former garrison marched out of the town, the knights of Rufus rode in with banners flying and trumpets sounding and raised the standard of the Red King on the Royal Tower, and on the forts of Mont-Barbe and Mont-Barbatule which had been built by the Conqueror to dominate the ancient city. The burghers of this much-disputed place, skilled by long experience in the art of simulating a joy which they assuredly did not feel, applauded the entry of Rufus into their city. Bishop Hildebert, at the head of a procession of priests and monks, marched before the King and conducted him to a Mass celebrated in the basilica of the martyr St. Gervais, and Rufus must have listened with grim satisfaction, concealing his ennui and his scepticism, at the Te Deums which the clergy had successively sung in honour of their conquerors and their liberators.

The rest of the story, and most of its dignity, belongs to Helias. The legitimate Count of Maine, released from his captivity at Bayeux under the terms of the treaty with Rufus, came to the King's court at Rouen and offered to serve under him, asking merely to conserve his former title and rank. He would not, he said, claim Le Mans and the other strongholds that he had lost until he should have merited them by his loyal services to the King. He aspired only after the King's friendship and asked to be given rank among the King's followers.

The first impulses of Rufus were usually generous, and he was willing to grant the request of Helias. But his principal minister, Robert, Count of Meulan, dissuaded him. Robert viewed with displeasure the advent among the King's servants of so powerful and attractive a figure as Helias, senior to himself in rank and eminence. Accordingly he warned the King against admitting into his intimacy and his secrets a crafty enemy who would seize the first opportunity of uniting with his adversaries against him.

Like all the Norman rulers, William Rufus had had bitter experience of treachery. He was impressed by the arguments of Robert of Meulan and he finally refused to admit Helias into the inner circle of the court. Piqued at his rebuff, Helias nevertheless made one more dignified attempt to conciliate the King, but again failed. Then he came a last time before Rufus and said: 'Lord King, I would have served you with a good heart if you had been willing, and I had found favour in your eyes. Henceforth do not hold it against me if I take my services elsewhere. I cannot bear the loss of my heritage in patience. Nobody can be astonished if I exert all my efforts to recover the possessions of my father.'

The reply made by Rufus showed a reluctant admiration for the candour of Helias. 'Go,' he said to the Count, 'and carry out all you can undertake against me.' Helias then demanded a safe-conduct across Normandy, and this being granted, he rode to the border of Maine. There he was warmly greeted by his supporters. He lost no time in putting his five castles into a state of defence. During the eight months from August 1099 to Easter 1100 Maine was left in peace. Rufus returned to England in the autumn of 1099 and at the following Easter Helias set his troops in movement. He began by raiding the villages on the Norman border and harrying the country beyond. Then, in the month of June, he marched with a strong force of enthusiastic followers towards Le Mans, forced the river Huisne and attacked the garrison of the capital. The Normans made a courageous sortie from the town and fought bravely but they were outnumbered. And when, strongly pressed by Helias, they attempted to retire behind the city walls, the friends of Helias inside the town prevented them from closing the gates. They fled across the town closely followed by Count Helias and succeeded in entering the fortresses of the Conqueror. Here they found abundant provisions against a long siege.

Helias was now master of his capital but not of the castles which dominated it. The commander of the largest fortress, called the Royal Tower, set his armourers to work making arrows, to which lighted rags and torches were tied. From the security of their battlements the Norman archers sent hundreds of flaming missiles over the houses in the town. It was midsummer and the roofs of the houses were dry as tinder. A strong wind aiding, the town was soon swept by a hurricane of fire which destroyed it utterly. The Norman commanders were in safety behind their thick defences, and in spite of all the attempts of Helias to storm the three castles, the defenders held fast.

In the meantime Robert of Bellême, who had strengthened the walls of his castle of Ballon, sent a messenger named Amalgis to England to warn the King of the loss of Le Mans. Rufus and his friends were hunting near Clarendon in the New Forest when the breathless messenger arrived. Rufus was in a high good humour and gaily he asked the messenger what news he brought. Amalgis said: 'My Lord King, Le Mans has been taken by treason, but my master holds Ballon, and your troops stand fast in the places you have entrusted to them. They ask for aid against the enemies who attack them from all sides.'

Rufus showed no great concern, but he acted promptly. He said merely: 'We go across the sea to aid our subjects.' Then he turned in his tracks and spurred his horse. He rode to the coast jumped into the first vessel he found, an old and not very seaworthy ship, and ordered the seamen to row him to Normandy. The next morning, after a stormy passage, he landed at Touques. There he found a concourse of Normans of all classes who had crowded to the harbour at the sight of a vessel coming from England, and waited to hear what news it brought. Their first question was about the King, and Rufus himself answered it. He talked to them gaily. He had always had a way with the common people, and the crowd responded with enthusiasm. Then the King borrowed a horse from a priest and followed by a large crowd of peasants on foot he rode to Bonneville, where his father had built a castle.

At Bonneville Rufus called together his vassals and their knights and prepared to reconquer the county of Maine. Before he crossed the border he was visited by the Bishop of Le Mans, Hildebert, who came to implore him to pardon the recent insubordination of his subjects. Rufus greeted him cordially, having heard that the Bishop had no part in the capture of the capital by Helias. Meanwhile the followers of Helias, hearing of the imminent arrival of the King, fled from Le Mans, still desolate from its recent destruction by fire and once again plunged into flames as Helias and his men rode out of the city. Rufus did not deign to occupy the ravaged capital. He set up his tents in the meadows beyond the river Huisne. He found the towns and villages destroyed by fire like Le Mans. Helias had left nothing for the Normans to loot or to burn. Not a house, not a bed was left for the invader. The castles of Vaux and Ostilly had been set on fire, but Vaux was saved for the King to occupy by the timely intervention of his army commander Robert of Montfort, who rode ahead with 700 knights and extinguished the flames.

As the Easter feast began Helias, with the greater part of his forces, awaited the King at Château-de-Loir, where he had elected to give battle rather than in Le Mans, where the Normans held all the strong positions, and where he would have been hampered by the presence of a multitude of famished and homeless citizens. On Good Friday the King laid siege to the town of Mayet and ordered for the following day an assault on the castle. But listening for once to counsels of piety and prudence, he cancelled all operations during the feast of the Church and gave Helias a truce until Monday. The men of Helias spent the truce in strengthening their defences. The Anglo-Normans and mercenaries of Rufus had piled up great quantities of brushwood and kindling to fill the moat around the walls and provide a bridge for their grand assault on the castle. When Monday came the men of Helias threw over the walls all kinds of vessels filled with hot coals, cauldrons of burning tinder and boiling pitch. The faggots and tree-branches in the moat, dry in the heat of the early spring, caught fire and burned. On both sides there were heavy losses. While Rufus watched the assault, clearly visible to the men in the castle, one of the defenders standing on the battlements threw a large stone at the King. It narrowly missed Rufus, and struck instead a Norman soldier standing near him, dashing out his brains. A mocking laugh greeted the spectacle. A man on the ramparts shouted derisively: 'Here is fresh meat for the King. Take it to your kitchens and serve it up to him at his dinner.'

At dawn the next day Rufus raised the siege, on the advice of his counsellors, and marched to Luce. The fortress of Château-de-Loir was too strong to be taken by the force that Rufus had under his command. Its stone walls were thick, its defenders full of courage and well provisioned. Without a lengthy blockade, which the King was doubtless in too great a haste to undertake, a castle manned by resolute soldiers and well supplied with arms, food and water could not be forced to surrender to an army camping in the open plain. Unlike the early Norman castles of the first years of the Conqueror, the walls of Château-de-Loir were proof against the favourite Norman tactic of incendiarism. Rufus contented himself accordingly with ravaging the countryside. The vines and fruit-trees were cut down, houses and farm-buildings were looted and destroyed. In July Rufus returned to Le Mans, and thence travelled to England, leaving Count Helias still unconquered with his valiant supporters in Château-de-Loir.

VI

ST. ANSELM

Two remarkable archbishops served the first two Norman Kings. The great Lanfranc, administrator as well as spiritual adviser of William the Conqueror, was succeeded by the no less great Anselm, who became Archbishop of Canterbury under Rufus. The future St. Anselm had already made a brief appearance in England during the reign of the Conqueror, when as abbot of the famous Norman monastery of Bec he had come to consult Lanfranc concerning the revenues of the lands held by the abbey in England. Lanfranc was then in the thick of his dispute with the monks of Christ Church, Canterbury, provoked by his decision to eliminate a number of English saints from the calendar. Among them was the venerable Archbishop Ælfeah, who had been killed by the Danes for refusing to order his flock to pay the financial tribute demanded by the invaders. Anselm had wisely urged Lanfranc to retain the name of Ælfeah in the calendar, as a worthy man and a heroic martyr, and was in consequence venerated by the English monks for his successful intercession.

Like his great predecessor, Anselm was an Italian. He was born about 1034 at Aosta at the foot of the Great St. Bernard. His parents were well-to-do and his early years, until he left home to become an itinerant student of theology, were spent in comfortable circumstances. After wandering in Europe for several years Anselm heard of the fame of Lanfranc, as years before Lanfranc had heard of the pious Herluin, founder of the abbey of Bec in a lonely Norman valley near Brionne. Anselm became in his turn Prior of Bec, and then its Abbot. By the austerity and purity of his life, the wisdom of his teaching and the ripeness of his learning he soon gained a reputation for saintliness, and like Lanfranc before him had become renowned as the foremost scholar and theologian of his age.

In 1093, when Lanfranc had been dead four years and Rufus had refused to appoint a successor to the vacant Primacy, the King fell so seriously ill as to be thought, and to think himself, dying. He lay in the abbey of St. Peter at Gloucester with his sins heavy upon him, and for the first time seemed to show any fear or misgiving at his contemptuous disregard of the laws of the Church. The Abbot Serlo, the same friendly abbot who was to warn him some years later on the eve of his mysterious death, now urged the King to agree to the election of a successor to Lanfranc. By a curious coincidence Anselm, whose name was uppermost in the minds of the English clergy, was in England at the time, and even in the vicinity of Gloucester. He had come to England, it was said, at the urgent request of Hugh, Earl of Chester, whose spiritual needs were at least as great as those of the King. The consent of Rufus to the appointment of Anselm was almost dragged from him. And later, Anselm himself allowed himself to be almost physically dragged to the archiepiscopal throne. He insisted, like Lanfranc before him, that he had neither the claim nor the desire to be invested with the office. He was a monk cut off from the world, and for thirty years he had lived a life of study and contemplation. In the end, still violently protesting, he had practically to be carried to the investiture.

Anselm was a gentle and mild-mannered man, in striking contrast to the violent and blasphemous Rufus, but like many such men he could at times be fiercely obstinate and unreasonable. He was now thrust into the office of Primate and principal adviser to the King, with many temporal responsibilities as a great feudal vassal. These duties he was temperamentally unfitted to discharge. And in the conflict which now began between the saintly monk and the cynical and lawless Rufus, both the Archbishop and the King showed the worst defects of their character.

The dispute between them broke out as soon as Rufus had recovered from his illness, and he discarded all the promises of good conduct and good government which he had made at Gloucester. The King and Anselm met at Rochester, where the new Archbishop presented the three conditions of his acceptance of the office in which he had been so violently and unwillingly inducted. First, the lands which belonged to the see of Canterbury, and which had been exploited by the King's agents since the death of Lanfranc, must be restored to their state when Lanfranc was alive. Secondly, in all spiritual matters the King should accept Anselm's guidance. Thirdly, the Archbishop should be permitted to recognize Urban II as the rightful Pope.

Rufus conceded the restoration of the lands. On the second condition he would say neither yea nor nay. But the third he violently rejected. Full of his sincere filial respect for the Conqueror, who had refused to recognize Urban, he would not act contrary to the wishes of his father. Opinion in Western Europe was still divided between the two rival Popes, Urban II, the choice of the Reform party in the Church, and Clement III, the candidate of the Emperor. Anselm inclined towards Urban II, whom he had already acknowledged when he was Abbot of Bec. However, he agreed to let the matter drop for the moment and consented, although still with reluctance, to accept the archbishopric. He did homage to the King for his temporalities at Winchester, and was enthroned at Canterbury on 25 September 1093. Finally, on 4 December, he was consecrated by Thomas, Archbishop of York, although Thomas, reviving the subject of a previous dispute with Lanfranc, insisted on investing Anselm not as Metropolitan of all England, but merely as Primate and as Metropolitan within his own province.

The relations between Anselm and Rufus were soon embittered. Although the King had accepted Anselm's stipulation that the lands belonging to his see should be restored, their restoration was not carried out immediately, and in the meetings between the King and his saintly but obstinate Archbishop Rufus frequently lost his always uncertain temper. In 1094 he bitterly reproached Anselm with the poor quality of the knights he had furnished for the King's campaign in Normandy, and Anselm rebuked him solemnly for the gross immorality of the court.

On the eve of his embarkation for Normandy Rufus lost his temper completely and roundly abused the Archbishop, for whom he expressed his loathing and contempt. Nearly a year later, when Rufus returned to England, the King's attitude had not improved and Anselm decided on his own departure. His motive, ostensibly, and probably primordially, was his desire to go to Rome to be invested by the Pope with his pallium, without which he could not consecrate a bishop or hold a council. This again raised the question of the recognition of Urban II. A meeting of the King's Council was held at Rockingham on 25 February 1095, and to it Anselm submitted the old and never really resolved question whether obedience to the Pope was not incompatible with the fealty he owed to the King. In his position as principal adviser and great vassal of the crown he did homage and pledged his faith to the King, but as Lanfranc had already admitted in his own case, Anselm in his spiritual capacity was the vassal and servant of the Pope.

The scene at this historic Council of Rockingham was vividly described by Eadmer, the friend and biographer of Anselm. The Council lasted four days and settled nothing, but it afforded a brilliant illustration of the manner in which the kings from Edward the Confessor's day, by the method of promoting to bishops' sees the most submissive of the clerks in the royal chapel, however uncultured, ensured their obedience to the royal will. At Rockingham the bishops in servility carried out the orders of Rufus, and in the debate unanimously supported him against Anselm. One of them, William of St. Calais, Bishop of Durham, even argued that Anselm should be deprived of his see and banished from England. This was the very bishop who six years earlier had rejected the competence of a royal court to try him on a secular charge, i.e. treason, and had himself committed, in appealing to Rome, the offence of Anselm in recognizing Urban before the Pope had been acknowledged in England.

Rufus had now made the fateful decision which was reached seventy years later by Henry II in the case of Thomas Becket. He was resolved to get rid of this obstinate Archbishop who would not bow to his will. But he hesitated before taking the final step, in spite of his contempt for Church law and custom. He realized that the Archbishop could only be deprived of his see by a decision of the Pope. Now the Pope recognized by Western Christendom, except for the Emperor and his satellites, was Urban II. Rufus thereupon sent two of the most pliable clerks in his chapel to Rome on a secret mission. They were Gerard, who afterwards was rewarded with the bishopric of Hereford, and subsequently became Archbishop of York, and William Warelwast, who afterwards became Bishop of Exeter. The envoys were ordered to offer on behalf of Rufus his recognition of Urban II on condition that Anselm be deposed. They were also instructed to bring back a pallium which Rufus himself would grant to Anselm's successor.

There is no evidence that Anselm was even aware of the intrigue now set on foot against him. But in the end he emerged triumphant from the ordeal. More skilled in diplomacy than the clerks of the Red King's chapel, the churchmen of the Curia in Rome manœuvred with great subtlety. When the two envoys of Rufus returned to England early in May 1095 they were accompanied by a Papal Legate, Cardinal Walter of Albano. They landed at Dover and went straight to the King at Windsor, arriving there just before Whitsunday, 13 May. The Cardinal astutely began his conversation with the King by announcing that the Pope conceded to Rufus a principle refused to his father the Conqueror. He accepted in substance the justice of the Conqueror's mandate that no Legates or Papal letters be sent to England without the King's authority. Thus conciliated, and confident that the Pope would grant his request for the deposition of Anselm, Rufus immediately ordered the public proclamation in all the English churches of Urban II as the canonical Pope.

Now came the master-stroke of Roman diplomacy. The main purpose of the Cardinal had been accomplished. His Pope had been officially accepted in a country which rivalled in importance and exceeded in wealth the dominions of the Emperor, Urban's principal enemy. He now had no longer any need to defer to the King. When Rufus presented his request for the immediate deposition of Anselm, the Cardinal refused point-blank. The King, who had planned to humiliate his Archbishop of Canterbury, was now himself humiliated in his turn. He could not even justifiably complain that Anselm had acknowledged a Pope without his authority, for he himself had just acknowledged the same Pope. Rufus suffered a further humiliation when he attempted to invest Anselm with the pallium brought by the Legate from Rome. Anselm refused this investiture. Two weeks after the opening of the Legate's negotiations with the King, the Archbishop received the pallium, the symbol of the Pope's confirmation of his office, in his own cathedral of Canterbury, with all the customary sacred rites.

But even although victorious in his struggle with the King, Anselm felt himself degraded and humiliated by the whole intrigue. He had been studiously kept in ignorance of the Legate's negotiations. He could not, in any case, have sympathized with the conduct of the Cardinal in taking and offering bribes, in refraining from comment on the King's exploitation of the churches, or on the moral depravity of Rufus and his court. In the following year, 1096, another Papal Legate, the Abbot Gerunto of the monastery of St. Benignus at Dijon, visited England. His mission, as we have seen in an earlier chapter, was to reconcile Rufus with his brother Robert and to promote Robert's desire to pledge Normandy to the King for three years for the sum of 10,000 silver marks, in order that Robert might join the Crusade. Gerunto was also instructed to attempt to bring about a reform of the abuses committed by Rufus and his officers in the handling of Church finances. Gerunto succeeded in the first part of his mission, which could not be other than welcome to Rufus, but he failed in the second part, to which Rufus objected violently. It has been suggested that the King sent an agent with bribes to the Curia in Rome to have the Legate withdrawn, and in fact a messenger arrived shortly from the Pope with letters cancelling the Abbot Gerunto's commission.

Anselm was thus left alone to carry on his dispute with Rufus. In 1097 it again came to a crisis. The see of Canterbury, as was customary, had been required to send a contingent of knights and men-at-arms to the

E

King's Welsh war. As had already happened during a previous campaign in Normandy, the Archbishop's troops were insufficiently armed and trained, or at least the King so complained. This was a charge against him in his capacity as the King's vassal, and Anselm could quite properly be summoned to appear before the royal council. He did not answer the summons, but requested instead permission to travel to Rome, whither Pope Urban had repeatedly invited him. Rufus stubbornly refused to grant the request. In November 1097 Anselm decided to go without the King's consent. He left Canterbury secretly without the usual armed escort of an archbishop, and crossed the Channel in the company of a solitary priest. He was received in the churches and monasteries of the Continent with enthusiasm. But by leaving England in defiance of the King he had forfeited his archbishopric. Rufus promptly proclaimed the see of Canterbury vacant and appropriated its revenues to himself. The King had won the long struggle with Anselm in the end, and in the only way that mattered to him.

Anselm's reception in Rome made ample amends for his scurvy treatment by Rufus. The Pope invited him to be his guest at the Lateran and treated him as almost equal in rank to himself. Was he not the Pope and Patriarch of the lands beyond the sea? The English visitors and pilgrims to Rome, of whom there were a multitude all through the Middle Ages, called him the 'Holy Man', and if he had permitted it they would have kissed his feet. Anselm passed his days between attendance at the Pope's councils and tranquil retreat at the monastery of San Salvatore at Telese near Benevento. There, in peace and contemplation, he completed his celebrated treatise *Cur Deus Homo*.

Nearly a year after his departure from England Anselm appeared in October 1098 at the Council of Bari, at which he was given the seat of honour. At Bari, and at the following Easter Council at Rome in 1099, Anselm was again covered with praise. He heard and perhaps took part in the long debates on lay investiture, simony and clerical marriage, which were the principal features of these two Councils, and he could take satisfaction in the decrees passed by the Councils against all three offences.

Nevertheless the cause of Rufus still triumphed at the Papal court. The King's agent, William Warelwast, succeeded so well in his arguments, shrewdly supported by bribes, that although Rufus was threatened with excommunication, the threat was never carried out. Pope Urban was statesman enough to sacrifice the principle when the necessity seemed to him paramount. He would not agree to antagonize a powerful King who had recognized him in the churches of England and whose friendship would counter-balance the hostility of the Emperor. Anselm was therefore caressed, flattered and venerated, but his cause was not heard. In some vexation he left Rome and travelled to Lyons, where he was the honoured guest of his friend the Archbishop Hugh. At Lyons and in the monasteries of Dijon he spent the following year. Then he returned to England. But before his return his cynical and implacable enemy William Rufus had been buried under an unmarked stone in Winchester.

VII

RANULF FLAMBARD

AFTER Rufus himself, the most scandalous character of his reign was his all-powerful minister Ranulf Flambard. The nickname of Flambard or Passe-Flambard was given to him, according to one account, by William the Conqueror's cook, who resented the flamboyant elegance of the King's clerk. Ranulf himself was of humble origin. His father, relates Orderic Vital, was a small priest of the region of Bayeux in Normandy. In early youth he gave evidence in minor affairs of the extraordinarily malign astuteness and competence he was afterwards to show in affairs of state. Later he was promoted by the Conqueror to be a clerk in the royal chapel. He became one of the King's chaplains and keeper of the King's seal. When the great Domesday survey was ordered in 1085 he possessed five small estates in various English shires. One of them was granted to him in the days of Edward the Confessor, from which it would seem that that saintly King had the dubious merit of introducing Ranulf Flambard into England.

But it was Rufus who gave Ranulf full play for his powerful and malignant genius. The new King employed him in his financial and administrative affairs and even, when absent in Normandy, appointed Ranulf as Grand Justiciar, or chief executive officer in England. Eadmer, the biographer of Anselm, describes him as 'the chief agent of the King's will'. It was possibly Ranulf Flambard who was the prime mover behind the scenes in all the King's disputes with Anselm. It was certainly Ranulf who conceived and carried out the ingenious exploitation of the churches and abbeys of England for the benefit of Rufus.

Ranulf hit on the idea of applying the feudal principle of royal wardship to vacant ecclesiastical lands and buildings as if they were the property of a lay baron. The King, always in need of ready money for the pay of his mercenaries, greeted the innovation with enthusiasm. As and when sees and abbeys became vacant on the death of their beneficiary, their revenues were confiscated in the name of the King, on the ground that the services due from them as from a lay vassal were no longer performed. There were many vacancies in the reign of Rufus. The Norman bishops and abbots appointed by the Conqueror were already aged, and their English colleagues who remained in office were even more venerable. In the course of natural law abbots and bishops died during the new reign, and Ranulf Flambard took care not to recommend the appointment of a successor. At the end of the reign of Rufus eleven of the richest English abbeys and three bishoprics were vacant and exploited by officers of the Crown. The monks were awarded a meagre pension.

If a candidate for office offered a large enough bribe, however, Rufus yielded. Thus in 1091 the scholarly Herbert Losinga purchased the see of Thetford for a very large sum of money. Later he repented of his sin of simony and went to Rome. There he resigned his bishopric into the hands of Pope Urban II and received it back from him again. On his return to England he found himself in fresh difficulty, for Rufus had not yet recognized Urban. The King ordered that Herbert be deprived of the bishopric for which he had paid Rufus in gold, and kept the see vacant for a time. Finally Herbert was restored to his see, and he seized the opportunity of moving it from Thetford to the flourishing city of Norwich, where he built a fine cathedral.

In the case of vacant abbeys, the secular clergy was not eligible for election, and the large sums demanded by Ranulf Flambard were above the possibilities of many monks, even if they had been willing to pay. The Norman Abbot Thurstan of Glastonbury had been deposed by William the Conqueror after a scandalous scene in his church. He had ordered the archers of his escort to shoot down on the steps of the altar the English monks who had refused to abandon their Gregorian chants in favour of the abbot's Norman innovations. Thurstan was readmitted by Rufus to the abbey of Glastonbury on payment of 500 pounds of silver. But other monasteries remained vacant, and the King's officers took over the management of their affairs and exploited their lands for the benefit of the royal treasury.

The feudal principle could possibly be stretched to the point of treating the interim revenues of a vacant see or abbey as belonging to the King, but it could not be justly evoked in the worst cases of Ranulf Flambard's administration. Thus on the death of the aged English Bishop Wulfstan of Worcester, the friend of King Harold, Ranulf demanded and obtained financial reliefs from the under-tenants of the see. And in the last days of the venerable Abbot Simeon of Ely he pensioned the monks with a miserable pittance and seized the balance of the revenues of the abbey for the King.

But this Norman precursor of the modern Chancellor of the Exchequer did not often act without instructions. Rufus was behind him, ever avid for gold and silver to squander on his minions, or to bribe the equally avid barons of his brother's Norman duchy whom he designed to win over to his cause by this means rather than by force of arms. It was Rufus who conceived, and Ranulf who operated, a manœuvre which brought 10,000 pounds into the King's treasury in 1094. Rufus was in Normandy and presumably engaged in consolidating his positions in preparation for the eventual conquest of the duchy. He sent a messenger to Flambard in England ordering him to mobilize 20,000 English militia-men for service abroad. Each man was to be provided by his lord with a sum of ten shillings for his subsistence, and to embark at the port of Hastings.

When the men had assembled at the port and were ready to embark, Flambard received another message from the King. He was ordered to collect the subsistence money from each man and send the sum thus realized to the King in Normandy. The soldiers were then dismissed. A ten-shilling head tax had thus been neatly and painlessly extracted from 20,000 soldiers or their immediate lords.

In 1096 when Rufus needed money to pay the 10,000 marks of silver for which his brother Robert had pledged Normandy to him, he resorted to a more exorbitant measure. He asked for, and the barons reluctantly granted, a geld of four shillings on the hide of land. On this occasion, the Church was not exempted from the geld as hitherto, and the ecclesiastical writers of the day were accordingly bitter. Either Rufus or Ranulf Flambard had already ransacked the treasures of the churches, or the revenues of the clergy were remarkably meagre during the reign of Rufus, for some of the bishops found themselves obliged to sell their church plate to pay the geld. And Archbishop Anselm himself was reduced to borrowing the amount of his contribution to the national levy from the monks of Canterbury, to whom he offered his manor of Peckham as security.

The geld of four shillings a hide imposed to pay for the pledge of Normandy was twice the normal rate of two shillings practised both before and after the Conquest. It is true that the Conqueror had ordered a tax of six shillings on the hide of land when the national emergency arose in 1084 over the threat of invasion by the three Scandinavian kings. But Rufus imposed no other geld during his reign. It may be surmised that for his national and personal expenditure he was sufficiently provided by the normal operation of the feudal reliefs on vacant lordships and by the appropriation of ecclesiastical revenues which he practised on a large scale.

However bitterly Rufus and Ranulf Flambard were censured in their own and in subsequent ages, they were but acting in accord with contemporary practice in other countries. The simony, or the sale and misappropriation of church benefices, for which they were condemned, was still widely current in France, Germany and Italy, despite the thunders of Gregory VII and subsequent pontiffs. King Philip I of France was the arch-sinner of Europe in this and other respects. And the successors of Rufus, both Norman and Plantagenet, were equally unscrupulous in seizing the revenues of vacant sees and neglecting to appoint a successor.

Crafty and corrupt as he was, there is no doubt that Ranulf Flambard enjoyed the complete confidence of the King during the reign of Rufus. Honours and rewards were heaped upon him. In 1088, the year after Rufus came to the throne, he was made Abbot of Hyde at the Council of Winchester. In 1099, the year before Rufus died, he was given the great bishopric of Durham, which he exploited so shamelessly that in the following year, when Henry I had succeeded his brother, Ranulf was deprived of his honours and was committed to the Tower of London— the first recorded of a long series of notable prisoners to be confined in William's tower. The new King granted the monks of Durham special privileges 'on account of the injuries and violence which Ranulf the Bishop did to them in his lifetime'.

VIII

THE FATAL FOREST

No adequate reason has ever been given for William the Conqueror's decision to create the New Forest in Hampshire for his own hunting, when so large a part of the forest land of the entire country was already reserved for the King's pleasure. It may be that on many occasions when he waited on the English coast for favourable winds to cross the Channel, he had regretted the absence of a deer forest within easy reach of the ship. Or perhaps in England he was visited by nostalgia for the great Norman forests in which he had hunted all his life. Whatever the real reason, the creation of the forest, and the depopulation of a large part of a fertile shire which it involved, proved singularly fatal to members of the Conqueror's family.

In 1081, during William's lifetime, his second son Richard, a youth who alone of the four sons was said to resemble the Conqueror in looks and even in character, and who was not yet old enough to bear the arms of knighthood, met his death by accident in the New Forest. In the spring and summer of 1100 the forest was to witness the death of two other members of the royal house. A younger Richard, the son of Duke Robert by one of his mistresses, had lived at the court of Rufus since his father's departure for the Crusade.

Richard's mother is said to have been the beautiful concubine of a venerable priest. Robert Curthose, then a young man and in the fever of his first rebellion against William the Conqueror, had met her in a village on the border of France and Normandy, had wooed her and carried her off. She bore two sons to Robert, named Richard and William, and educated them carefully until they were of age, by which time the father had become Duke of Normandy. Then this long-forgotten mistress presented herself with her sons at Robert's court and invited him to recognize them. Although she gave him undoubted proofs of their past

72

intimacy, Robert is said to have entertained doubts of his paternity of the two sons.

Whereupon, it is related, the courageous woman offered to undergo the ordeal of hot iron, and the challenge being accepted, she bore in public a white-hot bar of metal without showing signs of burning. Her two sons were then recognized by the Duke as his children and the grandchildren of the Conqueror. One of them, William, ultimately died in the Crusade after distinguishing himself as his father had done. The other, his elder brother Richard, was killed in the New Forest by an arrow intended for a deer. The companion who had unwillingly caused his death fled on the spot to the monastery of St. Pancras and took the vows, thus evading the vengeance of the dead youth's kinsmen.

Rufus at this time was heavily engaged in Normandy and in France. He was preparing to resist the intention of his brother Robert, now on his way back from the Crusade, to regain his Norman duchy. And he was planning, with the aid of Duke William of Poitiers, Lord of Aquitaine, to extend his dominions from the Firth of Forth to the river Garonne. Duke William, fired by the brilliant exploits of Robert of Normandy and Raymond, Count of Toulouse, in the deliverance of Jerusalem, was eager to embark on a second Crusade. He planned to raise an army of 300,000 men, and for this force, huge by mediaeval standards, and immeasurably costly to equip and maintain in the field, he needed a large sum of money. To obtain this he was willing to pledge his lands. It says much for the wealth of England at this time, and for the extent of the extortions of Rufus from laity and clergy alike, that the King, after having paid the pledge on Normandy, could seriously contemplate raising a much larger loan on the duchy of Aquitaine.

In July 1100 Rufus had assembled an army and a fleet to take possession of his new dominions in France. He had also collected a great mass of gold with which to pay the loan to the Duke of Aquitaine and to hire mercenaries, if he should need them. For the French King was not likely, without at least a perfunctory recourse to arms, to suffer an attempt to transfer one of his vassal states to the government of Rufus.

While he waited for a favourable wind to France Rufus and his court were installed in the castle at Winchester, and the King spent the days in hunting. As always when great movements of men and arms occurred, the superstitious saw everywhere signs and portents of impending doom. Many monks had visions of disaster, and Serlo, the venerable Abbot of Gloucester, whom the usually cynical Rufus held in some degree of respect and even friendship, wrote a letter to the King recounting a particularly impressive apparition witnessed by a monk in his community. On 1 August the aged Norman Abbot of Shrewsbury, one Foulchered, preached a sermon denouncing the vices of the court, and foretelling an imminent Divine act of vengeance. He even described, in a strikingly prophetic metaphor, the image of a bow stretched in Divine anger, and an arrow ready to slay.

The sequel was Homeric in its simplicity. On the morning after the Abbot's sermon the King prepared to set out for the day's hunting. As he was pulling on his boots, an armourer appeared and presented him with six newly forged arrows. The King took them in his hands, felt their suppleness and complimented the man on his fine craftsmanship. Then he selected four arrows for himself and gave the remaining two to his close friend Walter Tyrrel, saying to him with a smile: 'Sharp arrows for the best marksman,' and adding, according to another account: 'Be sure to aim at the mark.'

Lord of Poix and Pontoise, a wealthy and distinguished French knight, Walter Tyrrel was the King's constant companion. He was a valiant soldier, and in war as in peace Rufus kept him by his side. While the two men jested together, surrounded by the members of the royal hunting party, a monk of the abbey of St. Peter in Gloucester came to the King and gave him a letter from the Abbot Serlo. The King read it and laughed, and said to Tyrrel lightly: 'Walter, take good care to carry out the orders I gave you.'

Walter Tyrrel, whether he comprehended the King's meaning or not, made answer: 'Yes, my Lord.'

Whereupon Rufus recited the contents of the Abbot's message. 'I am astonished,' he said, 'that my Lord Serlo should have had the fantasy to write such things. I have always taken him for a good Abbot and an old man of ripe wisdom. In his simplicity he recounts to me, in the midst of my other troubles, the dreams of sleeping men, and he tells me that he is reporting them in letters to other countries. Does he think I shall imitate the English who abandon their journeys or their business according to the manner in which an old woman dreams?'

The King thereupon rose to his feet, mounted his horse and rode into the forest, followed by his brother Henry, by William of Breteuil, the son of his father's oldest friend William FitzOsbern, by Walter Tyrrel and by other members of the court. The hunting party then dispersed into various parts of the forest. The King, his friend Walter Tyrrel and a few others who usually hunted together, took up their accustomed positions in a part of the forest near Brockenhurst. The King and Tyrrel seem to have been separated by the space of an open clearing, for a large stag suddenly appeared between them. The King aimed at once but his bowstring snapped. He is said to have cried to Walter to shoot. Tyrrel aimed, and his arrow, one of the new weapons offered him by Rufus, sped across the animal's path, grazed the deer slightly without wounding it, and struck the King mortally. Rufus fell to the ground, and died almost immediately. There is no record that he spoke after his fatal injury.

News of the King's death spread consternation among his followers. There were some among them, like Walter Tyrrel, who had been his intimates. There were some doubtless who had been the associates of his vices. There was also his brother Henry, the youngest son of the Conqueror, who had long cherished his designs upon the throne.

As had happened on the death of William the Conqueror, the followers of the dead man dispersed in panic, each man going to his own place and putting his treasure in surety. The corpse of the Red King was left in the forest clearing where he had fallen. Later it was found by woodsmen, covered with humble garments and transported in a farm-cart to Winchester. A procession of monks and priests, poor widows and mendicants went out to meet the dead King. He was hastily buried in the old monastery of St. Peter at Winchester, and the stone which covered his grave had no inscription. The prelates of the Church which he had humiliated and exploited took their revenge on him after his death. They had not sufficiently condemned his sins, and he had scornfully refused to do penance for them. They now refused him absolution, and in many churches of his kingdom the bells were not tolled at his demise. Rufus had reigned for nearly thirteen years, and was about forty-three years old when he died.

Meanwhile Walter Tyrrel, innocent or guilty of causing the King's death, had not waited to be judged. Mindful perhaps of the timely evasion of the man who had been the cause of the recent death, in the same forest and in similar circumstances, of Richard the young nephew of Rufus, Walter rode as fast as his horse could carry him to the coast. There he found a fishing-boat and the weather being now favourable, he crossed the Channel to France. Once outside the borders of England or Normandy he could count on the protection of his own friends and his own sovereign lord Philip I. Walter had married Adelaide, the daughter of Richard, a member of the great Norman house of Giffard, of which the founder Walter Giffard had borne the Conqueror's standard when Ralph of Tosny relinquished it at Hastings. Some time after the death of

Rufus, Tyrrel went on a pilgrimage to Jerusalem and died in the Holy Land.

The case of Walter Tyrrel has always been one of the deepest mysteries of English history. After his return to France he repeatedly affirmed on oath, in the presence of the Abbot Suger, the minister and biographer of Louis VI, that he was innocent of the death of Rufus. He even maintained that he was not in that part of the forest and that he did not even see the King on the fatal day. Those who reject the theory of accident have seen the possibility of complicity between Tyrrel and other members of the hunting-party. His wife was related to the house of Clare, and her two brothers Gilbert and Roger of Clare were among the courtiers who accompanied the King. Henry I, who had most to gain by the death of Rufus, showed marked favour to the Clare family when his throne had been assured.

The greatest suspicion against Walter Tyrrel seems to have been attached to him because of his flight. But it may also be reasoned that in that age suspicion fell on the innocent as readily as on the guilty. And it may be argued in favour of his innocence that as the closest friend and companion of Rufus he had more to gain by the King's survival than by his death.

Henry's first act on learning of his brother's fate was characteristic of his capacity for swift and ruthless decision. He rode to the castle of Winchester, where the royal treasure was guarded, and demanded as the heir to the vacant throne that the keys of the treasury be surrendered. Soon after him, in breathless haste, came William of Breteuil, son of William FitzOsbern and brother of Roger, Earl of Hereford. William of Breteuil was a friend of Henry's brother Robert, then still absent from Normandy but already reported to be returning from the East. William protested vigorously against Henry's action in seizing the royal treasury. He maintained that the crown belonged to Robert, as the eldest son of the Conqueror, according to the agreement signed by Rufus and Robert. Henry, like himself, had sworn allegiance to Robert, and his brother had a prior claim to the throne of England.

A large crowd had gathered and an angry altercation ensued. Henry drew his sword and swore that no other hand than his should wield the sceptre of William the Conqueror. The firmness of the young prince, the popularity he had acquired among the English by reason of his English birth and speech, and his prestige as the first Norman to be born of a King and Queen crowned at Westminster, won over the support of the majority. The castle of Winchester and its treasure were surrendered to

Henry, and he placed his own men to guard them. Then, in the company of his friend and future minister Robert, Count of Meulan, the youngest son of the Conqueror rode from Winchester to London. On 5 August 1100, in the astonishingly short space of three days after the death of his brother, Henry was crowned at Westminster. No archbishop officiated at this ceremony. The Primate, Anselm of Canterbury, was still in exile. Thomas, Archbishop of York, had just died. The new King was crowned by Maurice, Bishop of London. Henry was thirty years old.

IX

THE RETURN OF ROBERT CURTHOSE

IN THE month which followed the death of King Rufus his elder brother
Duke Robert of Normandy returned from the Crusade. He had been
absent from his duchy for four years. He had seen his restless uncle Bishop
Odo of Bayeux buried in Palermo and had won renown on the battlefields
of the Orient. Robert's smiling face, his generosity, his short sturdy figure,
so solidly planted in the saddle that neither Christian nor Saracen could
unhorse him, made him loved and admired among the usually quarrel-
some and vainglorious leaders of Christendom in arms. As Duke of
Normandy he marched on an equal footing with the other chiefs of the
first Crusade, with Godfrey of Bouillon, Duke of Lorraine, with his
cousin Robert, Count of Flanders, and with Raymond of St. Gilles, Count
of Toulouse. He took part on equal terms with the other Christian princes
in the councils of war which were of frequent occurrence during the slow
and painful progress of the Crusaders. By short but far from easy stages
they had reached the Eastern Emperor's court at Constantinople. They
had crossed the Bosphorus to land in Asia Minor, and after long delays,
many sordid quarrels and fruitless battles they had come at last in sight of
their goal of Jerusalem.

Robert won fame in several of the notable sieges which were laid to
the Saracen cities. In the siege of Jerusalem he is said to have captured the
silver standard of the Saracen chief and to have placed it in the church of
the Holy Sepulchre. As a result of his prowess, or perhaps because he was
preferred to the other rival leaders, he was offered the crown of Jerusalem,
which he refused. During the siege of the city Robert made a strange
encounter. A brown-skinned man dressed as an Arab, but speaking
French, came to him and offered his services. He was, he said, Hugh
Baduel, the son of the Norman knight Robert of Saugei. Many years
earlier he had been violently dispossessed of his lands by the Countess

Mabel of Bellême and had murdered her in revenge. After the murder he had fled to Italy with his three brothers, had sojourned first in Apulia, then in Sicily and finally had taken shelter in the dominions of the Emperor Alexis of Constantinople.

But the arm of William the Conqueror was long. His agents and the spies of the great house of Bellême searched everywhere, even in the lands of the Orient, for the murderer of Mabel. To escape recognition, he had changed his dress and his name, had renounced the Christian religion for that of Islam, and for twenty years he had lived as an infidel Turk. Duke Robert listened to the tale in sympathy. The son of Mabel, the equally ferocious Robert of Bellême, was his own vassal, but he had no reason to love him. He took the brown-skinned Hugh of Saugei into his own service, where his knowledge of the infidel armies, their language, stratagems and tactics, proved of great value to the Norman Crusaders.

In the summer of 1100, after the capture of Jerusalem, Robert returned to Sicily to be treated for a wound. During his convalescence he met and married the lovely and intelligent Sybil, daughter of the Norman Geoffrey, Count of Conversano. With Sybil Robert acquired a handsome dowry, and with the money or the loot in gold and jewels he amassed in the wars of the Crusade he was preparing to return to Normandy to redeem his pledge to Rufus when the news of his brother's death reached Sicily. The terms of a charter signed by Robert in Sicily about this time suggest that he already claimed the title of King of the English. His treaty with Rufus gave him some right to the succession.

He returned to Normandy with as much haste as his leisurely temperament would permit. He reached his duchy late in the month of September 1100, about seven weeks after the coronation of his brother Henry. Robert's first act was to go with his wife Sybil to the abbey of Mont St. Michel, in which some years earlier he and Rufus had besieged their brother Henry. There, on the rock of the Archangel Michael in Peril of the Sea, he gave thanks for his safe return from the Crusade. And there, says the chronicler, his son William, afterwards called Clito (Ætheling or Prince), was conceived.

Soon after his return from Jerusalem Robert learned that he had lost Le Mans, the capital of Maine, to Count Helias. The valiant descendant of Herbert Wake-Dog, as shrewd in diplomacy as he was courageous in battle, had succeeded in regaining the city of his ancestors without striking a blow. With a small force of followers he entered Le Mans and was greeted by the citizens with enthusiasm. But the Normans placed in the citadel by Rufus still held the Royal Tower of the Conqueror. They were

well supplied with arms and provisions and could hold out almost in-
definitely. The garrison and the townspeople were on friendly terms, or
at least assumed them when it suited their purpose. From their battlements the Normans talked freely to the men of Helias. They exchanged
threats but also jests.

Aimeri of Mori and Walter of Rouen, who commanded the castle,
promised security to Helias on condition that he approached the fortress
clad in white. Confident in their good faith, Helias came frequently thus
attired, and the spirited conversations he carried on with the chivalrous
enemies within his gates are said to have excited the admiration of his
contemporaries. One day the Norman defenders of the tower told Helias
that although they were in a position to send stones and arrows among
the inhabitants of the city, and did not fear the reprisals of their siege
batteries, they had too much friendship for the Manceaux to take advantage of their situation. Moreover, since the death of Rufus and the return
of Duke Robert they did not know for which master they were fighting.
They had therefore sent a messenger to Duke Robert and to King Henry
to inform them of their intentions, and in the meantime they offered
Count Helias a truce.

The envoy of the Normans in Le Mans found Duke Robert in the
midst of his preparations to claim the throne of England. He was indis-
posed to divert his efforts—never very strenuous—in order to assert his
authority over the capital of Maine. He therefore urged the envoy to
return to his friends and invite them to make their peace with Helias.
The envoy, instead of returning to Le Mans immediately, crossed the
Channel and went to the court of King Henry. The King listened carefully to his account of the situation and then decided to defer the reconquest of Maine to another occasion. The messenger returned to Le Mans
and reported to the Norman garrison the meagre results of his double
mission. Walter and Aimeri, by the voice of a trumpeter, thereupon
invited Count Helias to don his white tunic. When he arrived before the
tower they told him that if they had wished to resist longer, they had the
arms and the food supplies required to hold out. But in exchange for a
large sum of money they were willing to hand over the fortress to Helias
and thus make him the veritable master of Maine. Helias immediately
accepted the proposal and with an escort of 200 knights conducted the
Norman garrison safely through a population which had bitter memories
of the burning of their houses by the Normans during the previous year.

After the surrender of the Norman fortress Helias made treaties of
friendship with both Duke Robert and King Henry, but in fact he proved

an ally to Henry alone. He was notably to play an important role in the decisive battle of Tinchebray. Helias gave his daughter Eremberge in marriage to the younger Fulk, son of his overlord Count Fulk of Anjou.

Geoffrey Plantagenets father he married Mathilda

The return of Robert Curthose from the Crusade had been hailed by all the enemies of his brother Henry as his return from exile on the death of the Conqueror had been welcomed by the enemies of his brother Rufus. It was now the opportunity for all the men who had lost power and wealth at the accession of Henry I, and chief among them the Grand Justiciar of Rufus, Ranulf Flambard, who was shortly to escape from the Tower of London.

At the instigation of Flambard the barons in England and Normandy who had most to fear from the resolute government of Henry now supported Robert. Those who feared a return of the disorder and lawlessness which had reigned in Normandy under Robert's earlier government gave their support to Henry. As in the case of the revolt of Bishop Odo and his brother Robert of Mortain against Rufus, the clergy and the people sided with the King. Many of the barons who had lands in both countries, such as Robert of Bellême, his two brothers Roger of Poitiers and Arnulf, William of Warenne, the young Walter Giffard, Yves of Grandmesnil and others, joined the party of Robert. Robert rewarded his supporters lavishly. He gave to Robert of Bellême, already the most powerful baron in Normandy, the wealthy bishopric of Séez, the town of Argentan and the immense forest of Ecouves. To Thibault-Pain, in return for a night's hospitality, he gave the great castle of Gisors.

The prodigality of the Duke was a byword in Normandy. He made many promises which he would have been unable to carry out, even if he became King of England. He soon dissipated, in largesse and extravagance, the mass of treasure he had brought from the East, and the dowry of his wife Sybil did not last any longer. He spent his days surrounded by courtesans and buffoons, to whom he gave fantastic presents. He was soon reduced to such penury that on several occasions he is said to have actually lacked bread, in the midst of a prosperous duchy. Often he did not leave his bed until late in the day for lack of decent garments to wear. His followers robbed him of his linen and he had no suitable clothes to wear to Mass.

This was the gay and indulgent Duke who was now to make, or to allow to be made for him, a second attempt to acquire the throne of England, which he considered to have been usurped by his youngest brother. This time Robert set out for England in person. In the summer of 1101 he assembled at Le Tréport an army of knights, archers and foot-soldiers. The English fleet had not been a reliable force since the days of Earl Godwin. The sailors were proud and independent of the King. A number of them were induced or bribed, probably by Ranulf Flambard, to convoy the army of Robert safely into Portsmouth.

In England meanwhile there was a momentary alarm like that which the country knew in 1084 when an invasion fleet was assembling in the ports of Scandinavia. Curiously enough the least warlike man in England, Archbishop Anselm, alone kept his head. Like Archbishop Lanfranc at the beginning of the reign of Rufus, he rallied the clergy to the King. The English militia of the shires, together with the mass of the people, were loyal to Henry. The King is said to have inspected them in person, riding or walking among the assembled foot-soldiers, and teaching them how to defend themselves against mounted knights.

With the traditions of his father's invasion of England still vivid, although Henry was not born until after the Conquest, the King had expected his brother to land on the famous beach at Pevensey, where the castle had been defended against Rufus by the rebels of Odo and Robert of Mortain. Accordingly he awaited Duke Robert there. But Robert landed instead at Portsmouth and marched towards London. He did not halt at Winchester, out of a delicate regard for his sister-in-law, Henry's Queen, who had just given birth to a child there. The two brothers eventually met at Alton. But no battle followed. In the presence of his brother Robert felt the prompting of family ties. He had once interrupted the siege of Mont St. Michel to allow his brother access to the water of which the defenders stood in sore need. And now he again yielded to the bond of fraternal affection. But at first the two brothers, at the bidding of their counsellors, exchanged the preliminaries of mutual defiance. Henry sent an envoy to ask why Robert had marched into peaceful England in arms. Robert replied: 'I have come, with the lords who are attached to me, into the kingdom of my father, and I claim it as my due as his first-born son.'

For several days delegates went to and fro between the armies, and some of them at least traduced the words and intentions of the lord whom they affected to serve. At last Henry, realizing that he would have a greater chance of conciliating Robert if he saw him face to face and alone, suggested a meeting with him and without followers. Robert agreed, and the two brothers met in the middle of a wide circle made by the two armies. They had not exchanged more than a few words before they fell into each other's arms, embraced and were reconciled.

Without any assistance from their normal advisers, the King and the

Duke now made an agreement between themselves. Under it Robert abandoned his claim to the throne of England and released Henry from the allegiance which he had hitherto claimed from him for his possessions in Normandy. Henry for his part agreed to make his brother an annual payment of 3,000 pounds sterling, and to abandon to him the lands in the Cotentin peninsula and elsewhere which he held in Normandy excepting only the town and castle of Domfront, which he had sworn to the citizens to defend as long as he lived. The treaty was signed by the brothers and ratified by the oaths of twelve nobles from each side. It was typical of Robert's generosity that later he renounced the pension of 3,000 pounds a year in favour of his sister-in-law Matilda.

Robert spent two months in England as the guest of the King, and on the approach of winter he returned to Normandy. With him he took a number of the Norman barons with possessions in England, among them William of Warenne, Earl of Surrey, who had openly or secretly supported him in his claim on the throne. Henry had determined to get rid of the principal Norman intriguers against him, and he now found pretexts for bringing them before his court and fining or expropriating them for breaches of the law. One of these offenders was his cousin William of Mortain, son of the Conqueror's half-brother Robert. William had succeeded his Uncle Odo as Earl of Kent. In 1104 he was deprived of his English lands and honours by a judicial sentence and banished from the country.

The chief intriguer against Henry was naturally Robert of Bellême, who had proved a thorn in the side of both of his brothers, now supporting one against the other, now opposing both. Two years before the death of Rufus, Robert of Bellême had acquired for 3,000 pounds—an enormous sum in that age—possession of the lands inherited by his late brother Earl Hugh of Chester from the great Roger of Montgomery, the husband of Mabel of Bellême. Robert had thus become one of the most powerful barons in England, as he already was in Normandy. In addition to his thirty-four castles in the duchy he was now master of the great earldom of Shrewsbury and the lordship of Arundel, besides many manors in other English shires.

With characteristic patience and pertinacity Henry now proceeded to achieve the overthrow of his dangerous and treacherous adversary. He had always maintained an army of spies and informers. He now set them to work in earnest. For a whole year they quietly and industriously collected evidence against the baron. In 1102, when the testimony was complete, Robert of Bellême was arraigned on forty-five separate charges in the King's court. A verdict against him was inevitable, and Robert, having heard the accusations, asked permission to leave the court on the plea that he must call his respondents together and prepare his defence. But he did not reappear to stand his trial. Instead he rode to one of his strongholds after another and ordered his followers to resist the forces of the King.

Henry was not slow in answering the challenge. After summoning Robert again in vain to appear before his court, he denounced him as a public enemy and led an army in person against the baron's castles. The King's men besieged Arundel for three months until the garrison begged for a truce, for the purpose of consulting their master whether to resist further or to surrender. Robert was then engaged in building his great castle on the Severn at Bridgnorth. He listened to the message from Arundel with scorn and anger, but could send no reinforcements and finally permitted his men to yield.

At some point in Henry's campaign against Robert of Bellême a number of other barons, rendered anxious for their own safety by the King's success in reducing his castles, urged the King to agree to a reconciliation with his rebellious vassal. While the barons were engaged with the King in his tent a crowd of 3,000 people assembled on a hill overlooking the royal forces and cried loudly to the King not to spare the traitor and not to parley with his secret sympathizers. Thus encouraged by his subjects, Henry continued in his efforts to master the rebel.

The strong castle of Bridgnorth held out against the King for three weeks, and surrendered only to a mixture of diplomacy and guile. The Welsh chiefs, on whom Robert of Bellême had counted for assistance, were bought off by William Pantol, a former victim of Mabel of Bellême who had passed into the King's service. The burghers and unarmed citizens who had taken refuge inside the castle were similarly bribed. The mercenaries were allowed to leave the castle unmolested, carrying their arms. When Robert of Bellême, in his almost impregnable castle at Shrewsbury, learned of the fall of Bridgnorth he gave way to rage and despair. The King was advancing on him slowly and methodically with a great army, cutting a path for his troops through a dense forest and building a road as he came. Without waiting for the inevitable conflict, Robert sent messages to Henry begging for clemency and proposing to negotiate. But the King was now resolved to humiliate the proud baron into surrender. When the royal army was under the walls of Shrewsbury castle Robert finally gave way, came to Henry and handed him the keys of his great fortress.

The King punished him for his treason and arrogance with the loss of his possessions in England and a sentence of perpetual banishment. Robert spent the rest of his active career of brigandage in France and Normandy. But he had not come to the end of his crimes or his intrigue. He allied himself to Duke Robert, and in the winter of 1105–6 he came to England with the Duke on a mission of conciliation which resolved nothing. But in due course the ultimate retribution of Henry overtook him. When he finally returned to England it was as a prisoner in chains which he never shook off. But now his first banishment sufficed to fill the English with joy. Ballads were sung in the streets to celebrate his departure. During his few years in England as a powerful baron the son of Mabel the poisoner had created his own legend of cruelty.

X

HENRY I

THE youngest son of William the Conqueror was King at last. From
what we know of Henry's character and of his father's judgment of his
son, it may be believed that since the Conqueror's death he had known
that only the unpredictable Robert and the childless Rufus stood between
him and the throne. Henry I, the first of his name to wear the English
crown, had probably been named by his mother after her grandfather
Henri I of France. He was unlike his father and his brothers Robert and
Rufus in character and temperament. Like his father and his brother Rufus
he was strong and thickset and of moderate height. His black hair fell over
his brows. His eyes had a soft and pleasant expression. Like all the men of
his family he had an inordinate love of hunting. In his private life he presented a notable contrast both to his father and his brother Rufus. The
Conqueror was both pious and continent, irreproachable in his conjugal
fidelity. Rufus mocked at religion and disdained to acquire either wife or
mistress. Henry was both pious and profligate. He was married twice,
he had a large number of mistresses, and is known to have had about
twenty illegitimate children. He was affable in manners and pleasant in
speech.

His learning, which had gained him the surname of Beauclerc, was
doubtless magnified by the chroniclers of the day, but unlike both
William I and William II he could read a letter in Latin—he is stated to
have deciphered a message in that tongue from Philip I of France—and
could converse in English. The latter was his native language, for he was
born in his father's conquered realm in the second or third year after the
Conquest. Another and perhaps better founded trait in his character was
his interest in animals. His father had loved the tall deer, and naturally,
like all his race, had a passion for horses. Henry extended his affections,
or at least his curiosity, to the whole of the animal creation. He organized

86

in his park at Woodstock what was probably the first zoological garden in England, to which other European rulers contributed.

Like many men with a passionate love of animals, Henry had only a limited interest in his fellow human-beings. Yet in that ruthless age he was distinguished by a certain humanity. He had no love of war. He preferred the arts of statecraft and diplomacy. He was praised for his restraint in the unnecessary shedding of the blood of his subjects. Nevertheless like the other members of his race he was capable of acts of cruelty and unbridled passion. He had not yet succeeded to the throne of one brother or seized the duchy of another when he hurled the insurgent burgher Conan from the highest window of the Tower of Rouen. He was later to order, or at least to permit, an insensate act of cruelty against his own grandchildren, the daughters of his illegitimate child Juliana. In all he seems, like his brother Rufus, to have been a man of infinite contradictions. Probably less cruel than Rufus, he did not share his brother's obsession with the traditions of chivalry. In everything he did he showed a strong practical element of calculation and foresight. He had inherited, indeed, the Conqueror's weakness of avarice. Without possessing the impressive and awe-inspiring personality of his father, he displayed the Conqueror's instinct for authority and good law. After the disorders and extravagances of the reign of Rufus, that of Henry seemed to his contemporaries a period of good law and government, and the King was even praised as the 'Lion of Justice'.

Henry's first step after his accession was to assure his new subjects of his intention to rule wisely and honourably. In a famous charter which was the precursor of Magna Carta itself, he disowned the oppressive measures and unjust exactions of his brother Rufus, and promised to maintain law and justice and the liberty of the Church. He pledged himself to restore the good laws of King Edward 'with those amendments with which my father improved it on the counsel of his barons'.

Copies of this Charter, signed by the King on the day of his coronation and witnessed by Maurice, Bishop of London, the Bishops of Rochester and Winchester and six barons, were sent to each of the English shires.

A picture of the feudal system and of the relations, real or ideal, between the King and his barons, the Charter of Henry I, known as *Institutiones Henrici Primi*, has been translated thus in Thomson's *Historical Essay on Magna Carta*:

'In the Year of Our Lord's incarnation MCI, Henry the son of King William after the death of his brother William, by the grace of

God, King of the English, to all his faithful subjects, greeting. Know ye that because through the mercy of God and the common council of the barons of all England I was crowned King of the same, and because the kingdom hath been oppressed by unjust exactions, for the honour of God and the love which I have towards you all, I have firstly set at liberty the Holy Church of God, so that I will neither sell, nor let out to farm, nor upon the death of any archbishop, or bishop or abbot, will I take anything from the lordship of the church or its tenants until a successor shall have been admitted to it. And I also take away all evil customs with which the kingdom of England has been unjustly oppressed, and which are here in part set down. If any of my earls, or barons, or others who hold of me shall die, his heir shall not redeem the estate as he was wont to do in the time of my brother, but shall relieve it by a just and lawful relief. In like manner shall the tenants of my barons relieve their lands of their lords by a just and lawful relief. And if any of my barons or other tenants will give his daughter, sister, niece or kinswoman in marriage, he shall treat with me about it; but I will neither take anything of his for that licence, nor will I prevent him giving her in marriage, unless he be willing to join her to my enemies. And if upon the death of a baron or other of my tenants, there remain a daughter and heir, I will give her in marriage, together with her lands, by the counsel of my barons. And upon the death of a man if his wife be left without children, she shall have her dower and marriage-portion; and I will not give her again in marriage excepting by her own consent. But if the wife be left with children, she shall then have her dower and marriage-portion while she lawfully preserves her body, and I will not dispose of her in marriage, but according to her own will. And of the lands and children there shall be appointed guardians, being either the wife or some near kinsman, who ought to be just. And I also command that my barons conduct themselves in like manner towards the sons, daughters and wives of their tenants. The common mintage of money which was accustomed to be taken in cities and counties, though not paid in the time of King Edward, I do wholly forbid to be taken for the future. If any coiner or other person shall be taken with false money, due justice shall be done upon him. All pleas and debts which were due to my brother I forgive, excepting my just farms; and excepting those things which were convenated for concerning the inheritance of others, or for those which properly concerned other men. And if any have engaged anything for his own inheritance, that I forgive; with all reliefs which were agreed upon for lawful inheritances. And if any of my barons or tenants lie sick, and he will give, or designs to bequeathe his money, I grant that it shall be disposed of accordingly. But if, being prevented by war or sickness, he should neither give nor dispose of his money, his wife, children or relations, and his lawful tenants, shall divide it between them for the good of his soul, as it shall seem best to them. If any of my barons or tenants shall forfeit, he shall not give a pledge in forbearance of the fine, as was done in the time of my father and brother, excepting according to the manner of the fine; so that it shall be satisfied as it was wont to be before the time of my father, in the time of my other ancestors. But if he be convicted of perfidy or any other wickedness, he shall make a due satisfaction for it. Also I pardon all murders, from the day in which I was crowned King; and those which shall hereafter be committed shall have satisfaction according to the laws of King Edward. I have, by the common council of my barons, retained in my hands all forests in the same manner as they were held by my father. I also grant of my own free will to knights who defend their lands by their habergeons (that is to say, tenants by military service), that their demesne lands and carriages shall be free from all gelds and payments to works; so that being so greatly relieved they may the more easily provide themselves with horses and arms, better fitting my service and the defence of my kingdom. I also establish firm peace in the whole of my realm, and command it to be held for the future. I also restore to you the law of King Edward, with those amendments with which my father improved it by the counsel of his barons. If any man hath taken anything of mine, or the goods of another, since the death of King William my brother, the whole shall speedily be restored without any other satisfaction; but if he shall retain anything, he shall pay a heavy recompense for it.

'Witnessed by Maurice Bishop of London, and Bishop Gundulf, and William, Bishop elect of Winchester; and Earl Henry, Earl Simon, Walter Giffard, Robert of Montfort, Roger Bigod and Henry of Port.

'At London, when I was crowned.'

On 11 November 1101, three months after his coronation, Henry adroitly enhanced the prestige of his English birth in the eyes of his non-Norman subjects by a marriage with Edith, the great-granddaughter of Edmund Ironside. Edith was one of the children of the late Malcolm of Scotland and Margaret, the sister of Edgar the Ætheling. To conciliate the

Norman barons in England, the new Queen adopted the name of Matilda which had been that of the wife of the Conqueror. Since the death of her parents Edith had been living in the convent of Romsey in the care of her aunt the Abbess Christina, another sister of Edgar the Ætheling. She had been sought in marriage by several noble subjects of King Rufus. Alain of Brittany, Lord of Richmond in Yorkshire, had asked for her hand, but had died before Rufus could either grant or refuse the request. William of Warenne, Earl of Surrey, who afterwards married Gundrada, a real or fabled daughter of the Conqueror's Queen, had also vainly desired to marry her.

Some of the Normans opposed to the King's marriage with Edith objected that she had already taken the vows as a professed nun and had been seen wearing the veil. But now an impressive champion appeared in defence of Edith: no less than Anselm, Archbishop of Canterbury. Recalled by Henry from his exile, self-imposed or compulsory during the reign of Rufus, Anselm had returned to England soon after Henry's coronation. He was now asked to celebrate the marriage of the Norman King and his Anglo-Scottish bride. Since his first visit to England in the Conqueror's reign Anselm had always shown goodwill towards the conquered nation, and now warmly encouraged Henry's marriage project as a gesture of conciliation. When confronted with the grave objection that the future Queen was already consecrated to God, the holy Anselm replied that nothing should induce him to make a nun break her vows, but before he proceeded further with the marriage he decided to interrogate the bride.

The descendant of Edmund Ironside replied with candour and dignity. She denied that she had ever been consecreated a nun. She admitted, however, that she had sometimes in her early youth appeared veiled, but only on the insistence of her aunt the Abbess Christina, and to defend herself from the libertinage of the Normans.

Anselm then convened an assembly of bishops, abbots and lay barons at Rochester. Two Norman archdeacons had been sent to the convent at Romsey to inquire into the truth of Edith's statements. They deposed before the assembly that the nuns of Romsey confirmed her denial. Anselm discreetly withdrew while the assembly discussed this weighty matter. On his return, it was announced that the assembly found the girl free to marry and quoted as precedent the famous decision taken by the great Archbishop Lanfranc when he released from their vows those Englishwomen who at the time of the Conquest had taken shelter in religious houses from the Norman invaders.

A few days later Anselm celebrated the marriage of Henry to the last female descendant of the old line of English kings. But before he pronounced the nuptial benediction, the Archbishop resorted to an extraordinary device to save the religious reputation of the bride. A platform had been erected before the door of the abbey church at Westminster. Anselm ascended it and in full view and hearing of the people announced the verdict of the assembly at Rochester. He recited the allegations which had been made against Edith, now newly named Matilda. And he dismissed them as unworthy after reading the solemn judgment of the Council of Rochester that the bride was free to marry.

Henry had decided, or more probably had been summoned by Anselm, to abandon his mistresses on his marriage, and this, to general astonishment, he did. For a while he lived in domestic harmony with his English wife and, to outward appearances at least, was faithful to her. The first months of his reign were promising. He had received the recognition of King Philip I of France, who sent to England his son and deputy, Louis called the Fat, to attend Henry's first court at Christmas.

A strange story is recounted by Orderic Vital concerning this visit, though it finds no place in the Abbot Suger's subsequent history of Louis the Fat. The father of Louis, the voluptuary Philip I, had scandalized France and the Pope by taking as his second wife, without troubling to divorce the first, the lovely and intriguing Bertrade of Montfort. Bertrade, a daughter of the first Simon of Montfort, was reputed to be the most beautiful woman in France, as she was certainly one of the least scrupulous. She had married, out of personal ambition, one of the most licentious of kings. Her first husband was Count Fulk of Anjou, a vassal of Philip I. Four years after her marriage to Fulk, fearing that one day he would replace her in his affections as he had already replaced his two previous wives, she decided to anticipate the separation. The French King had already met and admired her at Tours. She now sent a secret message accepting his advances but making the stipulation that she should become his Queen.

Philip promised this and Bertrade thereupon deserted the bed of Fulk for that of his overlord. Philip repudiated his existing queen, Berthe, daughter of Florent I, Duke of Holland, sent her to languish in a dungeon at Montreuil, and elevated Bertrade in her place. He even demanded the Papal blessing on his new union. The Pope refused indignantly, and no French prelate would agree to perform the marriage ceremony, but two Norman bishops, one of them the famous Bishop Odo of Bayeux, had been found willing to pronounce the benediction of the Church, and were suitably rewarded with the gift of churches in Mantes.

Two successive Popes, Urban and Paschal, maintained France under an interdict during the fifteen years that Bertrade and Philip lived together. Pope Urban sent legate after legate, bull after bull, to admonish and threaten the adulterous monarch, but Philip remained under the spell of Bertrade. However, he refrained during this time of interdict from wearing the royal crown and the royal purple. No church bells were rung when he entered a town, and the priests ceased to chant the psalms. However, Philip's bishops still owed him temporal allegiance as his vassals, and they accorded him a private chaplain who said Mass for the unrepentant King and his household.

Meanwhile Fulk of Anjou had not accepted without protest the affront put upon him by his overlord. He demanded the return of Bertrade and threatened reprisals, no small threat since Anjou at that time was at least as powerful as the small realm of France. But the audacity and charm of Bertrade succeeded in promoting a reconciliation between the two rivals. They sat down together at a splendid banquet organized by her, and it is said that afterwards, replete and satisfied, they slept in a bed in the same room.

Bertrade had two sons by Philip I. She persuaded the King to recognize them, and she even planned to replace the lawful heir to the throne, Louis the Fat, by one of her own sons. Now comes the strange story of Orderic Vital. When Louis appeared at the court of the newly crowned Henry I as the envoy of the French King, he was closely followed by a secret messenger from his stepmother. The messenger brought to the King a letter purporting to come from Philip I and sealed with the royal seal. Henry read the message and promptly called his barons together in council. He then revealed the astonishing contents of the French King's supposed missive. It was nothing less than a request that Henry should arrest his son Louis and keep him in lifelong captivity.

Cruel as he could be on occasion with his own subjects, Henry had a strong paternal sense. He was as much revolted by the conspiracy against Louis as embarrassed by the diplomatic quandary in which he was placed. The council of barons supported him in his decision not to accede to the request. The council was still sitting when a French knight of the escort of Louis, William of Buschelei, who had sensed or discovered something of the plot against his Prince, appeared uninvited at the door of the council and as if in jest took his seat among the English barons.

Henry saw his opportunity and grasped it. He told the Frenchman to persuade his master to return to France in peace. William of Buschelei obeyed and undoubtedly informed Louis of the reasons for this request.

Philip's heir arrived in his father's court and indignantly related the whole story of the conspiracy. The King denied any part in the plot, whereupon Louis turned his wrath against his stepmother. This curious Hamlet-like situation continued for some years, with alternate efforts of the Prince and the adulterous Queen to destroy each other. In an attempt to kill Louis the Fat, Bertrade is said to have had the assistance of two sorcerers, who were betrayed by a third, their rival. Then she resorted to professional poisoners who succeeded in making the King's heir so ill that his life was despaired of. But he recovered and eventually pardoned Bertrade. If the story of his adventure at the court of Henry I is true, and stranger events than this occurred in all the courts of the Middle Ages, Louis the Fat did not bear Henry eternal gratitude for having spared him. When he followed Philip I on the throne of France and Henry had become his nominal vassal as Duke of Normandy, Louis and Henry were frequently at war.

Henry's first acts on his accession had won him immediate popularity. He had sent for Anselm and had promised to abide by his counsel. And he had seized and thrown into prison the arch-instrument of his brother Rufus, the hated and feared Chief Justiciar Ranulf Flambard, Bishop of Durham. Henry had an unfailing memory and he remembered the slights and insults he had received from Ranulf in the days of Rufus, when he had been a landless younger son. He was careful, however, to accord his prisoner a comfortable residence in the Tower of London, and he appointed William of Magneville as his custodian. The circumstances under which Ranulf made his extraordinary escape from the Tower suggest either that he was insufficiently guarded or that the King did not regret his evasion.

Out of his subsistence allowance, and with the aid of friends outside the castle, Ranulf was in the habit of entertaining his guards daily at his table. One day he received from his friends a cask of Falernian wine in which a rope, possibly of silk, was coiled. The bouquet of the wine seems not to have been changed by the presence of the rope, for the guards drank generously from the cask. After their libations they fell into a deep sleep. Ranulf then tied the rope to the central pillar of the window of his chamber in the Tower, and seizing his pastoral staff (he was still Bishop of Durham) he slid down the rope. But he had forgotten to wear his gloves. The rope was rough to his cleric's soft hands and they were sadly abraded. Moreover the rope was too short, and the Bishop found himself dangling at its end, at some distance from the ground. He jumped, or fell, the last few yards of his descent, and was picked up in a sorry state. His friends awaited him at the foot of the Tower with fast horses, and in spite of his bruises he managed to make the journey to the coast of England. He crossed the Channel safely and arrived in Normandy, where Duke Robert, lately returned from the Crusade and eager to contest his brother Henry's possession of the English throne, was glad to make use of his services. Ranulf rapidly acquired in Normandy a position hardly less powerful than that he had enjoyed in the England of William Rufus.

Ranulf Flambard succeeded on his escape from England rather better than his aged mother. The avarice and cunning of this ancient crone had given her the reputation of being a witch who communed frequently with the Devil, in whose intimacy incidentally she was said to have lost an eye. She made the crossing to Normandy in another ship and was accompanied by her son's treasure horde. Her eccentric appearance and behaviour caused her to be treated with derision by her fellow-voyagers, but her worst mishap befell later when some of the numerous pirates in the Channel boarded the vessel, seized the gold and silver which had been amassed by Ranulf Flambard during his long years of exploitation in England, and landed the pretended sorceress on the shores of Normandy, stripped like the crew and the other passengers of all her possessions, even her clothing.

Flambard had forfeited his bishopric of Durham by his escape from England, even if he had not been already deposed before that. In Normandy he soon obtained the indirect control of the bishopric of Lisieux after the death of its aged incumbent Gilbert Maminot, the Bishop skilled in medicine who had tended the dying William the Conqueror. Ranulf first induced Duke Robert to grant him the see of Lisieux for his brother Foulcher, who was employed as a clerk in the Duke's chapel. Foulcher was almost illiterate and moreover in poor health. He died seven months later, and Ranulf then solicited the vacant see for his own son Thomas, a boy of twelve years. For the next three years Ranulf ruled the diocese as a lay administrator. Finally he accepted a large bribe from William of Pacy in exchange for the bishopric, but the new Bishop was speedily charged with simony first by the archiepiscopal court at Rouen, and then by the *Curia* at Rome. He was then deprived of his see. As the result of the intervention of Ranulf, the diocese of Lisieux, for long a shining example of good government in Normandy, was without a spiritual ruler for five years.

But in the meantime this masterly intriguer had been restored to his bishopric of Durham, absolved by the archbishops of Canterbury and York and placed again in possession of his large English estates.

Duke Robert's invasion of England, which was to end farcically for

Robert himself, resulted in a reconciliation between Ranulf and the King who had thrown him into the Tower. It is probable, however, that the reconciliation was not complete until five years afterwards, when Robert had been crushingly defeated at Tinchebray and had become a prisoner of Henry, leaving his brother in possession of his own duchy of Normandy as well as the kingdom of England. Ranulf Flambard thereafter played no outstanding role either in English or in Norman history. The unscrupulous minister of Rufus was now an old man. He had survived three kings of England, Edward the Confessor, William the Conqueror and William Rufus. His end was obscure.

XI

THE ENGLISH CONQUEST OF NORMANDY

A S THE conquest of England had been largely achieved by the Normans in the mixed invasion force of William I, the conquest of Normandy was largely achieved by the English in the mixed invasion force of Henry I. It may well be imagined that the dying prophecy of the Conqueror had inspired Henry's systematic acquisition of his father's dominions. England was already his. Normandy was soon to fall into his hands. Since the return of Duke Robert from the Crusade, Henry had been kept secretly and regularly informed of the state of affairs in the duchy. All his adult life he had been careful to conciliate the ecclesiastics in England, indeed he owed his speedy election to the throne largely to their support. Those of Normandy were his surest sources of aid and intelligence.

The Norman churches were the especial prey of Robert of Bellême, and they found no competent defender in Duke Robert. He made weak efforts from time to time to check the reign of terror and anarchy established by Robert of Bellême, but in each successive trial of strength with the baron he was invariably defeated and forced to negotiate an uneasy peace. Among the most pressing appeals which Henry received to intervene in Normandy, was one from Ivo, Bishop of Chartres, a diocese on the borders of Normandy. Bishop Ivo wrote to the King's chief minister, Count Robert of Meulan, to complain of the scandalous state of the Norman churches, notably those of the diocese of Lisieux which the Duke had left spiritually vacant and under the dubious government of Ranulf Flambard.

Since his coronation Henry had taken measures to secure himself in advance against the retaliation of his continental neighbours in the event of his seizure of Normandy. He had been promised the friendship of Philip I of France. In 1101 he made a treaty with Count Robert of Flanders by which the Count, in return for an annual subsidy of 500 pounds, undertook to provide the King with 1,000 knights and their men-at-arms. Probably about the same time Henry made sure of the support of Normandy's other neighbours, Maine, Brittany and Anjou, all of whose rulers promised him troops when he should call for them. In the meantime, by the same methods of bribery and intimidation which had succeeded so well when employed by William Rufus, the King set to work within Normandy itself to create a party of barons hostile to his brother Robert. The Duke eventually found himself reduced to asking the aid of men like William of Mortain and Robert of Bellême, who had lost their lands in England and had been banished by Henry.

In 1104, two years before the campaign reached its climax, Henry visited his lordship of Domfront and saw to its defences. He placed his own men in the castles of the Norman barons whom he had won over to his cause. And to punish his brother for having become reconciled with Robert of Bellême, contrary to the terms of the Treaty of Alton, he forced the Duke Robert to surrender to him the county of Evreux, the men of which had been conducting their own private war with the neighbouring county of Breteuil.

In the following year Henry began his campaign for the acquisition of Normandy in earnest. In Holy Week, 1105, he landed at Barfleur on the Cotentin peninsula. This region had been his first possession in Normandy, purchased with a part of his legacy from the Conqueror. His influence in the region was strong. On the eve of Easter Sunday he arrived in Carentan, where the venerable Bishop Serlo, who had reason to complain of the sorry state of the churches in his own diocese of Séez, hastened to greet the King and invited him to celebrate the Easter feast in his presence. When Serlo entered the church of Carentan, clad in his richest vestments, the Bishop was astonished at the scene which met his gaze. The church was piled high with the rustic furniture, the farm implements and personal effects of a large crowd of peasants. Driven from their devastated farms by the quarrelling barons, they had taken refuge in the church, and even the altar was inaccessible amid the mountains of heaped-up farm-gear.

The King and his companions were seated amid the baskets and wicker-paniers of the refugees. The worthy Bishop delivered a remarkable sermon addressed to the King personally. He denounced the misdeeds of Robert of Bellême, who in the Bishop's own diocese had set fire to the church of Tournay and caused the death of forty-five persons of both sexes. He spoke of the negligence and disorderly life of the King's brother Duke Robert, who did not govern but submitted to the evil influence of

G

his brother-in-law William of Conversano, of the Governor of Rouen, Hugh of Nonant, and his nephew Gunhier. The Duke Robert, complained the indignant prelate, dissipated in frivolous extravagance the wealth he drew from his once prosperous duchy, but was himself compelled to fast for lack even of bread. The greater part of the time he dared not rise from his bed, for lack of clothes to wear, and could not go to church for lack of shoes. The buffoons and courtesans who accompanied him everywhere stole his clothes at night while he slept heavily after an orgy of drinking, and only laughed at his discomfiture on awakening. The Bishop then adjured the King to take up arms, not out of personal ambition, but in the interests of Normandy.

The King consulted the barons around him, and with their accord told the Bishop that he was willing to do so. Thus fortified, Serlo resumed his sermon and this time turned his critical attention to the King and his courtiers. He accused them of wearing long hair like women, a custom introduced by the companions of William Rufus and directly contrary to the teaching of St. Paul. They also, said the Bishop, let their beards grow long, refraining from the use of the razor lest their perfunctorily shaven cheeks be resented by the mistresses whom they caressed. They wore garments of silk, and long shoes (a fashion introduced from Italy) which terminated in points curled like the tails of scorpions.

The Bishop then invited the monarch to set an example to his subjects. A scene worthy of the highest comedies of the Middle Ages was then enacted. Profiting by the momentary confusion caused by his unexpected denunciation, the prelate drew from a sleeve of his gown a large pair of scissors and sheared first the long locks of the King and then those of his minister, Count Robert of Meulan; finally he cut off the hair of the King's courtiers who meekly allowed themselves to be shorn.

After this strange opening, the drama of the English conquest of Normandy followed stage by stage. The immediate object of the King was the recapture of his two castles at Bayeux and at Caen. Bayeux was commanded by Gunhier of Aunai who held as prisoner in his dungeon a powerful supporter of Henry, Robert FitzHamon. On the King's arrival before the walls of Bayeux Gunhier boldly sallied forth to meet him. He greeted the King courteously and surrendered to him his prisoner Robert FitzHamon, but the town itself he would not yield. Henry then made a determined attack on Bayeux, and with the aid of the followers of his ally Count Helias of Maine, he set fire to the town and its castle and captured Gunhier and his garrison.

The inhabitants of the neighbouring town of Caen, intimidated by the fate of Bayeux, surrendered without fighting. When they learned that Henry was marching on their city and threatened it similarly with destruction, they hastened to send envoys to the King. They offered to hand over the keys of the castle and to expel its guardian, Enguerrand FitzIlbert. This they did, and the four principal citizens of Caen were rewarded by the grateful King by the gift of the English town of Darlington, which then brought into the royal treasury an annual revenue of eighty pounds. The English-born Orderic Vital, a contemporary who records the gift, says that Darlington was thenceforward known among the Normans opposed to Henry as Traitors' Town.

From Caen, vanquished without a blow, Henry next marched on Falaise, the birthplace of his father the Conqueror. Here, in its already powerful castle, Duke Robert seems at that time to have made his headquarters. But Henry did not attack the town. His forces were weakened by the temporary defection of Count Helias of Maine. Some fighting took place around Falaise, nevertheless, in which a valiant knight, Roger of Gloucester, was killed.

When the Whitsuntide feast came the two brothers Henry and Robert met near Falaise at Cintheaux, and during two days of feasting and argument attempted to patch up their quarrel. But in view of Henry's designs on Normandy it was clear that no agreement could be reached, and the burning and pillaging of the countryside, its towns and villages, was indifferently continued by the soldiers of one party or another.

It was proably at this time that the Abbot Robert of St. Peter on the Dives made a treacherous attempt to capture King Henry in the interests of his brother. After confiding his intentions to Duke Robert at Falaise the Abbot rode to Caen, spoke to the King and offered with all the appearances of friendship to place him in possession of a stronghold which he possessed on the banks of the Dives. The Abbot suggested that the King accompany him with only a small force of troops, to prevent the alarm from being given to the defenders of the town, in which Robert claimed to possess a small number of devoted followers.

Henry put on his mail, mounted his horse and with 700 men set out after nightfall. At dawn he found himself near the abbey of St. Peter on the Dives. Meanwhile, 140 knights owing allegiance to his brother, and led by Rainauld of Warenne and the Abbot's natural son, the young Robert of Estouteville, had installed themselves in the castle adjoining the abbey. Other parties of knights hostile to the King had set out to intercept him from Falaise and other places in the region. Henry soon realized the danger which threatened him on all sides and saw that his only chance of escape lay in an immediate attack on the castle. His men succeeded in setting fire to it and in destroying also the adjoining abbey of St. Peter. Rainald and Robert, the two commanders of the castle, and the other fighters in Duke Robert's cause were captured. Many others perished when the church tower was burned down. The knights who were on their way from Falaise and other places to reinforce the garrison of the castle, seeing it already in flames, rode hastily back. The King pursued them a certain distance, but once they had reached the shelter of the walls of Falaise castle they were in safety, and Henry had not sufficient force to lay siege to so powerful a stronghold.

But the treacherous Abbot Robert had been captured. He was roped like a sack of grain across a horse's back and brought into the presence of the King. Henry looked at him scornfully and said: 'Traitor, leave my lands. If I did not respect the sacred order whose habit you wear, I would have you torn in pieces this instant.' The perfidious monk was thereupon released. He fled across the border of Normandy into France, where he was born, and obtained from Philip I the post of tax collector of Argenteuil. Within a year he was killed by a peasant from whom he had attempted to collect an unjust tax payment.

In the winter of 1105–6 both Duke Robert of Normandy and his nominal vassal Robert of Bellême visited King Henry in England, and once again proposed a settlement of their quarrel. But Henry was now weary of negotiations which only ended in fresh disputes. In the summer of 1106 he crossed to Normandy with the determination to make an end of the anarchy into which his brother's duchy had fallen. Convinced that his cousin William of Mortain and Robert of Bellême were at the head of the opposition to him, he began by attacking the Count of Mortain's stronghold at Tinchebray, about forty miles east of Avranches.

In preparation for a long siege, Henry built a small castle outside Tinchebray to contain the defenders, and placed it under the command of Thomas of St. Jean. Meanwhile William of Mortain, a nephew of William the Conqueror and a courageous soldier, had succeeded in sending into the besieged castle of Tinchebray a considerable quantity of provisions both for men and horses, including forage cut from the green crops of the region. He even entered the castle himself, together with a number of his followers, under the eyes of the besieging army. When he learned this Henry flew into a violent rage and hastened to bring up his main body of troops to reinforce the besiegers.

William of Mortain appealed for aid to Duke Robert and Robert of Bellême. They arrived near Tinchebray with William of Ferrières, Robert of Estouteville and other rebel lords. The Duke then challenged the King either to raise the siege and depart peacefully or to accept battle. While the leaders debated the question the two armies faced each other in the plain outside the castle of Tinchebray, in a silence broken only by the admonitions of the monks, who appealed to them not to indulge in needless bloodshed. Henry is said to have made a final appeal to his brother, inviting him to surrender all his strongholds, and to hand over one-half of the duchy and the profits of the administration of justice. In return Henry would pay to Robert the yearly revenue of the lands under his government. But on the advice of his counsellors Robert rejected the offer, and Henry's envoys returned to the King to announce their failure. The conflict was now inevitable, and both sides made ready for it.

The battle of Tinchebray was to prove a landmark in the relations between England and Normandy. Before it began Henry delivered the customary harangue to his troops. He also took the risk of setting free those of Duke Robert's followers, including Rainald of Warenne, whom he had captured in the burning castle and abbey of St. Peter on the Dives. He also made a solemn vow to rebuild the ruined abbey.

The royal army contained a greater proportion of mounted troops than that of Duke Robert. The King had also a larger group of notable barons in his army—four counts, Helias of Maine, William of Evreux, Robert of Meulan and William of Warenne, and with them a number of powerful barons of Normandy, including Ranulf of Bayeux, Ralph of Tosny, Robert of Montfort, Robert of Grandmesnil and others, with their followers.

Henry divided his army into three corps. The first was commanded by Ranulf of Bayeux, the second by Robert of Meulan and the third by William of Warenne, whose brother Rainald had just been liberated by the King and who in gratitude urged his followers to fight valiantly. A fourth body of volunteers from Brittany and Maine, under the command of Count Helias, was placed by the King in reserve. Henry himself took command of his English infantry, which as at Hastings was to play an important part in the battle. Foot-soldiers outnumbered the cavalry in the army of Duke Robert and many knights on both sides, including the King himself, dismounted when the battle began and fought on foot.

Robert had divided his own force into two corps, the first commanded by William, Count of Mortain, who had left his castle to fight in the open, and the second by Robert of Bellême. The troops of William of Mortain opened the battle by charging the knights of Ranulf of Bayeux. The first shock of the encounter plunged both attackers and defenders in an inextricable confusion, and while the main body of Duke Robert's cavalry was thus engaged, Helias of Maine, with his reserve troops, seized the opportunity to make a flank attack in which he killed 225 of the Duke's followers. Seeing Robert's cause already hopelessly lost the Duke's redoubtable vassal Robert of Bellême took refuge in ignominious flight, and with his followers deserted the struggling mass of victors and vanquished.

Duke Robert himself was captured by the King's chaplain, a warlike priest called Gauldri, who fought in the battle at the head of a small group of knights. Shortly after the battle Gauldri was appointed Bishop of Laon, where his aggressive temperament made him many enemies. On the eve of a religious feast they came upon him in an orchard and slew him, together with seven clerks of his church.

One of Duke Robert's two principal lieutenants, William of Mortain, was taken prisoner by the Breton mercenaries of King Henry and fell into the hands of the younger Stephen of Blois, a future King of England, who gave him into the power of the King. Among others captured by the royal army were Robert of Estouteville and William of Ferrières. Some of the prisoners were magnanimously released by Henry as having merely followed their feudal lords into the battle. Others, responsible for personal acts of rebellion against him, he condemned to perpetual imprisonment.

Sentimentally the most interesting prisoner taken by Henry that day was Edgar the Ætheling. The last male descendant of the old English kings, disillusioned by his long sojourn in Scotland as perpetual pretender to the English throne, had settled in Normandy at the court of Duke Robert, for whom he soon developed a sincere affection. He accompanied him on the Crusade, and fought with him in his minor battles in Normandy and Maine. Henry, who had married the Ætheling's niece, took him to England after the battle, and granted him a small pension, upon which the Ætheling lived for the rest of his days in a country retreat, solitary and obscure.

The battle of Tinchebray lasted little more than an hour, and most of the losses had been borne by Duke Robert. By a curious coincidence, on which the English chroniclers were quick to remark, this battle, which left Robert decisively, and as it proved permanently, in Henry's power, and which brought Normandy again under the rule of the King of England, was fought on 28 September 1106, the fortieth anniversary of the landing of William the Conqueror on Pevensey beach.

Robert, now a captive, and regretting bitterly the fatal influence of

Robert of Bellême and other violent counsellors, offered to place Henry in possession of their father's great castle of Falaise. He had left it in good hands, with orders not to surrender it to any other than himself or his vassal William of Ferrières. He now advised the King to send William, who had also been taken prisoner at Tinchebray, to Falaise to take over the castle in the King's name before Robert of Bellême could seize it. Henry did as his brother suggested, and soon after followed William, taking Robert with him for greater security. In Falaise Henry received the homage of the citizens and also met his nephew William, afterwards called the Clito (Prince or Ætheling), then a boy of six years. William was the son of Duke Robert by his legitimate wife Sybil of Conversano. As a grandson of the Conqueror, he was a potential rival to his cousin, also called William, the heir to Henry's throne. It was obviously to the King's interest to keep William Clito under close surveillance, if not in his own company. But Duke Robert had entrusted his son to the care of a brave and valiant knight, Helias of St. Saens, who had married a daughter of the Duke by one of his mistresses and had been made Count of Arques. Helias took good care to keep his charge out of Henry's hands.

News of the King's victory at Tinchebray had rapidly spread throughout Normandy and had been generally greeted with enthusiasm. Henry went to Rouen, accompanied by the defeated Duke, who ordered his vassal Hugh of Nonant to surrender the keys of the tower. In Rouen, Robert formally released his subjects from their oaths of fealty in favour of his brother. At the same time Henry swore to restore the laws of William the Conqueror and confirmed the city of Rouen in its ancient privileges.

In the middle of October, less than a month after the battle, Henry assembled all the barons and prelates of Normandy at Lisieux, and there ordered the restoration of all the lands of the churches and other legitimate owners as they were held at the death of the Conqueror. He re-attached to the royal domain all the lands which had previously belonged to his father, and he cancelled the over-generous or imprudent grants and donations which Robert had made to his friends. Finally he sent his captives under strong guard to England. William of Mortain and Robert of Estouteville were condemned to perpetual imprisonment, and the former is said in one unconfirmed account to have been blinded.

Robert Curthose was also condemned by his brother to spend the rest of his life in captivity. But he was humanely treated, and provided with food, clothing and even luxuries. He was held successively in the castles of Wareham, Devizes, Bristol and finally Cardiff. Here he succeeded in learning Welsh and even in writing a pathetic little poem in that language. Robert Curthose survived the battle of Tinchebray by nearly twenty-eight years. He died in February 1134 at the age of eighty, a memorable case of longevity in the Middle Ages. He was buried beneath the high altar of the abbey church of St. Peter at Gloucester, where an effigy in wood preserves to this day the memory of the unfortunate eldest son of William the Conqueror.

Meanwhile, Robert of Bellême had, as we have seen, succeeded in escaping capture at Tinchebray, and not long after the battle his formidable prestige and the greater part of his territorial wealth were still intact. For the moment Robert feigned submission to the King. He had appealed to Count Helias of Maine for aid against Henry, and Helias had refused to betray his ally. Then he had asked Helias to intercede with Henry on his behalf, and the brave Helias had consented. Thanks to his close friendship with the King and his own guarantee of Robert's future fealty, Helias persuaded Henry to restore to Robert of Bellême the great castle of Falaise and the lands which had been in the possession of his father, Roger of Montgomery.

XII

AFTER TINCHEBRAY

THE return of Normandy to the rule of the Norman King of England solved some problems for Henry I but created others. The barons with estates in both countries were no longer divided in their allegiance between King and Duke. Henry was King in England and Duke in Normandy. But Normandy, as a continental state, had problems of its own which now directly affected the English. The relations between the Normans and their neighbours in France, Brittany, Anjou and Maine created new obligations for the King of England who had become a Norman Duke. England was again directly involved, as during the reign of the Conqueror, in the affairs of the Continent. While Normandy was weak and divided, Philip I of France could watch indifferently the disputes between Duke Robert and his brothers, the anarchy of the barons, and the depredations of Robert of Bellême. But now reunited to a powerful and prosperous kingdom across the narrow seas, Normandy could deny the French access to the same seas, and could control the lower reaches of the Seine.

The duchy once more became a thorn in the side of the French King. The quarrels of the Normans with the French became the quarrels of the English. Thus were initiated, in the reign of Henry I, the long centuries of Anglo-French dynastic wars, wars caused by questions of feudal obligation, by marriages and successions. Henry I and his little army of mercenaries, English, Flemish and Breton, were engaged in Normandy or in France during more than half of the twenty-nine remaining years which remained to the King after Tinchebray. The wars were small wars, the battles were trifling affairs which sometimes occupied scarcely 1,000 men on either side, but they were incessant. The wars, moreover, were kept alive by the existence of a serious rival to Henry and his own heir in the young William Clito, the legitimate son of Robert and the Duchess Sybil.

William Clito, whom we have seen briefly at Falaise when the castle was surrendered to Henry after the battle of Tinchebray in 1106, was then six years old. After Henry's return to England in the spring of 1107 he seems to have realized the danger of leaving a grandson of the Conqueror at liberty, the child, moreover, of the Conqueror's eldest son. He thereupon sent orders to the governor of Arques, Robert of Beauchamp, to seize the boy. The events which followed curiously recall an incident in the threatened childhood of the Conqueror himself. Robert of Beauchamp arrived at the castle of St. Saens in the absence of the boy's guardian Helias. The young William was asleep and the followers of Helias were at Mass. Someone, however, had the presence of mind to conceal the child on the arrival of the King's envoy and carry him secretly from the castle until he could be returned to the safe-keeping of Helias. This brave and faithful follower of the captive Duke Robert escaped with the boy to safety beyond the border of the King's territories. Helias spent the following ten years in wandering from castle to castle in France, Anjou and Flanders with his cherished ward.

When he reached adolescence William Clito became an instrument in furthering the policy of King Louis the Fat, Philip's successor, and of other rulers hostile to Henry of England. Fulk V, Count of Anjou, promised William his daughter Sybil in marriage, with the reversion of the County of Maine (which had come into his possession on the death of Count Helias, the brave adversary of William Rufus, in 1110), but the bare threat of so dangerous a union between two great houses excited the wrath of Henry. The other William, his own legal son by Matilda, was almost of the same age as his cousin and if he succeeded to the throne of England might suffer from the existence of a rival grandson of William the Conqueror. Henry therefore exerted all his efforts to prevent the marriage of the Clito with Sybil of Anjou. He bribed and threatened, and at last bethought himself of that useful weapon, the Church's ban on marriages within a certain degree of consanguinity.

William and Sybil were in fact related, although distantly, by blood. Both descended from Gonnor, the wife of Duke Richard I of Normandy, and the beautiful ancestress of so many Norman dukes, prelates and nobles. Henry sent two of his cleverest dialecticians to the Count of Anjou to dissuade him from so embarrassing a marriage for his daughter, and their arguments, backed by Henry's gold and the fear of Henry's power, were decisive. The house of Anjou refused to sanction the marriage and withdrew its support from William Clito. The young man, after failing to find aid in several other quarters, was finally welcomed in the court of his young kinsman Count Baldwin VII of Flanders, who gave him generous assistance and hospitality during the few remaining years of his rule.

The long series of French interventions in Normandy against Henry I in the interests of William Clito led in March 1113 to a direct challenge from Louis to Henry to settle their differences by the old rite of judicial combat. They did not fight in person but each was represented by a champion. The details of the encounter are obscure, but the result was unfavourable to Louis, who was forced to recognize Henry's suzerainty over Maine, Brittany and the lordship of Bellême. Another version of the incident says that Louis challenged Henry to combat in the middle of a narrow bridge, over a river, but that Henry refused the challenge. Three years later, in 1116, the French King reappeared in the field against Henry, having managed to secure the alliance of Clito's friend Baldwin of Flanders. At the head of a force of Flemings, Baldwin invaded Normandy and advanced as far as Arques, setting fire to the adjoining village of Talou under Henry's eyes. The King watched it burn without betraying resentment and contented himself with fortifying the neighbouring village of Burel. He placed as defenders in this stronghold not his Norman troops, in whom he had little trust, but his English subjects and his Breton mercenaries.

The young Count Baldwin met his death in this campaign. While challenging the Bretons to combat outside the walls of Burel in 1118 he was wounded by one of Henry's knights. He returned to the castle of Stephen of Aumale to be nursed of his wound by Count Stephen and his wife Hedwise. On the following night, it is primly related by a chronicler, he ate of meat insufficiently mature, drank sweet wine and slept with his mistress. As a result of these excesses his wound was dangerously inflamed and he died ten months later. Baldwin VII was succeeded as Count of Flanders by his cousin Charles the Good, who promptly made peace with Henry and his other neighbours.

During one of the French King's subsequent campaigns against Henry the exiled William Clito met his cousin William the Ætheling in the field, in circumstances which cast a vivid light on the battles of the age of chivalry. In 1119 King Henry was in his castle of Noyon on the river Andelle, a tributary of the Seine. With him was his son William and a small force of 900 English and Norman knights. After hearing Mass in the church of Noyon he set out in the brilliant sunshine of August in the direction of the town of Andely, now a part of Les Andelys, ignorant of the fact that King Louis the Fat had arrived in that town. There was often a rustic element in the wars of the Norman kings. Henry had seen the ripe corn standing in the fields around the village of Etrepagny, on the road to Rouen, and he now ordered his men to dismount, cut the corn and load it in sheaves on the backs of their horses to be transported to the castle of Lyons, which was, then and later, his favourite hunting seat in Normandy.

Four knights left as sentinels on the hill of Verclive then informed the King that they had seen a company of French knights in armour, riding behind their banners in the direction of Henry's headquarters at Noyon. King Louis was in fact attempting to take the castle of Noyon by surprise. In both camps some of the royal counsellors timorously advised their leaders to refrain from giving battle. But both Louis and Henry were bent on fighting. They met on a plain called Brémule. Henry had mustered 500 English knights in full armour, and they presented a brave spectacle in the Norman sunshine. Besides his heir William the Ætheling Henry was accompanied by two of his natural sons, Robert and Richard, and by three of his great barons, Henry of Eu, William of Warenne and Walter Giffard. Other nobles who fought with the English King and his sons were Roger FitzRichard and his cousin Walter of Aufay, William of Tancarville, William of Roumare and Nigel of Aubigny. The King's standard was borne by Edward of Salisbury, who from his name was probably of English origin.

On the side of Louis the Fat, a brave soldier in spite of his corpulence, were his protégé William Clito, whom he insisted on regarding as the rightful heir to Normandy, and with him some of the most famous warriors of France. They were Matthew, Count of Beaumont, Guy of Clermont, Osmond of Chaumont, William of Garlande, commander-in-chief of the French army, Peter of Maulle, Philip of Mowbray and Burchard of Montmorency. Among the Norman exiles who fought with the French were Balderic of Bray and William Crépin.

The French knights and their Norman allies advanced boldly into the plain of Brémule and struck the first blows against Henry. But their advance was disorderly. Henry had instructed his archers to spare the nobles but shoot at their horses. Many French knights had their horses killed under them and were soon surrounded and taken prisoner. Another wave of Frenchmen, led by Godfrey of Sérans, rode against Henry, and at one moment the weight and impetuosity of their charge shook the English line of battle. But eighty French knights did not return from the encounter, and King Louis readily yielded to arguments that the day was lost. Accompanied by Balderic he rode from the field of Brémule. He had evaded a direct encounter with Henry of England as, in another Norman battle, William the Conqueror had evaded a personal combat with his liege-lord Henry of France. But the French King's ally William Crépin, who commanded the Norman contingent, is said to have nourished a violent hatred against Henry. He rode directly at the King, who as he had done at Tinchebray was fighting on foot with his English soldiers.

William Crépin struck the King on the head with a blow of his sword which only the King's helmet prevented from being mortal. William was then attacked by Roger FitzRichard, who unhorsed him and held him at his mercy. Standing over his prisoner he then had to defend the fallen man from the King's friends, who would have killed the aggressor. In the age of chivalry Kings wore their crowns into battle, and it was considered an unheard-of crime to do violence against a head crowned and anointed. Except for this incident the whole battle of 900 knights and several hundred foot-soldiers ended almost amicably, with the deaths of but three knights. The aim of the mounted men on each side seemed to be to capture an enemy and hold him to ransom, rather than destroy a source of revenue.

Meanwhile Louis of France, tall, pale and stout, wandered mournfully alone through the forest which separated the battlefield of Brémule from his headquarters at Andely. He seems to have left his companion Balderic on the road. The French King would also have been lost in the dense forest if he had not met with a Norman peasant and induced him, by the promise of a reward, to lead him by the shortest path to Andely. There the King's guards sallied out to greet him, and the peasant, only then realizing the identity of his charge, cursed the ill-chance which had caused him to fail to recognize, and take prisoner, so valuable a prize.

The battle of Brémule, fought in August 1119, is interesting for its display of courtesy on the part of the victors. Henry had purchased for twenty silver marks the standard of King Louis from the soldier who captured it. He kept the flag as a trophy. But the horse of Louis the Fat, with its magnificent trappings, he sent back to the French King on the day after the battle. Henry's heir, William the Ætheling, not to be outdone in generosity by his father, equally returned to his cousin William Clito the palfrey he had lost on the field. And on the counsel of his father he also made to his cousin a number of gifts 'necessary to an exile'.

Faithful to his habitual policy of conciliating his enemies by bribes or by magnanimity, Henry freely pardoned some of his prisoners, including Hervieu of Gisors and Burchard of Montmorency, on the ground that they owed allegiance to both kings and could not keep faith with both if their lords quarrelled. Guy of Clermont, who was also taken prisoner, died in captivity at Rouen. Osmond of Chaumont, a lawless baron who had personally protected the highway robbers and brigands in his territory, was kept in chains in the castle of Arques. Only one follower of Henry was captured by the French. He was the young Robert of Courcy, who had imprudently pursued the fleeing French knights into the town of Andely.

Soon after his ignominious defeat at Brémule, Louis the Fat made fresh efforts to further the cause of his protégé William Clito. They met with varying success. Finally he decided to attempt to gain by the arbitration of the Pope what he had failed to achieve by arms. A Papal Council was held at Reims in October 1119, and Louis appeared before it in person to plead for Clito. Pope Calixtus II, who before his elevation to the Papacy was Guy, Archbishop of Vienne, presided over the Council. He was a second cousin of King Henry. Both were descended from the famous Gonnor, wife of Richard I of Normandy, and he is said by Orderic Vital to have recognized his kinship to the English King in the course of a discreet speech in praise of Henry. The English bishops had been given permission to attend the Council, but Henry told them bluntly that he would not tolerate any intervention by the Pope in English affairs.

When the Council opened King Louis entered the cathedral of Reims followed by William Clito and the principal lords of France. He is said to have pleaded eloquently against Henry, accusing him of having invaded Normandy, a vassal of the French King, taken his brother Robert prisoner, and despoiled and banished Robert's heir, William Clito. Louis the Fat also protested against the imprisonment of Robert of Bellême, who seven years earlier had been sent by Louis on an embassy to Henry, and had been promptly seized by the English King and thrust into prison. (Robert of Bellême had fallen into Henry's hands in 1112, and was imprisoned for life. Presuming unwisely on his own great prestige and on his immunity as an ambassador of the French King, he had boldly appeared at Henry's court in Normandy and had been arrested. He was first confined at Cherbourg, and then at Wareham, where Duke Robert of Normandy may then have been also confined. Robert of Bellême was still living in 1130, when the sheriff of Dorset accounted for his food and clothing. It is not known whether he survived Henry I.)

Another complaint made against Henry at the Council of Reims was that he had instigated Count Theobald of Chartres, a vassal of Louis, to rebel against his overlord. And a host of other grievances, real or pretended, were alleged against Henry.

A Norman archbishop, Godfrey of Rouen, rose to defend Henry, but his speech was drowned in the outcry raised by Henry's adversaries. A convenient diversion was caused by the dramatic intervention of Hildegarde, Countess of Poitiers, who appeared before the Pope to complain in a loud and sonorous voice of having been abandoned by her husband. The Count of Poitiers had in fact deserted her to join Malberga, wife of the Viscount of Chatellerault. This tale of adultery captured the attention of the cardinals and bishops and the woes of Louis the Fat were temporarily forgotten. Finally the Pope promised to use his influence with King Henry. The Council was adjourned to permit of a meeting of reconciliation between Calixtus II and his arch-adversary the Emperor, which did not however take place. In the following month of November the Pope met his cousin Henry of England at the castle of Gisors, and informed him of the judgment of the Council of Reims. The Council had empowered Calixtus to request his cousin to set Robert of Normandy free and to restore to him and his son William Clito the duchy of Normandy.

Henry was well prepared for this request, and he had no difficulty in representing to the Pope the state of anarchy which existed in the Norman duchy under the rule or non-rule of his brother Robert. He also spoke of the depredations committed by Robert of Bellême and other barons against the abbeys and churches of the duchy, and the invitation which he had received from barons and prelates alike to restore good government in Normandy. He had taken Bayeux from Gunhier of Aunai, and Caen from Engerrand FitzIlbert. He had made war against the brigands and the perturbers of the public peace. He had invited William Clito to his own court and had even offered him three counties in England, but the son of Duke Robert chose to live in exile.

The Pope then readily agreed to listen no more to the grievances of Robert of Normandy and his son. But he now raised the question of King Louis, who complained that Henry had broken the treaty between them and had done great damage to Louis and his kingdom. To this Henry retorted that Louis had been the first to violate the treaty. He had instigated Henry's vassals to revolt against him. But if Louis would keep faith in the future, Henry was willing to hearken to the Pope's counsels. He was also willing to reconcile his nephew Theobald of Chartres with

Louis, and he renewed his offer of hospitality to William Clito. The other William, Henry's son the Ætheling, would do homage to Louis for Normandy as Henry's successor. With this gesture of friendship from Henry, Louis the Fat had perforce to be content for the time being. But Destiny had other intentions for William the Ætheling.

Robertus Dux Normannorum Partum Prosternit: Robert Curthose is seen un-horsing a pagan warrior in the great battle of the Franks against the Egyptian emir Malik el-Afdhal near Ascalon. This medallion, reproduced from Bernard de Montfaucon's *Les Monumens de la monarchie françoise* (Paris: 1729–33), is eighth in a series of ten dealing with the First Crusade in a stained-glass window at Saint-Denis, executed at the order of Abbot Suger and dating from *c.* 1144, when the church was dedicated. Most of the medallions, including this one, were destroyed during the French Revolution

Mont St. Michel, where Henry was besieged by Robert and William, and where Robert gave thanks for his safe return from Crusade

The Rufus Stone in the New Forest: 'Here stood the oak tree on which an arrow shot by Sir Walter Tyrell at a stag glanced and struck King William the Second, surnamed Rufus, on the breast, of which he instantly died on the second day of August anno 1100'

Fiona Wilkie

The Reredos and Rufus Tomb, Winchester Cathedral

Probably made in 1280, this effigy of Robert of Normandy was broken in pieces during the Cromwellian wars, but was repaired and returned to Gloucester Cathedral after the Restoration. It rests on a wood chest of the late fourteenth or early fifteenth centuries

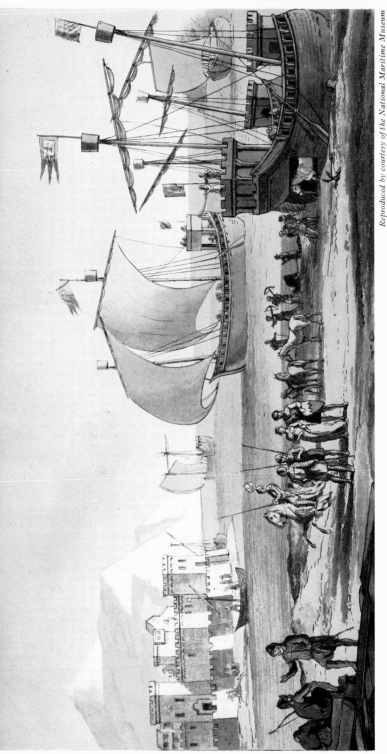

Shipping of the time of Henry I: an aquatint by Atkinson after C. H. Smith

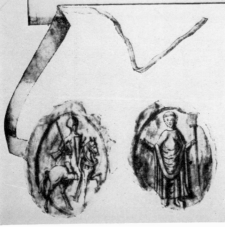

Reproduced by courtesy of the Clarendon Press from Sir Christopher Hatton's
'Book of Seals', ed. L. C. Loyd and D. M. Stenton, 1950

Notification by Odo, Bishop of Bayeux and Earl of Kent, that he has given land to Christchurch Canterbury in exchange for that which he has enclosed in his park of Wickambreux. The original is in the Cottonian Collection at the British Museum and measures $8\frac{1}{12} \times 5\frac{1}{2}$ in. left-hand side, $\times 4\frac{1}{2}$ in. right-hand side. Badly damaged by fire, it now lacks the red oval seal (*c.* $3 \times 2\frac{1}{2}$ in.), which showed on the obverse the Bishop on horseback, armed with sword and kite-shaped shield, and on the reverse standing, tonsured and holding a fan-shaped crozier

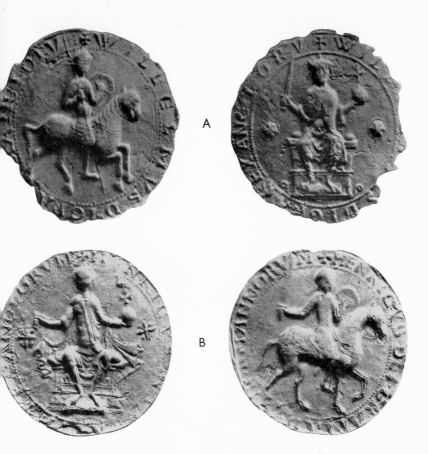

A

B

(*a*) First Seal of William II (diam. 3·25 in.). Seated on his throne, the King wears a crown of five points on which are crosses or trefoils, and from which hang two chin-straps. The straps, used for keeping the crown steady, appear in this seal for the first time, but appear on subsequent seals down to the First Seal of Henry II. The sword in his right hand has a deep central groove, and in his left he holds an orb from which proceeds a cross *pattée pommettée*. He wears an undercoat, with tight sleeves and skirts reaching below the knee, over which is a mantle, or cloak, fastened in front of the throat. Legend: ✠ WILLELMVS D-I GRA REX ANGLORV. On the reverse, the King gallops to the right, wearing a hauberk of mail and conical helmet; in his right hand is a lance with three streamers and in his left a kite-shaped shield. Legend: as on obverse

(*b*) Fourth Seal of Henry I (diam. 3·25 in.). The King enthroned, holding in his right hand a sword, very deeply grooved, and in the left an orb on which is a small cross surmounted by a dove. Legend: ✠ HENRICVS DEI GRACIA REX ANGLORVM. On the reverse, the King on horseback, pacing to the right, and clad in a hauberk of chain mail formed of large rings. In his right hand is a sword and in the left a kite-shaped shield. Legend: ✠ HENRICVS DEI GRATIA DVX NORMANNORVM

This Fourth Seal was adopted after the battle of Tinchebray in 1106, when Henry I took Robert prisoner and assumed the title of Duke of Normandy. The title DVX NORMANNORVM had not been borne by William Rufus, nor by Henry I previous to 1106

Second Seal of Stephen (diam. 3·6 in.). The King enthroned, a sword in his right hand and an orb ensigned with a cross and dove in the left. Legend: ✠ STEPHANVS DEI GRATIA REX ANGLORVM. On the reverse, he is on horseback, pacing to the right, and holding in his right hand a lance with a banner, terminated by two/four long streamers. The ties of the casque at the back of the head appear combined in a sort of queue. Legend: ✠ STEPHANVS DEI GRATIA DVX NORMANNORVM. This seal is a reminder that Stephen's reign was broken into two periods. His First Seal was probably lost or destroyed, or fell into the hands of the enemy, after his defeat at Lincoln in 1141, and it became necessary to alter the type after his restoration. The Second gives much longer and narrower proportions to the King's figure, is much larger, and of even ruder workmanship

Seal of Matilda (diam. 2·5 in.). The Queen is seated, wearing a crown of three points, trefoiled, and clothed in a long garment, the sleeves of which approach in shape to the heraldic maunch. In her right hand she holds a long sceptre topped by a fleur-de-lis. Legend: ✠ MATHILDIS DEI GRATIA / ROMANORVM REGINA. Much smaller than the Seals of other English sovereigns, it resembles those of German sovereigns of the period, and, like them, it has no design on the reverse. The legend recalls that she was Queen or Empress of the Holy Roman Empire by virtue of her marriage with Henry V, and that the troubled nature of her reign gave her no leisure to prepare a new Seal for use as Queen of England

XIII

THE WHITE SHIP

IN NOVEMBER 1120 Henry I reigned unchallenged over both England and Normandy. His son William the Ætheling, now seventeen years old, had been accepted as their future Duke by the temporarily docile barons. Louis the Fat had not attempted to renew his not very dangerous interventions in favour of William Clito. The French King's alliances had broken down to Henry's advantage. In Flanders a hostile Count Baldwin had been replaced by the friendly Count Charles the Good. And in Anjou the once-hostile Count Fulk V had married one of his daughters to William the Ætheling. Then, having mortgaged his lands and, possibly with financial aid from Henry in return for which he left Maine under Henry's overlordship, he had set out for Jerusalem, of which he was one day to become King. Henry's Queen Matilda, the English Edith who had taken refuge in Romsey abbey from the Norman invaders, had died in 1118, leaving no record of her tranquil life other than the reputation of having often interceded for her countrymen after her public vindication by Archbishop Anselm.

Two years after Matilda's death, another and far more serious blow fell on the King. For reasons of policy or of personal pleasure, or probably of both, Henry spent longer and longer periods in Normandy. England was peaceful. The most restive of his barons had been brought to heel, or thrown into prison. The lord of misrule himself, Robert of Bellême, had been held captive since 1112, and according to one account held in chains. At the end of 1120 Henry had spent four years in Normandy. And now the King and his sons, followed by the flower of the young Anglo-Norman nobility, were about to return to England.

The tale which follows is one almost of Biblical simplicity. On a day in November the King ordered his fleet to assemble in the port of Barfleur. On the eve of his departure a shipmaster named Thomas, the son of

Stephen, came to him and begged him to sail in his new vessel, which he had christened the *White Ship*. Thomas told the King, showing him a mark of gold, probably an inherited trophy of the invasion of England, that his father Stephen had piloted William the Conqueror's ship *Mora* on the memorable voyage from Dives and St. Valéry to Pevensey beach fifty-four years earlier. He asked for the honour of conveying the Conqueror's son to England.

The King replied that he had already chosen his own ship, but that he would confide to Thomas and his skill in seamanship his sons William and Richard, and his daughter Matilda, together with a number of his nobles. The shipmaster went away rejoicing and made ready to sail. The crew of the *White Ship* asked for wine to celebrate the joyous occasion, and William the Ætheling, flattered by the sailors' enthusiasm, ordered three casks to be broached. The sailors drank so heartily that they were soon in a state more zealous than proficient.

The *White Ship* was a large vessel for those days. Fifty men sat on its rowing benches besides the sailors who handled the sails and rudder. But now 300 passengers crowded on board, and with them were the King's treasure in gold and silver, the casks of wine and the provisions taken for the voyage. The ship was now seriously overladen. Nevertheless it was not this fact that was responsible for the disaster which followed. The sailors and their passengers, most of them young and over-confident Normans, the sons of the great barons, were flushed with wine.

William the Ætheling was barely seventeen years old and his brother Richard was even younger. They rejected with jeers and mocking cries the priests who came with holy water to bless the ship before she sailed. Some more elderly members of the King's court, disquieted by the general atmosphere of gaiety and wild enthusiasm on board, or in some cases taken ill by their excess in drinking, had abandoned the *White Ship* before she left the quayside. Among these were Edward of Salisbury, the King's English standard-bearer, Stephen, Count of Mortain, William of Roumare, a chamberlain called Babel and two knights.

The King in his own vessel had already left the harbour of Barfleur when the *White Ship* put out to sea on the evening of 25 November 1120. A fair wind blew from the south. The night was calm but cold. Thomas FitzStephen, the master of the ship, doubtless at the command of the young Ætheling, ordered his rowers to strain at their oars. He hoped to catch up with, and perhaps overtake, the King's ship, which had reached the entrance to the harbour. The sailors, flushed and excited by the wine they had drunk and the gaiety of the Ætheling and his companions, pulled vigorously at the oars. A following wind filled the sail. The tide was high. And then suddenly the *White Ship*, badly steered, or not answering her rudder, struck a concealed rock. Two planks were stove in, and the vessel filled and sank immediately.

The men on the King's ship heard cries, but did not realize their significance until the following day, when news of the disaster followed them to England. Of the more than 300 men and women on board the *White Ship* all save three were drowned when the vessel foundered. Two men, a butcher of Rouen named Bérold, and a youth of noble birth, Godfrey, the son of Gilbert of L'Aigle, clung to the mast and sail, which rose above the water for a time. The shipmaster Thomas, who could swim, came to the surface and saw the two survivors clinging to the mast. 'Where is the King's son?' he asked. The two men on the mast told him that he was drowned, together with all the others on board.

Thomas, the son of Stephen, is said then to have cried out: 'I dare not live to face the King!' Then he plunged beneath the waves and died.

Of the two survivors the young noble Godfrey, delicately clad, perished of the cold during the night. The butcher of Rouen, Bérold, owed his life to his rough sheepskin coat. He alone lived to tell the tale of the disaster.

The next morning the outgoing tide uncovered the fatal rocks and revealed the foundered *White Ship*. The fishermen of Barfleur dragged the wreck ashore and recovered the King's treasure intact. Some of the bodies of the drowned were swept ashore one by one on the new tide, but many were never found.

Three children of the King had perished in the wreck: his sons William and Richard, and his illegitimate daughter Matilda, the wife of Rotrou, Count of Mortagne. Fourteen other women of gentle birth were among the drowned. Among the dead nobles were the young Richard, Earl of Chester, and his wife, his brother Otver, the Ætheling's tutor, who seized the Prince in his arms and jumped into the sea with him. Thierry, the nephew of the Emperor, also perished in the fatal ship, and with him William Bigod, William of Pirou, the King's seneschal, Godfrey Ridel and Hugh of Moulins, Robert Mauconduit and the King's secretary, Gisulfe.

Henry's other personal virtues seem to have been few, but with the single exception of his natural daughter Juliana, he was undoubtedly a fond parent. None at first dared approach him with the news of the disaster. At last a child was deputed to deliver the sad message. Henry was prostrated by the calamity. The loss of the *White Ship* had not only bereaved him in his dearest affections. It spelled also the doom of his dynastic ambitions. The direct male line of the Conqueror ended with the death of the young Ætheling William. If the Ætheling had survived the course of English history might have changed. He was said to have treated his father's English subjects arrogantly, and the national unity gradually established by Henry I might not have endured under his son. Meanwhile the death of William created complications with Henry's capricious neighbour the ruler of Anjou.

The Ætheling had recently been married to his distant cousin Matilda, the eldest daughter of Fulk V of Anjou. But the bride was only twelve years old at the time and it is unlikely that the union was consummated. The King, as was the custom of the day, returned the girl-widow to her father's court and afterwards she entered a convent. But Henry did not follow contemporary custom to the point of returning the bride's dowry. When Fulk V returned in 1122 from the Holy Land, he thus had natural grounds of resentment against Henry, and their political alliance by marriage having collapsed, Fulk returned to his old policy of intrigue in the interests of William Clito.

Having failed with one of his daughters through no fault of his own or of hers, Fulk tempted fortune with the gift of his second daughter Sybil. He affianced her to the dead Ætheling's cousin William Clito, and settled on him the county of Maine, which had been in his possession since the death of Count Helias. It was now that Henry made his intervention, already mentioned in a previous chapter, to stop the marriage of the Clito. By his influence over his cousin Pope Calixtus II, who valued his friendship as a counterpoise to the enmity of the Emperor, he succeeded in having the marriage between the Clito and Sybil of Anjou annulled on the ground of consanguinity—that old canonical weapon of Papal diplomacy which had been wielded unsuccessfully against William the Conqueror and Matilda of Flanders. Thus the Clito was at once deprived of his bride and of the county of Maine, which might have served him as a stage towards the reconquest of his father's duchy of Normandy.

Until the disaster of the *White Ship* Henry I had not been tempted to indulge in a second marriage. His first wife had died two years before the wreck at Barfleur, and while the Ætheling lived the King saw no reason to assure himself of a second legitimate male child. His two legal children, his many mistresses and his large brood of illegitimate offspring gave him sufficient occupation for his genuine family sentiments. But the loss of the

Ætheling drove him hastily to contract a second marriage in the hope of
begetting a legitimate successor.

Two months after the foundering of the *White Ship* Henry married
again. His new wife was a German, Adelisa of Lorraine, the daughter of
Duke Godfrey of Louvain, a great vassal of the Emperor. Henry had
already sought to find in a German alliance a check to the mounting ambitions of the French kings, too narrowly confined for their comfort in
the meagre territories of the Île de France. He also wished to defend himself against the hostility of the Counts of Flanders, who were inter-
mittently hostile to the English, despite the interests of the wool trade,
which eventually drove them to an uncertain alliance with the King. In
1109 Henry affianced his infant daughter Matilda to the young Emperor
Henry V. The effect of this gesture on Flemish policy was not long
delayed. The Flemings renewed in 1110 their treaty of friendship of 1101,
which had been allowed to lapse. Nevertheless, a year later Count Robert
of Flanders joined King Louis the Fat in an attack on Henry and paid for
it with his life. He was thrown from his horse on the bridge of Meaux and
killed.

When the marriage of the Emperor and Matilda, five years after their
betrothal, was celebrated at Mainz on 7 January 1114, the bride was
accompanied by a host of Norman courtiers, avid of honours and gifts.
But the Emperor's ministers, recalling perhaps a similar invasion of
Normans in the train of Edward the Confessor, and its historic consequences, pointedly invited the guests to return to their own land after the
marriage. The Norman courtiers obeyed, but the German escort of
Adeliza of Lorraine remained in the adopted country of their princess,
and some of them obtained rich rewards. Her chancellor Godfrey received
from King Henry the bishopric of Bath, and the bride's half-brother
Jocelyn of Louvain was given the great baronial honour of Petworth.

During the years which followed the marriage of Matilda and the
Emperor, relations between England and Germany grew steadily closer.
In 1117 Ralph, the successor of Anselm as Archbishop of Canterbury,
spent a week with the Emperor in his camp outside Rome. And we have
already remarked the presence among the notable personages drowned off
Barfleur of the Emperor's nephew Thierry, who has been identified as
the son of Henry V's sister Agnes and Frederick of Swabia.

All these circumstances suggest that except for their different policies
towards the Pope an alliance based on common interest was gradually
maturing between the Emperor of the Germans and the King of England.
Their friendly relations even resulted in the summer of 1124 in a plan to

make a joint attack on Louis VI. An imperial army was mustered and marched against France as far as Metz, but there the news reached the Emperor that King Louis was waiting to receive him at Reims with a superior force. Moreover, behind his back the burghers of Worms were in open revolt against him. The Emperor prudently retired and the planned joint campaign against Louis the Fat came to nothing. But it succeeded in diverting French attention from Normandy.

A few months earlier Henry's followers had inflicted a severe reverse on the supporters of William Clito in a brief but sanguinary skirmish at Bourgthéroulde, near Rouen, and the revolt against Henry was for a time checked. In his court at Rouen King Henry sat in judgment on the rebels captured in the battle. He sentenced Waléran of Meulan, the insurgent son of the King's friend and counsellor Count Robert of Meulan, to a long term of imprisonment. Hugh of Montfort was similarly punished. Two other barons who had broken their oath of fealty were condemned to lose their eyes. One of the most interesting among the accused was a poet, Luke of La Barre, who had never sworn allegiance to the King and in theory should have escaped severe punishment. But he had composed and circulated a number of indecent verses cruelly satirizing Henry, and the King's wrath had been aroused against the author. Henry's ally, the good Count Charles of Flanders, soon to die assassinated like his father, while he knelt at Mass, was by chance at Rouen during the trial, and he pleaded for mercy for the poet. But he pleaded in vain, and is even said to have allowed himself to be convinced by the arguments of the King or his ministers. Luke of La Barre, when he heard of his condemnation to be blinded, dashed out his brains against the walls of his prison.

To the end of his brief career William Clito continued to be a central figure in Henry's political and diplomatic struggle with the French King. Louis the Fat was anything but lacking in courage or in persistency, in spite of the corpulence which might have induced him to display the lethargy of his father Philip I. He was an able and ultimately a successful administrator. He had gradually extended his authority over his own vassals in France. He was now bent on weakening Henry's power in Normandy by any and every means available to him. In 1127 he gave to William Clito in marriage his sister-in-law Jeanne, the half-sister of Queen Adelaide of France. At the same time he made the Clito his effective vassal (the young man had presumably already sworn allegiance for the duchy of Normandy, which he did not possess) by giving him the French Vexin, the long-disputed region on the Norman border which had been the indirect cause of the death of William the Conqueror. The three great strongholds of Mantes, Chaumont and Pontoise accompanied the gift.

Louis was intelligent enough to realize that the installation of the Clito in this powerful fief on the confines of Henry's Norman duchy would inevitably force the English King to open a new and definite campaign against him. But an unforeseen event now placed a greater territory, if only briefly, in the hands of the Clito. This event, as already mentioned, was the murder of Charles the Good, Count of Flanders.

Charles was a descendant of the great King Cnut. He had refused the Imperial crown on the death of Henry V, and equally the crown of Jerusalem on the capture of King Baldwin II. On 1 March 1127, like another Cnut of Denmark, he and his followers were set upon and killed by Bouchard of Lille and thirty-two of his knights, as the victims knelt at Mass in Bruges. Charles left no direct heirs, and a multitude of pretenders claimed the succession. Henry I of England, as the grandson of Baldwin V of Flanders, through his mother Matilda, was among the claimants. But Louis the Fat, as sovereign lord of Flanders, moved swiftly for a man of his weight. He arrived in Flanders with William Clito and a small force of knights. He laid siege to the castle of Bruges in which the murderers of Charles the Good had taken refuge, and when the garrison surrendered, he hurled the assassins from the battlements of the castle to their death. Then he named William Clito, the great-grandson of Baldwin V, as legitimate Count of Flanders.

A number of Flemish nobles supported the Clito, and he reigned for thirteen months. He showed an unexpected vigour for the son of Robert Curthose. Although he conducted an inconclusive expedition against King Henry's vassal and successor Stephen of Blois, Count of Boulogne, he condemned to death 111 of the conspirators against his predecessor Charles the Good. The rest of the Clito's brief career as a ruler was as tumultuous as his earlier life. The kinsmen of the executed conspirators retaliated by raising another revolt against the new ruler. They called to their aid Thierry, Count of Alsace, who had already claimed the county of Flanders on the death of Charles. The Clito was surrounded by intrigues, fresh conspiracies and threats to murder him. One night at Ypres, while he visited a young mistress, his life was in immediate danger. Four separate groups of his enemies had laid an ambush for him. The rest of the tale is touching in its simplicity. The Clito's young mistress was aware of the conspiracy. She was in the habit, when he visited her, of washing his long hair, and while doing so she began to weep. When her lover demanded an explanation of her tears she confessed the plot against his life. The

Clito jumped to his feet, seized his arms and without waiting to comb his long locks, took the girl to the castle of his friend and companion-in-arms William of Poitiers. He begged William to find an honourable marriage for the girl, as if she were his own sister, and this duty his friend promised and performed. Then the young Clito went out to fight his way through the ambush laid for him.

The end of William Clito came in July 1128, during the siege of Alost. William was an intrepid leader, and was often reproached by his friends for exposing his life recklessly among his soldiers. One day as he was engaged in rallying a company which had turned to flee before the insurgents, William seized the head of a lance held by one of the fugitives. The point of the weapon pierced his hand between the index finger and the thumb. The wound became septic and he died five days later. His friend and guardian, the heroic Helias of St. Saens who had saved him as a child from his uncle Henry I, and who had since then remained his inseparable companion, temporarily concealed the Clito's death from his Flemish subjects. When the commander of the castle of Alost sued for peace, Helias conducted him to the dead ruler's tent. There he showed him the corpse of the young Count and said to him sternly: 'Behold what you have done. You have killed your master.' The insurgent commander is said to have burst into tears. Helias then ordered him to arm his knights and to conduct the dead man in solemn state to the abbey of St. Bertin, where he was buried next to the tomb of one of his predecessors, Count Robert the Frisian.

News of the Clito's death was brought to King Henry by his cousin Jean, a natural son of the famous Odo, Bishop of Bayeux. Jean carried with him a number of sealed letters from the dying Clito in which the young man begged the King's forgiveness for the harm he had done him and asked him to pardon the companions of his lost cause who had followed him into exile. Henry was always eager to conciliate his adversaries, and he readily consented to receive into his favour those of the Clito's Norman supporters who wished to return to England or to Normandy. Others, disconsolate at the death of their leader, or doubtful of the King's sincerity, took the Cross and left for the Holy Land.

William Clito died in the twenty-eighth year of his uncle's reign over England. Courageous, gallant and generous, he showed many of the qualities of his father Robert Curthose, and some of his characteristic weaknesses, notably that of instability. His death became naturally the subject of myth and conjecture. His father, then confined in the castle of Devizes, was said to have seen in a dream a lance which struck him in the right arm, and to have cried out on awakening: 'Alas, my son is dead,' although the news of the Clito's death had not then reached England. Six years later Robert was himself to die.

Flanders passed at William Clito's death into the hands of his adversary Count Thierry of Alsace. The new ruler, on the death of his own wife, was induced by Henry of England to marry the widow of his dead rival, Sybil of Anjou. Thus the Clito, in dying, succeeded in reconciling his Uncle Henry not only to the followers of Robert Curthose but also to his Flemish neighbours, and even, for a time at least, to his old adversary Louis the Fat.

XIV

HENRY THE STATESMAN

THE long reign of Henry Beauclerc brought order and peace to England after the disorders of the reign of William Rufus. There is no doubt of his competence as a ruler. Men saw for the first time the Normans and the English living together as one nation, both firmly governed by a rigorous but on the whole impartial hand. Yet in spite of his English birth, his Anglo-Scottish wife ('Cedric and Godiva' sneered the Norman barons at his marriage with Edith), and his many English mistresses, he did not love the English, as may be seen from the comment of the Englishman Eadmer, the friend and biographer of Anselm. But he could flatter them when it suited him, and the English, at least at Tinchebray and in his early wars, composed the bulk of his armies.

Henry has been charged, and rightly, with personal cruelty. His reputed blinding of his rebellious cousin William of Mortain, taken prisoner at Tinchebray, the long confinement in prison of his brother Robert Curthose, and, worst of all, his treatment of his grandchildren, the two daughters of his natural daughter Juliana, are doubtless responsible for the accusation. One of the most appalling tales of cruelty, attributed directly or indirectly to Henry, concerns an incident in the disorders in Normandy during 1119. The King had married Juliana to Eustace of Breteuil, a great Norman baron who possessed several castles in the valleys of the Eure and the Andelle. He claimed the return of another of his strongholds, the tower of Ivry, which the King had granted to a knight called Ralph Harenc. To ensure peace between the baron and the knight, Henry had given to Eustace the son of Ralph Harenc as a hostage, and Eustace had given in exchange his two daughters by Juliana. But on the persuasion of his friend and familiar demon Amauri of Montfort, Eustace clamoured for the return of the tower of Ivry.

When this was refused him, he ordered the blinding of his hostage and sent the son's eyes to his father.

This revolting act was followed by an even more revolting reprisal. Ralph Harenc, with the King's consent, avenged his son by putting out the eyes and cutting off the tips of the noses of the two daughters of Eustace and Juliana. Eustace then broke out into open revolt against the King. He fortified his castles at Lire, at Glos, at Pont St. Pierre and at Pacy, and sent his wife Juliana a body of knights to defend his great castle at Breteuil. But the burghers of the town were not anxious to incur the King's wrath, and they opened their gates to the royal troops. Henry entered the town and found his daughter barricaded in the fortress, to which he immediately laid siege. Juliana is said to have sent her father a message asking for a meeting, and when he appeared at the rendezvous, to have hurled a javelin at him. But she missed her mark, and Henry, incensed at this filial treachery, ordered the drawbridge of the castle to be destroyed.

Juliana was now alone in her tower, surrounded on all sides by a deep moat. It was the third week in February, and the moat was flooded by that month's heavy rains. The King declared that no hand should release Juliana from the tower and that if she wished to escape she should climb down from the battlements. Henry's army of mercenaries then had the strange *divertissement* of seeing the King's daughter, half-nude and clad only in a shift, slide down the walls of the tower, and plunge trembling and half-frozen into the icy moat. Juliana was then permitted by Henry to rejoin her husband Eustace of Breteuil, who continued to hold out against the King in his castle at Pacy. In the grim comedy of her disgrace the twin tales of horror which preceded it were almost forgotten.

If Henry was capable of occasional acts of cruelty, his policy as a ruler was on the whole humane. He had, nevertheless, revoked the Conqueror's decree prohibiting capital punishment, and he had restored the death penalty for thieves and highway robbers of every class. For other offenders he maintained the lesser punishment, as it was then considered, of blinding and the mutilation of limbs. Sometimes the innocent suffered with the guilty, as in the case of the punishments inflicted by the Justiciar Ralph Basset in the year 1124. Forty-four thieves or reputed thieves were then hanged, and six others blinded or otherwise mutilated. Some of them, according to a chronicler, were generally believed to be innocent.

Mutilation was also the punishment of the false moneyers, and twice during Henry's reign, with the full approval of the mild Archbishop Anselm, the King's hand fell heavily on the minters of base coin, against whom their victims complained loudly. Another measure taken by Henry met with the approval of the people as well as that of Anselm. This was the stern justice meted out by the King against his immediate followers, and even against high officials of his court, who were found guilty of theft or abuse of power.

In spite of his enforcement of the forest laws of Edward the Confessor, confirmed and strengthened by William the Conqueror and his son Rufus, Henry escaped the curse associated by popular resentment and superstition with the New Forest. He had notably profited by the last of the mysterious deaths to occur in the Forest, and during his own reign the fatal chain seemed to have been broken. The Anglo-Saxon Chronicler even eulogises Henry's reign inside and outside the forest in the words 'Peace he made for man and deer.' But he maintained the *lawing*, or mutilation by the cutting off of three claws of the right fore-paw, of all dogs kept in the vicinity of a royal forest.

Henry's decree that all hunting in the royal forests of his kingdom was reserved to himself was doubtless more keenly resented by his barons than by the disinherited mass of his subjects. The great Blackstone even commended the forest laws of the Norman kings in preference to the Game Laws which succeeded them in later centuries. 'The Forest Laws,' he wrote wittily in his *Commentaries*, 'established only one mighty hunter throughout the land. The Game Laws have raised a little Nimrod in every manor.'

The greatest achievement of Henry I was no doubt his silent welding together of Normans and Englishmen. The chroniclers of his French wars no longer refer to Normans and English in the armies which fought the French Kings, but generally use the word 'English' even when the quarrel is one involving Henry as Duke of Normandy and the King of France. If only temporarily he broke the power of the great barons in England, and with more difficulty that of the barons in Normandy. By ennobling many men of inferior social position he created a class of judges and administrators in opposition to the hereditary aristocracy of the descendants of Rolf. It is even possible to see, in his selection of Count Robert of Meulan for the greatest post of authority in the realm, the desire to take the government of England out of the hands of the Normans whose fathers had served the Conqueror and occasionally rebelled against him. Robert of Meulan was not strictly a Norman. He was born in the French Vexin and was a vassal of King Louis the Fat until he transferred his allegiance to Henry. Among the other men chosen by the King to serve him several others were not Normans. It is probable too that Henry's use of English, Flemish and Breton mercenaries both at Tinchebray and later, was determined by his desire to play off other national groups against the monopoly of power hitherto enjoyed by the Normans.

Unlike his brothers Robert and Rufus, both impulsive and unreflecting in their respective characteristics of lazy generosity or of unbridled passions, Henry was slow, deliberate and calculating. But when his life or his immediate interests were in danger he could move with feline stealth and rapidity. He normally measured his actions according to a pattern planned in advance. He had a prodigious memory. He supplemented it by a prodigious intelligence service. As we have already seen his agents spent a whole year in collecting proofs and testimony for the charges of conspiracy brought by Henry against the powerful and treacherous Robert of Bellême. The chronology of the campaigns in Normandy suggests that Henry reflected long before attacking his brother Robert at Tinchebray and taking possession of his duchy. His capture and imprisonment of Robert constituted, by feudal as well as by chivalrous standards, a grave offence against the political ethics of the day. It directly provoked the long hostility of the French King, and under a less partial or less harassed Pope than Henry's kinsman Calixtus II it might have brought the Papal anathema on Henry's head and the Papal interdict on England.

Profiting perhaps by the example of his father, the Conqueror, before the invasion of England, Henry took care to involve the plight of the churches in the country to be conquered as his justification for invading it. Before he proceeded on the ultimate campaign to bring Normandy under his rule, Henry had received, or had solicited, the support of the Norman bishops. They appealed to him to intervene in their interest against the brigandage of the quarrelling barons and the supineness of the reigning Duke Robert. In the end Henry had succeeded in convincing the Pope of the justice of his cause, in the teeth of the opposition of the Council of Reims and in spite of the fact that his representative, the Archbishop of Rouen, had been literally shouted down by the other dignitaries present.

This notable diplomatic success, followed as it was by the elimination of William Clito as a serious rival to Henry in Normandy, is evidence of the great subtlety and patience shown by Henry in his relations with other states. In the art of government he was infinitely superior to his brothers Robert and Rufus. Robert never succeeded in becoming more than a gallant and unfortunate soldier of fortune, a knight in adversity, and at the last in captivity. Rufus was a good soldier, perverse but chivalrous, with no dignity or constancy as a King, completely indifferent to the welfare of the people he misgoverned. Henry alone of the three brothers was more statesman than soldier, more King than warrior. Like his father William the Conqueror he realized that the foundation of good government was good law and he strove to secure it.

It is also characteristic of his intelligence as a ruler that he knew how to select and train in his service the most able mind of the day. His great Chancellor, Roger of Salisbury, who for many years controlled the administration of the country, was a humble priest of Avranches whom he brought to England and covered with honours. It is said that one day before his accession to the throne Henry saw the priest during Mass in a church near Caen, and was impressed by the rapidity with which he despatched the office. After his coronation Henry made Roger his chancellor and two years later, in 1102, Bishop of Salisbury. He afterwards appointed him Justiciar. Roger of Salisbury had a natural son by his mistress Matilda of Ramsbury called Roger le Poer. He trained his son to follow him as Chancellor and also associated his two nephews, Nigel, Bishop of Ely and Alexander, Bishop of Lincoln, in the administration. This all-powerful family retained its power and wealth into the first years of the next reign, when its members fell into disgrace.

The court during Henry's reign was an itinerant spectacle which afforded entertainment as well as imposed heavy financial burdens on the King's subjects. The King and his household, his troop of mistresses and their children, were almost always in movement. He no longer, like the Conqueror, limited his ceremonious public appearances to the three crown-wearing feasts at Winchester, Gloucester and Westminster. He held one court at Durham, where Ranulf Flambard had once dispensed scandalous hospitality at the expense of his church, and another court at Carlisle, where a great new border fortress had arisen since Rufus conquered the region. In the later years of his reign Henry is said to have renounced, at least in part, the splendour and magnificence of the crown-wearings in the reign of his father and brother. He appeared at one time or another at Northampton, at Norwich, at Dunstable, at Brampton and at St. Alban's. When he was in England he spent much time at Oxford and at Woodstock, where he kept a zoological garden, the first to be created in England. In Normandy we hear of him at Rouen, his capital, at Lisieux and at Evreux, where he rebuilt an abbey which had been burned down during the private baronial wars. He especially favoured a hunting lodge in the great Forest of Lyons, in which he was to spend the last days of his life.

During his reign Henry enjoyed friendly relations with the Kings of Scotland, and for a period an unusual peace descended on the northern border. King Edgar, one of the three sons of Malcolm and the English Margaret, had been placed by Henry on the throne. Henry had married one of his natural daughters to Alexander, another son of Margaret. Under the reign of the third son, David, Anglo-Scottish relations became even closer. David was the brother of Henry's first wife Edith-Matilda, the uncle of two other Matildas, and the husband of a fourth. He had married the daughter of Waltheof, the last old English Earl, unjustly executed for his supposed share in the Norman conspiracy against William the Conqueror. Through her David had inherited two of Waltheof's earldoms, Northampton and Huntingdon. He was in addition Earl of the Anglo-Scottish shire of Lothian, and as such owed formal allegiance to the King of England. But whether as King or Earl he did his homage without reserve, and appeared frequently at Henry's court as his most honoured vassal.

In Wales Henry achieved if not a general pacification, at least a degree of submission unknown before his reign. One of his methods anticipated a political measure thought in modern times to be an innovation. He settled a number of Flemish colonists, probably taken from among his mercenaries of that race, in the wilds of Pembrokeshire. They were hard-working and courageous. They brought new crafts to the rural settlements in Wales, and they were not slow in inter-marrying with the native Welsh and in creating a mixed population beyond the border. Henry also appointed two Norman bishops in the sees of South Wales, Urban in Llandaff and Bernard in St. David's. They were more successful in their relations with their Welsh flock than another Norman, Bishop Hervey, whom the Red King had appointed to the wilder see of Bangor. Hervey 'agreed ill with the Welshmen' and hastened to place himself outside their borders. He was ultimately transferred to England to become the first Bishop of the new see of Ely. In 1111 the Anglo-Norman power in Wales was extended as far as Cardiganshire, which was finally conquered by Gilbert of Clare, a member of a house with which Henry had been friendly even in the time of Rufus and which played a great part in the affairs of Ireland as well as those of Wales and England.

Henry twice played a personal role in Welsh affairs. He led two expeditions into the country, the first in 1114. It was perhaps during this campaign that he became enamoured of a Welsh beauty, Nest, the daughter of the great prince Rhys ap Tudor. By Nest the King had a son named after himself. Nest afterwards became the wife of a Norman knight, Gerald of Windsor, who commanded the castle of Pembroke. Her kinsman Owen, the courageous son of Cadogan, fell in love with her and succeeded in abducting her from her Norman husband's castle. Owen was a typical Welsh border chieftain, making alternate war and peace with his neighbours on the slightest caprice. He was often in rebellion against King Henry, and was finally killed in a battle in 1116 in which Welshmen, Normans and Flemings were engaged.

Henry's second Welsh expedition was made in 1121, after his re-marriage. The loss of Richard, Earl of Chester, who went down in the *White Ship* with the Ætheling William, and the consequent extinction of the great house founded in the Conqueror's reign by Hugh (the Wolf) of Avranches, had encouraged the men of Powys to rise in revolt against the Anglo-Normans. Henry marched as far westwards as Snowdon and during the march was struck by an arrow. He owed his life to the steel breast-plate he wore, but the origin of the arrow, whether despatched by a Welsh rebel or by a traitor in his own ranks, was never determined. The King marched back from Snowdon after receiving the submission of the Welsh chiefs. He brought with him many hostages from among their children, and for some time thereafter the submission of Wales, for which he has generally gained credit, was no longer in question.

There is no evidence of any intervention by Henry in the affairs of Ireland, and he did not indulge in that direction the dreams of his brother Rufus. There was a connection between the churches of Ireland and England, and Bishop Gregory of Dublin, and possibly others, were consecrated in England. The ecclesiastical relationship was also maintained between England and the Norse-settled Orkneys. The Bishop of Orkney, although strictly a suffragan of Trondhjem in Norway, acted also as a suffragan of York. With Paul, the Earl of the Orkneys, who had accompanied his father in the famous invasion of England by Harold Hardrada, and who continued to be a vassal of the King of Norway, Henry maintained friendly relations, and there is a record of the Earl's gifts to Henry's zoo at Woodstock.

The death of a Norwegian King, Magnus Barefoot, brought unexpected advantage to Henry. On his second voyage around the north coast of Scotland Magnus had landed in Ireland and founded several colonies of Norsemen there. One of the Irish chiefs appealed to the Normans for aid against Magnus, and Arnulf of Bellême, brother of the notorious Robert, responded to the appeal. But the Normans and the Irish together were no match for the intrepid Magnus in open fighting, and they had recourse to treachery. Envoys were sent to the Norse King urging him to leave his ships and march inland with a small force, whereupon, they pretended, the country would submit to him. Showing an unusual credulity for those suspicious times, Magnus listened to the arguments of the envoys, and fell into the trap. When he had marched two miles inland with a handful of warriors, he was suddenly attacked by a force many times stronger. Magnus disdained to seek safety in flight. He fought desperately for his life, standing with his back against a tree and covering himself with his shield. But in the end he fell, covered with wounds.

Arnould, the Norman ally of the Irish chief, fell out with his associates. The Irish leader had given Arnould his daughter in marriage, but later he recovered her by force and married her again to one of his cousins. Arnould fled from Ireland to Normandy and lived there as an outlaw for twenty years. In his old age he became reconciled to King Henry and took a wife. The day after his marriage-feast he fell asleep at his banquet-table and did not awaken. The guests who came to his wedding stayed to celebrate his funeral.

The death of Magnus profited Henry twofold. In the first place he had no longer to fear an invasion by that restless and daring navigator. In the second the great treasure accumulated by Magnus fell into his hands. Magnus had entrusted his household goods and his gold and silver to the keeping of a wealthy burgher of Lincoln, who furnished the King of Norway from time to time with such articles from his great hoard of gold and arms as he called for. When he learned of the death of Magnus the burgher of Lincoln hastened to place the hoard in security, and became a very rich man in consequence. But Henry's intelligence service was highly competent. His spies were everywhere, and the envious fellow-townsmen of the newly enriched citizen undoubtedly supplied the monarch with all the information he needed. Some time after the death of Magnus Barefoot, Henry pounced on the custodian of his treasure and ordered him to disgorge. The man denied that the hoard was in his possession, whereupon Henry, who had all the proof he needed, threw him in prison and declared his wealth confiscated. The King's treasury was by this means enriched by the value of 20,000 pounds of silver, an enormous sum in those times.

I

Henry is said to have had about twenty illegitimate children by his many mistresses, in addition to his legal son and daughter. The best-known of them was undoubtedly Robert, Earl of Gloucester, born in Caen and the son of a Frenchwoman whom Henry knew in Normandy before his accession. Another natural son called Robert was born to an Englishwoman, Edith. The same Edith, or possibly another royal mistress of the same name, gave birth to a daughter named Matilda, who was drowned with the loss of the *White Ship*. Her half-brother Richard, who was also drowned, was the son of an Englishwoman called Ansfrida, the widow of one Anskill. Henry also had an illegitimate son called Reginald, who later became Earl of Cornwall. He had a daughter by Elizabeth, the child of his minister, Robert, Count of Meulan and the sister of Count Waléran of Meulan. This daughter was afterwards married to Gilbert, Earl of Clare.

XV

THE LAST YEARS OF HENRY I

A CRISIS in the English succession was opened in 1125 by the death of Matilda's husband, the Emperor Henry V. The Emperor had been steadily influenced by the successful methods of government employed by his father-in-law in England and Normandy. Towards the end of his life he is said to have attempted, on Henry's advice, to raise a land-tax in the Empire on the model of the Danegeld. The death of the Emperor offered a new solution to the problem of providing a successor to his father-in-law. King Henry's marriage to Adelisa of Lorraine had not resulted in the hoped-for birth of a son. The fact that the King's natural son, Robert of Caen, afterwards Earl of Gloucester, was not even considered a possible heir to the throne, in spite of his great qualities, suggests that the feeling of the Church against illegitimacy had grown in strength since the reign of William the Bastard.

Yet Earl Robert of Gloucester, courageous and intelligent, would probably have made a better King than many of his father's successors. He was, as we have noted, half French by his mother. He married Mabel, a daughter of Robert FitzHamon, the conqueror of Morganwyg, and a rhyming chronicler of Gloucester, also called Robert, recounts that his wife, when the marriage was first proposed to her by the King, objected that Robert did not possess a surname and that on this account people would scorn her as having married a man of inferior birth. The story goes that Henry then told her that he would give Robert a surname, that of Fitzroy, and that he would also create him Earl of Gloucester, with which concession the bride was perforce content.

Robert of Gloucester was the favourite among Henry's natural sons, and Matilda, although the King's only legitimate daughter and since the death of the Ætheling his only legitimate child, had a stubborn and arrogant character which caused her father many misgivings in his last years. Matilda, however, was not only a descendant of William the Conqueror but also, through her mother, of Edmund Ironside and the old English kings. The passion for legality and the forms of justice which may be considered to be Henry's leading characteristic was now extended to the problem of the succession. And this, rather than any predilection for his daughter Matilda, caused him to take a step which led directly to the nineteen years of turmoil which in English history are generally referred to as 'the Anarchy'.

When Henry returned to England in the autumn of 1126, after the defeat and judgment of William Clito's supporters at Bourgthéroulde, he was accompanied not only by the convicted rebel leaders but also by his daughter the Empress Matilda. She was said by the chronicler Roger of Hoveden to have brought with her not only the Imperial crown, which was returned eventually to the Imperial treasury, and the title of Empress, which she used all her life, but also a notable relic, the hand of St. James, to provide a fitting home for which, as well as to ensure his own spiritual salvation, the King founded the abbey of Reading.

Matilda was now a childless widow and free, in theory at least, to inherit the throne of England and to remarry. It is true that there was no historical precedent for a woman ruler, either in Saxon England or in Normandy. But the concepts of monarchy were rapidly changing. The hereditary principle was gradually supplanting the tradition of elective kings. Matilda, it was hoped, would unite in her person the duchy of Normandy and the kingdom of England. The legitimate Duke of Normandy, her Uncle Robert, was still alive and a prisoner in the castle of Devizes, from which he would shortly be transferred, for greater security, to the castle of Bristol under the charge of Robert of Gloucester. It is also true that many Norman barons, in England and in Normandy, were bitterly opposed to the notion of being ruled by a woman, especially a young and marriageable widow. A second marriage, it was feared, might create an entangling alliance from which England had just escaped by the death and childlessness of the Emperor.

It is a sign of the unchallenged and autocratic power wielded by Henry, in this the twenty-sixth year of his reign, that he was able at the end of 1126 to obtain the recognition of his daughter as his successor, and to induce his barons to swear an oath of allegiance to her. The Council which created this notable precedent in English history was held by Henry first at Windsor, during the Christmas feast, and then at Westminster during the feast of the Circumcision. The barons took the oath of allegiance to Matilda on 1 January 1127, but fearing the consequences of a second marriage by Matilda they attempted to forestall them by adding a proviso that she should not marry outside the country without their consent.

The first of Henry's vassals to take the oath to Matilda was King David of Scotland, the maternal uncle of the Empress. A contest in precedence then arose between Earl Robert of Gloucester and the King's legitimate nephew Stephen of Blois, Count of Boulogne. Stephen's rights were considered the stronger and he took the oath immediately after the King of the Scots. Robert of Gloucester, who was afterwards to prove a valiant champion in the interests of his half-sister, swore allegiance after Stephen who was the first to renounce it.

When he had summoned the widowed Empress to join him in Normandy, some months earlier, Henry had probably already conceived his grand design of a marriage which would bring not only England and Normandy, but also Maine and Anjou, under one crown. His old adversary Fulk V, Count of Anjou, had a young son Geoffrey Martel, the descendant and namesake of a traditional adversary of the early years of William the Conqueror. Within six months of the barons' oath of allegiance, but as far as is known without their consent, Matilda was secretly betrothed to Geoffrey Martel. Geoffrey is better known in history as Geoffrey Plantagenet, from the broom (*genêt*) which he planted to improve his hunting coverts, and the flower of which his son Henry II is also said to have worn in his cap. Henry knighted his prospective son-in-law and hung around his neck a shield of golden lions, the forerunner, it is believed, of the royal arms of England first used on the seal of Richard Cœur de Lion. A year later, on 17 June 1128, Geoffrey and Matilda were married at Le Mans. Count Fulk, the father of the groom, had already left for the Holy Land and at seventeen years of age Geoffrey was ruler of Anjou.

The Empress was not liked in England. She had left the country when she was eight years old to become first the betrothed and then the bride of a man whom she had never seen. In Germany, however, she seems to have won respect and even affection. After the Emperor's death she visited England on several occasions without endearing herself to the people. Her second marriage, designed by her father to overcome the mutual antipathy between the Normans and the Angevins, seems only to have exacerbated it. The Norman barons especially resented the alliance. In England also the marriage with Geoffrey was unpopular. A chronicler noted: 'All the French and English thought ill of it.'

There was a disparity of eleven years in their ages, and to the bride's disadvantage. Otherwise, in their arrogant and autocratic temperaments they were evenly matched. They quarrelled incessantly, and after a year of this ill assorted union Geoffrey returned his wife to her father's court at Rouen. The separation of the couple was solemnly discussed by the King's barons at Northampton in 1131. Then, probably at Henry's demand, Geoffrey relented and sent for his wife. They lived together for some years in outward calm. Matilda's first two sons were born during the last years of the King's life: the future Henry II on 5 March 1133, and his brother Geoffrey in the following year. A third son, William, was born in 1136. The birth of Henry Plantagenet seemed to his grandfather to secure the English succession to Matilda, and on 2 August 1133 he crossed the Channel to Normandy to welcome his first legitimate grandson, the continuator of the ruling houses of England, Normandy, Anjou and Maine.

This voyage to Normandy was Henry's last. It was marked in the memories or the imaginations of the native chroniclers by an eclipse of the sun, and is poetically recorded in these words, 'The other day that he lay on sleep in the ship, then westered the day over all lands, and was the sun swilk as if it were three night old moon, with stars about him at midday. Then were men in great wonder and dread, and said that mickle things should come thereafter.' Two years elapsed, however, before the portent seen in the eclipse by the Peterborough chronicler was to be realized.

Henry reached Rouen in August 1133 and settled down in contentment to his new joys as a grandfather. He may well have wished to spend his last years in the duchy which had seen the birth and death of his father William the Conqueror. Henry was now sixty-five years old. He was temporarily at peace with the neighbouring rulers whom he had conquered or reconciled. During this last stay in Normandy he made three attempts to return to England but was on each occasion prevented by disputes which required for their settlement his presence and his authority. Two years after his arrival in the duchy he was still busy suppressing minor revolts. The arrogance of his son-in-law, the hatred of the Norman barons for the Angevin-dominated court of Matilda, and the stiff insolence of the Empress provoked innumerable quarrels and disputes. But with all these preoccupations Henry permitted nothing to interfere with his indulgence in his passion for the chase.

On 25 November 1135 he arrived at his hunting lodge, the castle of Lyons in the great Norman forest of that name, and he summoned his huntsmen for the morrow. But in the evening he was taken ill with an acute attack of indigestion, said to have been caused by a meal of his favourite dish of lampreys, which he had eaten in spite of the strict injunctions of his physician. The next day he knew that his end was near. He sent for Archbishop Hugh of Rouen, the Primate of Normandy, and pardoned the barons who had rebelled against him, notably Roger of Tosny and William Talvas III, the latest to commit acts of defiance. He sent his natural son Robert of Gloucester to the Norman treasury in the castle of Falaise with orders to draw 60,000 pounds of silver, which he then distributed in alms to the knights and servants in his household. Then he ordered that after his death his body should be taken for burial to the abbey of 200 monks which he had founded at Reading.

Henry died as night fell on 1 December 1135. Five great barons were present at his deathbed; Robert of Gloucester, William of Warenne, Rotrou of Mortagne, Waléran of Meulan and Robert of Leicester. The two prelates present, Archbishop Hugh of Rouen and Audin, Bishop of Evreux, mindful perhaps of the scandalous scenes which had followed the death of William the Conqueror at Rouen, enjoined on the barons their duty not to abandon the corpse of their King, and to escort him honourably to the coast of Normandy on his passage to England.

The body of Henry I was first carried to Rouen, where it was laid in the cathedral. During the night it was taken to the Archbishop's house, where it was opened and embalmed. The King's heart was buried in the church of St. Mary at Emendreville, of which the construction had been begun by Henry's mother Queen Matilda, and had been completed by Henry himself. Finally the remains of the dead King were conducted to Caen, where the coffin was guarded for four weeks in the choir of his father's abbey church of St. Stephen until a favourable wind blew for the voyage to England. Henry I was finally buried early in 1136 in the church of the monastery he had founded at Reading.

He had reigned for more than thirty-five years over England, and for twenty-nine over Normandy. His contemporaries, even the great minister and biographer of his adversary Louis VI, the Abbot Suger of St. Denis, judged his reign and his character more favourably than might have been expected. The English chroniclers complained characteristically of his financial exactions, of which the burden had largely fallen on the churches and monasteries. Henry of Huntingdon mentions the King's three vices, avarice, cruelty and licentiousness, of which the last two were common to most of the rulers of his age. The continuator of William of Jumièges, Robert de Monte, extols his victories, records one or two cases of imprisonment and of blinding, and then praises Henry for the unexpected virtue of maintaining a large number of mercenaries. Under Henry I the mercenaries performed the functions of the house-carles under Edward the Confessor and Harold. They kept order and suppressed the incipient baronial revolts which had troubled the earlier years of the King's reign. But their retribution, which devolved on the monarch, must have been a heavy burden which could only be met by periodical levies on the King's vassals, lay or ecclesiastic.

Although his historians do not dwell on the sternness of the Forest Laws which Henry rigorously enforced, as had his father and brother, it is significant that the news of his death was greeted in England by a popular invasion of the King's forests. There was a spectacular national manifestation of the old folk-rights which had been long ignored or repressed. Men of all social classes and categories disported themselves gaily in the royal reserves. Not a wild beast which could be hunted was spared.

XVI

HENRY'S DISPUTE WITH ANSELM

I F IT were not for his troubled relations with Anselm and the long
dispute between King and Pope which has been sometimes, if wrongly,
described as the Investiture Struggle, the long reign of Henry I in England
at least might be regarded as largely without incident. As has been recorded, immediately after his coronation Henry invited Archbishop
Anselm to return from the exile to which the brutality and bad faith of
William Rufus had condemned him. The Archbishop lost no time in
complying. He arrived in England, after an absence of nearly three
years, on 23 September 1100. He was not in time to crown the new King,
but he gave his benediction to the marriage ceremony between the King
and his bride Edith-Matilda and intervened in spectacular fashion to
certify that the bride had not previously taken conventual vows. And
in the dispute between Henry and his brother Robert of Normandy, but
lately returned from the first Crusade to claim the throne of England,
as well as the duchy of Normandy, Anselm's support of the King was a
powerful factor in the ultimate triumph of Henry.

But as soon as the interests of the Church were challenged, Anselm
showed that he was a very different man from the Archbishop who had
fled secretly from England in defiance of the ban of Rufus. At that time,
backed by the diplomatic Pope Urban, Anselm had been willing to
negotiate. But after three years on the Continent, and attendance at the
meetings of the Lateran Council which had discussed the question of
investiture and the related question of simony, the saintly Archbishop
had returned with Papal authority to enforce the reforms initiated by
Pope Gregory VII, with all the power at his command, including that of
excommunication.

Unlike his brother Rufus, Henry I was firm but friendly in his relations with Anselm. Not once during the long dispute between them did
the argument descend to the low level it had reached in the reign of Rufus.

The King's position in regard to investiture was based on the ancient customs of England as recognized and enforced by his father William the Conqueror. 'No one before Anselm became a bishop or abbot who did not first become the King's man, and from his hands receive investiture by the gift of the pastoral staff.' Henry would grant to Rome what his predecessors had granted, but nothing that they had refused to grant.

The King's first act on Anselm's arrival in England was to demand that the Archbishop do homage to him on receiving again at his hands the temporalities of his see. His second demand was that the Archbishop agree to consecrate the bishops whom Henry had appointed before his return. Anselm refused both requests, although he himself had already submitted to the English custom, and had received his pastoral staff from the hands of Rufus.

Whatever the custom may have been in the countries of Western Europe, in which the Lateran Council now decreed the enforcement of the Gregorian programme, bishops and abbots in England, before and since the Conquest, were in a very different category. They were for the most part great officers of the Crown, escorted to the King's court and even to their own churches by an imposing retinue of armed knights and archers. They were in possession of extensive lands, granted out in knights' fees, and they had a statutory obligation to provide knights and men-at-arms for the King's service. It was natural that the sovereign should have some authority over the temporal functions of these power-ful prelates. William the Conqueror had rigorously exercised it, and his Archbishop Lanfranc understood the problem and even gave shrewd and apt counsel to the Conqueror when he faced the delicate problem of arresting his brother Bishop Odo, for abuses of his temporal power.

But Anselm was not a saint for nothing. He placed the question of principle on a higher plane than the merits or demerits of the particular case in hand. For him the judgment and authority of Rome were final. Henry therefore suggested an appeal to Pope Paschal II to relax the canons recently decreed by the Lateran Council in favour of the traditional custom of England. Anselm readily agreed, and an embassy was sent to Rome. But Paschal had none of the diplomatic temperament and skill of his predecessor Pope Urban, and he obstinately refused to make any concession. Two successive delegations were sent by the King to Rome, and each returned empty-handed.

At last Henry asked Anselm, as the Easter feast of 1103 approached, to undertake himself the journey to Rome. Anselm, although now nearly seventy years old, consented. But his journey was equally fruitless. The

King would not depart from his insistence on respect for the ancient customs of England. The Pope arrogantly refused to yield one iota of his demands. The result was that two and a half years after his return from his exile under Rufus, Anselm was still an Archbishop without authority. A member of the English delegation, on the King's order, suggested to Anselm that he should remain abroad for the time being. The saintly old man, so tolerant and accommodating in his personal relations, so inflexible and unyielding on matters of principle, took the hint, and willingly returned to Lyons to enjoy the hospitality of his friend and admirer Archbishop Hugh. The revenues of his vacated see of Canterbury once again were diverted to the royal coffers.

Anselm remained in France for two years, until in 1105 the Pope precipitated a crisis by excommunicating Count Robert of Meulun, whom as the King's chief adviser he considered to be mainly responsible for the deadlock. The Pope included in this terrible ban the bishops who had accepted investiture with the pastoral staff at the hands of Henry. Paschal even went so far as to threaten Henry himself with a similar sanction.

The King was not greatly concerned with the spiritual import of the threat, but Anselm's reputation was immense in Europe (he had been greeted in Rome as 'the Pope from over the seas') and even in England, although the English clergy as a whole do not seem to have supported the Archbishop in his rigid insistence on Papal investiture. And Henry may well have hesitated at the prospect of being excommunicated by his own Archbishop. In July 1105, when Henry was in Normandy, he met Anselm at the monastery of Bec (some accounts say the meeting was at L'Aigle) and offered terms of peace. He promised to restore the revenues of the see of Canterbury, and he asked Anselm to return to England, only stipulating that he recognize the three bishops, those of Winchester, Hereford and Salisbury, who had been invested by the King.

Anselm seems to have been willing for a settlement, but declined to act without Papal authority. Appeal was again made to Paschal II, who gradually was brought to realize that in this matter Henry would not grant away a control over the national church exercised by his predecessors. The argument dragged on for another year, and at the same time a parallel controversy raged in France, where it was finally settled by the conciliatory spirit of Ivo, Bishop of Chartres. A famous canonist, Ivo was on the friendliest terms with Henry's sister Adela, Countess of Blois, the mother of Stephen of Blois, and perhaps under her influence he had come to recognize the right of certain sovereigns, notably the

King of England, to be consulted in the appointment of bishops who were also wealthy temporal barons.

Thanks to the intervention of Bishop Ivo, the dispute in France was ended in 1107, and in August of the same year a Council held in London confirmed a settlement of the English dispute on the lines suggested by Ivo of Chartres. Under this agreement Anselm consented to do homage to the King and Henry promised not to stand in the way of his consecration. The King continued to exact homage from the bishops for their temporalities, but abandoned his part in the spiritual side of the ceremony, the rite of investing them with the pastoral ring and staff.

Henry also promised that the election of bishops and abbots should be made freely. In fact the elections were held in the King's court and under the King's influence. On some occasions, notably after the death of Anselm, the practice of simony was revived. The election was free, but the freedom of choice was paid for by a gift of money offered by the candidate. Henry left no doubt in the minds of the Council as to the candidate of his choice. The son of Henry II conveyed his wishes in writing. In a writ issued for an election to fill a vacancy at Winchester he said: 'Henry, king of the English, to his faithful members of the Church of Winchester, greeting. I order you to hold a free election, but nevertheless I forbid you to elect anyone except Richard, my clerk, the archdeacon of Poitiers.'

Anselm himself regarded the settlement virtually as a triumph for Henry I, although he was careful to present the matter to the Pope in a different light. In 1108 he wrote that Henry did not make elections of bishops and abbots according to his will alone, but accepted entirely the counsel of ecclesiastics. And in a letter to Thomas, Archbishop-elect of York, he made the compromise clear. 'Since it has pleased the King, with the counsel of his barons and with our consent, that you should be elected to the see of York . . .'

The King lost little or nothing by surrendering the right of investiture with the ring and the staff. He continued to choose the same kind of bishop and abbot, men in whom piety was of secondary importance to a sound sense of business, capable of administering their vast estates, of building churches and abbeys, of organizing their contingents of knights and men-at-arms for the fighting of the King's wars.

First and typical of this kind of statesman-bishop was Roger of Salisbury. Roger had entered Henry's service when he was still a humble priest in Normandy, and Henry was still a landless, or practically landless, prince. As mentioned earlier, it is said that Henry noticed and admired the rapidity with which Roger despatched a Mass. Two years after Henry's coronation Roger was named Bishop of Salisbury, but he was not consecrated by Anselm until after the settlement of the Archbishop's investiture dispute with the King. Roger had already acted as chief of the King's chancery. He proved to be a brilliant administrator, and through his nephews, also named bishops, he founded an ecclesiastical dynasty. Another churchman-administrator of the same order, who equally founded a line of able if unscrupulous clerics, was Richard of Belmeis, who after having acted as Sheriff of Shropshire was appointed by Henry, Bishop of London in 1108.

In Anselm's first synod in 1102, held in Westminster with the King's consent, three of the decrees published were of a moral rather than a constitutional order. One decree was aimed at the punishment of homosexuality, which had been the prevailing vice of the court of Rufus. All found guilty of this offence, whether clerks or laymen, were condemned to lose all rights and privileges in their respective orders. Another decree denounced the 'wicked merchandise by which men were used to be sold in England like brute beasts'. The necessity for such a denunciation shows that the succession of royal and ecclesiastical decrees issued down to the reign of William the Conqueror had been ineffectual in suppressing the practice of slavery. This latest pronouncement was the most comprehensive yet made. It seemed to apply not only to the traffic in slaves shipped to other countries, but to the principle of slavery itself.

The act of the Council of Westminster which provoked the greatest controversy was that which forbade clerical marriage. Since the reforms instituted by Pope Gregory VII, attempts had been vainly made to enforce celibacy among the clergy in the Western churches. Lanfranc had contented himself with a sensible compromise. No new marriages should take place, but parish priests, of whom the great majority were married, should not be compelled to put away their wives. But Anselm's synod, held after his long stay abroad and his attendance at the Lateran Council which had launched the new thunders against clerical marriage, went much further than Lanfranc. It ordered heavy penalties against the married clergy, and forbade marriage to all churchmen of the rank of subdeacon and upwards. This was the first time that celibacy was actually imposed on the lower ranks of the clergy in England.

The harsh new decree met with general opposition among its humbler victims. The higher clerics observed it in the letter and evaded it in the spirit. It was notorious that Roger of Salisbury, the greatest man in the realm after Anselm, who had played a prominent part in the synod and had been even consecrated as Bishop during its debates, lived openly with a mistress, Matilda of Ramsbury. One of his nephews, Bishop Nigel of Ely, was a married man, had a son Richard FitzNeal, by his wife, and had placed a married sacrist in his own cathedral. And the Papal Legate, John of Crema, was known to keep a mistress.

In the presence of this flagrant scandal in the highest orders of the clergy, the enforcement of the decree against marriage was difficult, especially among the lower orders. Illicit but undisguised cohabitation with women replaced the openly avowed married state. The new decree was exploited in characteristic fashion by King Henry himself. During his campaigns in Normandy he had frequent need of money, and he found ready means of procuring it by exacting fines from the priests who disobeyed Anselm's decrees against marriage. Anselm himself, to his credit, sternly rebuked the King for doing so, but he did not succeed in deterring Henry from the use of this expedient.

New enforcements of the law against clerical marriage were repeated at successive church councils, and in 1128 the Church authorities were actually authorized to sell the wives of married priests into slavery— an act which violated one canon of the synod of 1102 while purporting to uphold another.

Anselm did not long survive the settlement of the investiture dispute. He died in 1109, full of years and sanctity. He left in Canterbury to perpetuate his fame an extension of Lanfranc's fabric of Christ Church, and a tower which still bears his name. During his lifetime he had been venerated as a saint both in England and on the Continent, but his actual canonization did not take place until many years later, and then, strangely enough, at the hands of a Borgia, Pope Alexander VI.

After Anselm's death Henry's always precarious relations with Rome rapidly deteriorated. He soon lapsed into some of the financial practices for which the name of his brother Rufus was abhorred in Papal circles. The worst of these, in ecclesiastical eyes, was the sin of simony. On his coronation Henry had promised the independence of the Church in these terms: 'First I make the holy Church of God free, so that I will neither sell it nor place it to farm, nor on the death of an archbishop, bishop or abbot, will I take anything from the domain of the Church or from its tenants until a successor has been instituted to it.'

Henry began his fall from grace by repeating in respect of the see of Canterbury, vacant on the death of Anselm, the policy of his brother Rufus after the death of Lanfranc. He did not appoint a successor to Anselm for five years, and during this long vacancy the considerable revenues of the see were confiscated to the King. In his favour, however, it is said that he treated the tenants of the see with fairness and justice. Other vacant sees were similarly treated. The bishopric of Coventry, which fell vacant in 1126, was not filled until 1129. The see of Durham remained vacant for five years, from 1128 to 1133, and that of Ely for two years, from 1131 to 1133.

Henry further claimed, and exercised, as had his brother Rufus, a right to seize the personal chattels of a dead bishop in spite of the protests of Pope Honorius II. When Bishop Gilbert of London died, the venerable man's boots were filled with his gold and silver by the King's agents, and carried off to the royal treasury.

Henry continued his father's policy towards the Popes. He maintained that no Papal letters should be received in England, and no Papal legates heard, without his consent, and further, that no pleas or appeals should be presented to the Papal court in Rome. Pope Paschal II wrote in 1115 to protest against these restrictions, and also complained that the King transferred bishops from one see to another without reference to Rome. Nevertheless, the practice continued until Henry's death. The King exercised control over the speeches and actions of his bishops even in the Papal councils. In 1119 when the new Pope Calixtus II, Henry's distant cousin, held his Council at Reims and summoned bishops from the countries of Western Europe, Henry permitted the English bishops to attend, but warned them not to ventilate any grievances and not to introduce any new practices in England on their return.

In the matter of the privileges granted to the Papal legates on their visits to England, Henry resolutely followed the custom of his predecessors, both English and Norman. Of the nine legates who came to England during his long reign, one only, the famous John of Crema, with his stern views on the chastity of other churchmen and his personal self-indulgence, was permitted in 1125 to preside over a synod of the Church or to exercise any authority. Henry's insistence on the freedom of the English Church from Papal control was fiercely resented by successive Popes during his reign, but it was acquiesced in by Calixtus II, as freely as he eventually justified Henry's seizure of his brother's duchy of Normandy.

The English tradition since the days of St. Augustine was that the Archbishop of Canterbury alone was the rightful delegate of Papal authority in England. Pope Honorius temporarily settled the question in 1126 by commissioning William of Corbeil, then Archbishop of Canterbury, as his legate, and this precedent was followed for more than

100 years until in the thirteenth century the rule was formally laid down that the Archbishop was by virtue of his office the legate of the Pope.

Anselm had died leaving undetermined the old dispute between the two archbishops respecting the claims of Canterbury to exercise authority over the see of York. William the Conqueror had provisionally settled the matter in Lanfranc's lifetime by ordering that the Archbishop of York should make a profession of obedience to Lanfranc personally. In his last years Anselm had received a full profession from Gerard, the new Archbishop of York. But Gerard's successor, a stiff-necked kinsman of an earlier and equally independent Archbishop, Thomas of Bayeux, stubbornly refused on his appointment to York in 1109 to profess obedience to the Metropolitan of Canterbury.

The old controversy was revived in an acute form in 1114 when the King's secretary Thurstan was appointed to the see of York and loudly asserted the independence of his province from the authority of Canterbury. Thurstan refused to be consecrated by the new Archbishop of Canterbury, Ralph of Rochester, who had been appointed five years after the death of Anselm. At the Council of Reims in 1119 he received consecration at the hands of Pope Calixtus II and of certain French bishops. One of the most notorious characters of the reign of Rufus made a fleeting appearance at this Council. According to Roger of Hoveden the King sent Ranulf Flambard to Reims to forbid the consecration, but he arrived too late. Henry was so incensed at the action of his former secretary that he banished him from his dominions, in spite of the plea for reconciliation made by the Pope when the cousins met at Gisors. Afterwards, however, Thurstan succeeded in effecting a reconciliation between Henry and Louis the Fat, and was rewarded by being restored to his archbishopric.

Nevertheless the King continued to support the claims of Canterbury. Much correspondence was exchanged on the subject and there were frequent comings and goings between England and Rome. Successive Popes defended the cause of the Archbishops of York. In 1126, when Pope Honorius found a solution for the problem of the Papal legates in England, at the same time he found a salve for the wounded pride of Canterbury. For the claims of Canterbury to spititual authority over all England were found to be based on the palpably forged evidence produced by the monks of Christ Church in Lanfranc's day and offered by that Archbishop, wittingly or not, as proof of his claim. Judgment was finally given in 1126 in favour of the see of York, but William of Corbeil,

Archbishop of Canterbury, who had been appointed Papal Legate by Pope Honorius II in Rome, could nevertheless claim as legate absolute obedience from his rival.

In spite of his frequent disputes with Rome, Henry's reign witnessed important innovations in the life of the English Church, and notably in English monasticism. Without reference to the Pope the King created a new diocese at Carlisle in the recently annexed shire of Cumberland, and he gave the new see to an English bishop, Æthelwulf. And for the first time in more than a century an English diocese was reduced in size on spiritual grounds. The diocese of Lincoln, which extended from the Thames to the Humber, was divided under Anselm's authority and a new bishopric was created at Ely, where the existing great abbey in the fens became the church of Bishop Hervey, who had failed to win the respect of the Welsh at Bangor.

In the last years of the Conqueror's reign two new monastic orders had been introduced into England, the Cluniacs and the Austin canons. The Austin canons, the first reforming religious body established in England since the Conquest, founded the priories of St. Botolph at Colchester, St. Mary at Huntingdon and St. Gregory at Canterbury in the last years of the eleventh century. A number of other religious houses soon followed them in eastern and southern England. On the creation of the see of Carlisle in 1133, the cathedral, unique among the English cathedrals, contained a chapter of Austin canons.

Rufus, emulating his father's example, founded a Cluniac monastery at Bermondsey—the only benefaction recorded to his credit. The reforms in English monastic life begun under William I and Lanfranc, and inspired by the Cluniac reforms in the famous Norman abbeys of Jumièges and Fécamp, were continued under Henry I. The Constitutions compiled by Lanfranc for the direction of the monks of Christ Church, Canterbury, and founded on the customs of Cluny, were gradually adopted by the older monasteries. The King himself contributed to the building of the great church at Cluny. It had been begun by Alfonso VI of Castille. The nave was completed with the aid of Henry I, and was consecrated by Pope Innocent II in 1132. Henry gave the monastery an annual grant of 100 marks of silver, which his successor Stephen afterwards commuted for the gift of the manor of Letcombe Regis. Henry's daughter the Empress Matilda also made a number of gifts to the abbey, including a great bell cast in an English foundry. King Henry's nephew Henry of Blois had been brought up from childhood at Cluny and was later taken to England by the King, who appointed him Abbot

K

of Glastonbury and Bishop of Winchester. Henry of Blois remained all his life a firm friend and benefactor of the famous abbey. And when Henry I built a new abbey at Reading he established in it monks from the Cluniac priory at Lewes.

A wave of asceticism had spread to England from Cîteaux in Burgundy. The monastery of Cîteaux was founded in 1098, and soon afterwards it was joined by an Englishman, Stephen Harding. Harding had been a monk at Sherborne and then at Molesmes in the diocese of Langres. When the Abbot of Molesmes, desirous of attaining a greater degree of self-perfection and discipline, left his abbey to enter the new foundation at Cîteaux, Harding had followed him. There he was elected in 1109 the third abbot, and became one of the two founders of the greatness of the Cistercian order. Three years after his consecration he received into the order the famous St. Bernard, with thirty other monks, and the reputation of St. Bernard brought great prestige and popularity to the Cistercians.

The English Abbot gave the world of monasticism a famous Constitution, the *Carta Caritatis*, which was confirmed by Pope Calixtus II in 1119. By this constitution the Cistercians throughout the Christian world were bound together in one system of government. The observance of rites was made uniform, regular visitation of the houses of the order was prescribed, and the abbots were required to assemble in a general chapter every year to decide the needs of the rapidly growing order. Austerity and simplicity were laid down as the ideal of Cistercians, and the wearing of the splendid robes affected by many of the secular bishops and even the regular clergy were banned. The members of the order were required to dwell apart from populated places and in solitude.

The austere and Puritan-like simplicity of the Cistercians characteristically made an immediate appeal to the English. While Stephen Harding and St. Bernard were still living, the first scion of the parental tree at Cîteaux was planted at Waverley in Surrey in 1128–9 by William Giffard, Bishop of Winchester. Other houses soon arose on the borders of Wales, the famous abbey of Tintern, and a monastery at Neath. The most remarkable of the Cistercian foundations were established far from the milder and more fertile south of England, in the bleak and forbidding northern shires that first William the Conqueror and then his half-brother Bishop Odo of Bayeux had laid waste. The older order of the Benedictines had made little progress in these inhospitable lands. Their abbeys had usually been built in towns, or towns had grown around them. And those among them which were not utterly destroyed by the zealous Reformers of the sixteenth century have commonly survived in the form of the parish churches of today.

But the Cistercians, in addition to choosing the wildest and most forlorn sites for their new churches, built them with deliberate simplicity, shunning all architectural ornament and all interior painting. The original buildings were probably less impressive than their ruins. In these lonely northern dales these monastic searchers after solitude brought civilization and fertility to the wilderness, and their colonization resulted in permanent benefits to the countryside. Thus came into being, after much early struggle and unremitting effort, the famous northern houses of Rievaulx, Fountains and Kirkstall.

In other localities, less harsh and forbidding, the newcomers disturbed the existing peace by ejecting the villagers and condemning their cottages to fall into ruins. Even parish churches were sometimes destroyed when their existence threatened to endanger the solitude which the Cistercian monks demanded. In some places the inhabitants were ejected by force if they refused to go. In others their consent was first obtained, although this was practically made obligatory. In Lincolnshire, where Earl William of Roumare founded a Cistercian abbey at Revesby, the inhabitants of the village and those of two adjacent hamlets which subsequently disappeared from the map, were offered land elsewhere, and if they refused it were summarily told 'to go and dwell where they would'. Only seven accepted the land offered.

The only other foreign order which was introduced into England in Henry's reign or soon afterwards was the impressively named Premonstratensian order of canons regular. It was founded by Norbert, later Archbishop of Magdeburg. The canons first settled at Newhouse in Lincolnshire in 1143, but other houses of this order soon sprang up and their number steadily increased. Before the end of Henry's life came into existence the only purely English monastic order to be created since the Conquest, and it had the novelty of reviving the double monastery for both men and women which flourished in England in Saxon times. The new order was founded by Gilbert of Sempringham in Lincolnshire about 1131. Its beginnings were humble. The founder adopted a house attached to his parish church for the use of a small number of pious women. Lay sisters were employed to minister to their needs and lay brothers performed the domestic and agricultural duties needed to maintain the small community. Finally canons were added to act as priests. These Gilbertians, as they were called after their founder, gradually increased in number until they had twenty-seven other houses, but of these only eleven were maintained for both sexes.

In addition to the great growth in monastic institutions in the reign of Henry I, there was also a remarkable increase in the number of hospitals and leper houses. Before Henry died twenty-four of such institutions had been built in England, and during the civil war of the following reign many men attempted to atone for their sanguinary activities by providing for the aged and the sick.

XVII

ENGLAND UNDER THE NORMANS

IN 1099, the last year before his death in the New Forest, William Rufus had held his first court in his new hall at Westminster. The city in which he had been crowned, and which was rapidly approaching its later pre-eminence in the kingdom, had been walled by the Romans. After the Norman Conquest three strong castles had been built to dominate its mixed population of proud and stubborn Saxons and Danes. These were the Tower of William the Conqueror, built of white stone from the quarries of Allemagne near Caen, the castle of Montfichet, and Baynard's Castle, which controlled the Thames fisheries as far westwards as the bridge of Staines. Rufus had seen almost a new city rise upon the ruins left by the great gale of 1091, graphically described by William of Malmesbury. Six hundred houses had been destroyed, churches had been blown down, and the air was filled with flying beams and rafters. The great majority of the dwellings in London were then built of timber and plaster, and roofed with straw thatch. Nevertheless, the city impressed foreign visitors by its size and population, and especially by the large number of savage dogs that roamed by night in the neighbourhood of St. Paul's.

In the first year of the reign of Henry's successor Stephen, a great fire swept through London. It began at the wooden structure which, on the site of the present London Bridge, anticipated the stone bridge which would only be begun in 1176 and completed thirty-five years later. The fire burned down St. Paul's and the flimsy houses in Fleet Street and the Strand as far as the church of St. Clement Danes outside the city wall. In the new city which arose on the ashes of old London some of the inhabitants, wealthier or more prudent than the others, had their houses built of stone, as were also thirteen monasteries and 126 new churches.

During the Conquest London had escaped the savage looting and destruction which were the fate of other towns, by its prudent submission to William I. But the Conqueror and his successors were never entirely sure of the obedience of burghers who claimed the right to take part, as equals of the barons and the bishops, in the election of their kings, and whose mayor in the reign of King John was to be admitted to a seat among the barons of the Great Council. During the twelfth century other communities arose and flourished. The older towns outgrew their ancient walls; new townships were founded and both the King and his barons granted charters to the new towns. Some of these charters even attempted to lay down regulations for the planning and construction of the houses of the citizens. Rules for the size of dwellings and gardens were prescribed at Stratford-on-Avon, at Leek and on the new building site at Gloucester. Windows were not glazed, except in the houses of the very wealthy. Under Henry II there is a record of repairs to the glass in the windows of Rufus's palace at Westminster. But for the mass of the burghers linen curtains replaced glass.

The Thames opened up southern England to the sea-borne commerce with the Baltic countries, with Russia, Germany and Poland, and London had profited from the earliest times from its great river frontier. Like all prosperous cities in the Middle Ages, London took its pleasures seriously. Horse-racing, bull-baiting, bear-baiting, archery and other games of skill, wrestling and ice-skating in winter on the Thames and the frozen marshes near it, hunting in the Chiltern Hills, where the citizens had ancient rights, play-acting, feasting and drinking—these were the more familiar distractions of a people with which the Norman conquerors, at first haughtily aloof in their castles and walled palaces, became more intimately associated in the reigns of the successors of William I.

Three times a year the great bell of St. Paul's summoned together the ancient court of London, the Folkmoot, presided over by the Sheriff. This corresponded to the shire-court, and its existence had been wisely recognized by the Conqueror together with the rest of the local machinery of law and government which he had inherited from the old English kings. The civic business of London was managed by the aldermen at a weekly husting held at the Guildhall. In addition to their attendance at the husting the aldermen were responsible for their respective wards, and each presided over the wardmoot which corresponded to the hundred court of the shires.

William the Conqueror in his charter to London had exempted the citizens, in return for an annual payment, from the often capricious taxes imposed by his sheriffs elsewhere. The charter granted by his youngest son Henry I gave London for the first time a measure of local government. It exempted the citizens from the financial burden of the Danegeld, and from the collective fine for murders committed within their walls, as well as from road and harbour tolls and customs dues throughout the kingdom. It also relieved them from the Norman custom of ordeal by battle, and limited judicial fines to a maximum of 100 shillings.

But a more important concession was made to them. They were given the right to pay the 300 pounds annual farm of London and Middlesex direct to the royal exchequer, and to appoint their own Sheriff and their own Justiciar to keep the pleas of the Crown. In 1141 the famous Geoffrey of Mandeville exacted from King Stephen the posts of Sheriff and Justiciar, and for half a century London remained deprived of its newly won civic liberties. Not until the Plantagenet King Henry II was dead and his sons Richard and John proved willing to make valuable concessions to their subjects in return for money payments, did London win back the measure of local government it had achieved under the Norman kings. A month before John signed Magna Carta at Runny-mede he granted a charter to the city of London which not only confirmed its existing privileges but gave it the right to elect its mayor annually.

Although the new English boroughs, emulating the example of London, were moving tentatively in the direction of communal government, and following the precedent set by Rouen and other Norman cities had established the office of mayor, for some centuries the Norman passion for administrative progress ran side by side with old English conservatism. The Saxon custom of trial by compurgation, or the collective oath taken by the peers of an accused man as to his guilt or innocence, survived in many English towns after it was outworn elsewhere. In London, even as late as the middle of the thirteenth century, an oath taken on the grave of a deceased witness by a living witness was accepted in a court of law as the dead man's testimony. At Preston, in the twelfth century, law courts still followed the ancient English method of assessing damages for the infliction of wounds. They were paid for at the rate of fourpence an inch on the exposed parts of the body, and eightpence an inch on the covered parts.

The progress of the towns to prosperity and eventually to self-government is the surest indication of the order and justice generally achieved by the Norman kings in England until the advent of Stephen.

The towns were primarily organized for trade. When a Norman castle was built, a market was commonly opened in the shadow of its walls, at the lord's demand or not. The lord took his toll of the market transactions, but he protected them from other dangers. Around the market the township grew. The market was commonly held in the earliest times in England on Sunday. It was the weekly day of rest from labour and of popular distraction. But in 1200 Pope Innocent II ordered Abbot Eustace of Flaye to preach against the custom, and in a number of places the market-day was changed. Sunday, however, was far more convenient than a week-day and in 1207 the Earl of Clare petitioned King John to have his market at Rothwell in Northamptonshire on Sunday. Later, in the minority of Henry III, the Papal legates succeeded in ensuring that the Papal order was carried out.

Toll-gate and toll-bridge regulated traffic and the exchange of commodities all over England. To avoid the payment of the toll smuggling was evidently carried on on a national scale. The establishment of a primitive customs force of three men in a boat in the port of London was completed by an attempt to make the boroughs enforce the collection of toll-dues. Thus Henry I in his charter to Cambridge prohibited any boat touching at any hythe in Cambridgeshire except at the hythe of the town of Cambridge, or any barges to be loaded except at this hythe.

The annual fair, one of the greatest events in town and country life in the Middle Ages and long afterwards, lasted for several days and was usually held on the feast of the local patron saint. It was the great exchange and mart for luxury goods and exotic merchandise, and was attended by traders not only from the surrounding countryside but from distant and even from foreign parts. The King's peace protected the merchants from attack. And the example set even by the cynical William Rufus, in compensating from his own treasury the four Norwegian traders whose ships had been seized by the powerful Robert Mowbray, Earl of Northumberland, was sufficient to secure respect for the travellers. The King licensed the fair, on condition that it did not unfairly compete with a neighbouring market. Its yield in tolls and dues became frequently the property of the local bishop or abbot, who in this manner profited by the coincidence of the fair with a religious feast.

Sometimes one prelate's fair and market conflicted with the interests of another prelate whose fair was established some miles away. Legal disputes and even acts of violence frequently resulted and in one case under dispute the court's order against the Bishop of Ely for his market at Lakenheath was enforced by the abbot who owned the market rights at Bury St. Edmund's, sixteen miles away. The abbot sent his bailiffs to the rival fair at night with nearly 600 armed men, and they overturned the market stalls and the butchers' shambles.

William the Conqueror as Duke of Normandy had extended the Duke's peace and protection over all the Norman highways. Only four royal roads can be identified in Norman England. Three of them—Watling Street, Ermine Street and the Foss Way—were Roman in construction, and so well paved that after long centuries and frequent neglect they still served. The fourth was of prehistoric origin: the famous Icknield Way. In 1185, for digging up a portion of this great road the parish priest of Ebbesborne and three members of his flock were hailed before the justices and punished. Since Edward the Confessor these four great highways had been under the King's protection. An attack made against a traveller on them laid the offender open to a fine of a hundred shillings, then a very considerable sum. The highways must be kept wide enough for two waggons to pass, and for two oxherds to touch their goads across their width, or for sixteen knights in armour to ride abreast. Gradually, as other roads were built or improved, and trade and communications increased, all the important routes were taken under the King's protection.

In the absence or rarity of practicable roads, waterways played an important part in the country's economy. Transport by water was slow, but cheap and easy, and towns like London, Norwich and Chester owed their prosperity in mediaeval times in large part to their position on tidal rivers. In 1121 Henry I brought the commerce of the North Sea traders into the English Midlands by converting the Fossedyke. It had originally been built by the Romans to drain the fen country. Henry transformed the ditch into a navigable canal which joined the Witham and Trent rivers and brought Lincoln within reach of ships sailing on the Humber and the Wash.

The great architectural concepts of monks and bishops which began to be executed in England after the Conquest created a demand for large quantities of building materials. Stone and timber for the fabric of the new cathedrals and monastries, and lead for the roofs, were transported over great distances by road, river and sea. In England the Normans revived industrial production, which had been neglected under the old English kings, although the Domesday Book shows that iron, which had been exploited with coal and lead in Roman times, was still mined in various regions before the Conquest. The city of Gloucester, for example, was required to furnish the fleet of Edward the Confessor with 360 bars of iron and with 100 iron rods for the manufacture of nails. After the

Conquest the forges in the Forest of Dean worked to supply the King's army in Normandy with large numbers of picks and shovels, horseshoes and nails.

Under a later reign, when an expedition was sent to Ireland, and during the Crusade of Richard Cœur de Lion, a very large quantity of axes, picks, shovels, nails and horseshoes was sent from Gloucestershire. Apart from the smaller iron workings in the North, and until the emergence of the iron industry in the Weald of Kent and in Sussex in the thirteenth century, the Forest of Dean continued to be the main source of supply.

The lead and silver mines on Alston Moor on the Cumberland border, the lead mines in Derbyshire and Shropshire and on the Mendips in Somerset, were sources of profit to Henry I and his successors. Large shipments of English lead were sent to France for use in the building of churches and monasteries. The great abbey of Clairvaux was roofed with lead from English mines. In Devon and Cornwall tin-mining was a profitable industry during the twelfth century. England was still the principal source of tin in Europe, and even in Germany, where the native mines were not yet exploited, English tin found a ready market in the metal-working towns of the Rhineland, as it did in those of Flanders.

But mining and industrial operations were still limited in number and extent. Under the Norman kings, as under their Anglo-Saxon predecessors, coal was not mined, and the long interruption of coal-mining in England continued from the Roman occupation until the thirteenth century. The only fuel used apart from wood was charcoal. Coal, under the name of sea-coal, or in French *charbon de roche*, was not mentioned until 1200, when it figured in a Flemish record of exports from England to Flanders.

The chief source of the country's growing wealth in the twelfth century was wool. The monks introduced into England since the Conquest, and principally the Cistercians on the barren Yorkshire wolds and the Welsh hills, must be given the credit for the enormous expansion in sheep-farming. The wool was partly used for export to the weavers of Flanders, partly absorbed by the weaving industry in England.

The Norman era saw the introduction of the first guild system in England. In 1139, in the reign of Henry I, a guild of tanners existed at Oxford, and later it amalgamated with shoemakers in a cordwainers' guild which survived until the nineteenth century. Under the same Norman King the weavers of London, Winchester, Oxford, Lincoln and Huntingdon were granted royal sanction to incorporate themselves in guilds. For this privilege they paid an annual tribute. They were given in return the monopoly of weaving cloth within a radius of several miles which varied according to the town. The weavers of London paid two gold marks (£12) for the privilege, but those of Huntingdon only two pounds. Henry I prescribed that a standard ell should be used to measure cloth throughout the country. According to William of Malmesbury the ell imposed was the length of the King's right arm.

The cloth industry was not popular with other English workers, probably owing to the large proportion of foreigners engaged in it. As the inhabitants of the towns gained a measure of self-government they resented the existence in their midst of an organization like the weavers' guild which was outside their own control. When the mayor and citizens of London petitioned the King in 1202 to suppress the London weavers' guild he agreed on condition that the city pay into the royal treasury the equivalent of the weavers' annual tribute. On the city's failure to comply with this condition the King restored the guild, and seized the opportunity to impose an increased rent of twenty silver marks.

The hostility of the merchants against the weavers, manifested in London and in other towns, resulted in the end in the industry being crippled by an astonishing number of disabilities. The weavers were prohibited to sell cloth outside their own city. They were prevented from becoming freemen of their city, unless they first renounced their craft, and from attainting or bearing witness against a freeman. Under such humiliating conditions the weavers ultimately left the towns and established themselves in rural communities of the North and West.

Even as early as the twelfth century the English were a maritime nation. On their Eastern shores strong colonies of Danes and Norsemen were established. In London alone no fewer than six churches were dedicated to the Norwegian patron St. Olaph, and despite the defeat of Harold Hardrada and the triumph of the Normans the peaceful exchange of goods and merchandise continued to flourish between Eastern England and the Scandinavian ports. In the reign of Henry I the port of Grimsby was frequented by shipmen and traders from Norway and Iceland, Scotland and the Hebrides. The Norsemen regularly brought a supply of gerfalcons, of which a great number were used by Henry I in his favourite sport of hunting. They probably also brought pine timbers for the King's buildings at Clarendon, Marlborough and Woodstock. They sailed back to Norway with their holds full of English corn. The Scandinavians were permitted to stay in London and perhaps in other cities for a year, whereas the time limit for other foreign traders was forty days. In spite of this most-favoured-nation advantage, the Scandinavian predominance among the foreign traders rapidly declined during the twelfth century. The Danes in London sold their Hall of the Danes to the merchants of Cologne. The Swedes, who at one time held almost a monopoly of the traffic in furs with Russia and North-eastern Europe, gave way to the German traders who had established themselves in Novgorod and on the isle of Gothland.

The peace and order of the reign of Henry I resulted in the spectacle recorded by William of Malmesbury. About 1125 he described the wharves of London as 'packed with the goods of merchants coming from all countries, and especially from Germany'. When supplies in England were short owing to a bad harvest, he added, the German merchants supplied the deficiency. German traders, and especially those of Cologne, held a profitable role as middlemen in the commercial and financial exchanges between England and cities as distant as Constantinople. Gold and silver ware and precious stones were shipped to England from the capital of the Eastern Emperor by way of the Danube. Linen and coats of mail came from Mainz and Regensburg. Ultimately the growing political and commercial ties between the Germans and the English community were further encouraged by the marriage of Henry I's daughter Matilda with the Emperor Henry.

The only currency in common use in England at this time was the silver penny. It was the standard daily wage of a manual labourer, and for small change could be cut into halves or quarters. Money accounts were reckoned in pounds and shillings, or even in gold marks ($£6$) or silver marks ($13s. 4d.$) but the silver penny remained the unit of currency. A debasement in its purity and weight had serious consequences for the poor. In 1124 the false moneyers were so active that the Anglo-Saxon Chronicle notes: 'The penny was so bad that the man who had at a market a pound could by no means buy therewith twelve pennyworths.' A year later Henry I took strong measure to end the traffic. Coins were minted at this time in between fifty and sixty towns which enjoyed the King's privilege. Henry summoned all the moneyers to Winchester at the Christmas feast and ordered an inquiry into the scandal. Those who were found guilty of minting or issuing debased coinage had their right hands cut off and were also emasculated. Some of the guilty, however, seem to have escaped physical punishment by paying a heavy fine.

Since the marriage of Ethelred the Unready with the Lady Emma of Normandy, and even before that union, so fateful for the two peoples involved, trade had flourished between the English and the Norman ports. When the English and the Normans were ruled by the same sovereign, the commercial relations between the two nations grew even closer. The merchants of Rouen had long supplied London with wine and other commodities. Wine may have come down the Seine from the regions south of Paris, but Normandy itself then produced wine. Grape-vines grew in the Normandy valley of the Seine even into the twentieth century. And even in England as far north as Yorkshire grapes were grown and the wine they yielded was served in the great houses of the country for day-to-day use. The Norman shippers' wharf at Dowgate was busy for several centuries with their imports. Among the precious merchandise recorded as having been landed there it is curious to note the porpoise, then ranked as a royal fish like the sturgeon and the whale, and reserved for the King's table. Richard of Belmeis, Bishop of London, was however granted by Henry I the right to take porpoises, except the tongues which the King reserved to himself.

The import of French wines into England began under the Norman Kings. Rhenish wines entered in the reign of Henry II, the first of the Plantagenet kings, and by the King's order was sold at the same price as the French wines.

The herring and cod fisheries, and on occasion a little smuggling and even piracy, mainly occupied the coastal population of England under the Norman kings. Yarmouth was already a prosperous herring-port and the centre of a Herring Fair. Farther to the north, Scarborough and Grimsby were the centres of the cod fishery. Many of the fishing-boats at this time were of considerable size, and were manned by as many as twenty-six rowers, in addition to the steersman and the sailors who manned the sail. Such vessels could and did fare far into the western seas. Nevertheless the great English navigators came in a later period. The farthest-faring English sailors at this time seem to have limited their exploits to the coasts of France, Portugal and Spain and the Eastern Mediterranean.

They combined commerce with less reputable occupations. Piracy, religious pilgrimages, and in the intervals between them a little honest trade, satisfied the aspirations of many an English mariner. The English sailors had a greater share in the early Crusades than is generally thought. Thus in 1097, in the reign of William Rufus, an English fleet of thirty vessels captured Laodicea from the Turks, and considerably aided the land forces of the Crusaders engaged in besieging Antioch by main-taining the communications with Cyprus.

Early in the reign of Henry I, in 1102-3, a merchant with the very apt name of Saewulf made several voyages to the Eastern Mediterranean, and went as a pilgrim to Jerusalem. About the same time the future hermit and saint Godric, after sixteen years of voyaging as a merchant seaman, made two pilgrimages to Jerusalem. He has been identified, correctly or not, with the 'Gudric, the pirate from England' who went to the assistance of King Baldwin of Jerusalem after his defeat at Ramlah. On his return from his first pilgrimage Godric or Gudric halted to pray at the shrine of St. James of Compostella.

We have already noted the great part played by English sailors in 1147, on their way to the Holy Land, in the siege and capture of Lisbon at the request of Alfonso I, and their reward of trading privileges in Portugal. If the military glory gained in the Crusades largely enhanced the reputation of the Norman adventurers from France, England or Italy, a part of the sea exploits may be attributed to the sailors of the race conquered by William of Normandy.

XVIII

STEPHEN AND THE ANARCHY

THE loss of the Ætheling William in the *White Ship* had made Henry I the last of the legitimate male line of the Conqueror. The nineteen years which followed saw a struggle between the two surviving grandchildren of William I, between Stephen of Blois, the son of one of the Conqueror's daughters, and the Empress Matilda, the daughter of the Conqueror's youngest son.

Matilda, the widow of the Emperor Henry V, in 1127 had been imposed by her father on his reluctant barons as his successor on the throne. Matilda was doubly unwelcome to the proud Normans. She was a woman, and the Normans had had no experience of a woman ruler. She was arrogant and avaricious, an unpleasant woman to deal with either as subject or as ruler, and she had made the fatal mistake of marrying as her second husband a member of the house of Anjou, with which the Normans had been in almost constant conflict for two-thirds of a century. Matilda's subsequent quarrels and reconciliations with the young, hot-tempered and impetuous Geoffrey Plantagenet had gained her no sympathy from her father's barons. Indeed her intrigues against the Normans in the interests of her husband's ambitions had so exasperated Henry that he had frequently to admonish her. The rumour even arose that he had repudiated her on his deathbed.

As it happened there was an alternative candidate for the throne who possessed, equally with Matilda, the advantage of being a grandchild of William the Conqueror. This was Stephen of Blois, the third son of the Conqueror's daughter Adela and the elder Stephen, Count of Blois and Champagne. Stephen had sworn the oath of allegiance to Matilda with the other great barons of Henry I, but an oath in feudal times was lightly regarded. Stephen's eldest brother Theobald of Champagne and Chartres, had probably the better claim to the English throne, and he was in fact on the point of being elected as Henry's successor at a meeting of the Norman barons at the little town of Neubourg near Rouen when Stephen sent a monk to announce that he had crossed the Channel and was already crowned King. With a resignation uncommon in that age Theobald accepted the situation and thereafter served his brother loyally.

The adventure on which Stephen was now fully and at first successfully launched was to last nineteen years, and to bring England to the verge of anarchy, although no worse a condition than that which afflicted many other contemporary states. The suddenness and apparent ease with which Stephen overtook the Empress in the race for the English throne may be explained by his unique position at the court of Henry I. His mother Adela had been Henry's favourite sister, and since the death of the Ætheling William in 1120 he had been brought up almost as Henry's own son. In 1124 Stephen had married Henry's niece Matilda of Boulogne, the daughter of the younger Eustace of Boulogne and Mary of Scotland. Through his wife he held the county of Boulogne together with the great English estates that were attached to the county. He also held the great honours of Lancaster and Eye, and Henry I had granted to him the Norman county of Mortain.

Stephen was an attractive personality, brave and merciful, affable in manners and a striking contrast to the hard and grim Normans who surrounded the King. The anonymous author of the *Gesta Stephani* describes him as being bold and brave, judicious and patient, unassuming, generous and courteous. His simplicity and spirit of chivalry made him popular among both Normans and English. It is not impossible that Stephen's unexpected journey to England to claim the crown was instigated by the dying Henry himself. During the last months of his life his daughter Matilda and his son-in-law Geoffrey of Anjou had redoubled their efforts to bring all Normandy under Angevin domination and had demanded of the old King his surrender of castle after castle in the duchy.

In any event, Stephen acted for once without faltering, showing a surprising facility for swift and bold action that was sometimes denied him during the later crises of his career. He rode from the Forest of Lyons, where the King had died, to the Channel coast, attended by but a few companions, and crossed to England. He was refused admission by the authorities in Dover and Canterbury, but the citizens of London came out in enthusiasm to greet him, and used in his favour the prerogative they claimed to elect the King. Without waiting to be crowned Stephen hastened, like William Rufus and Henry before him, to seize the royal treasure in the castle of Winchester.

In this ancient town he possessed an ally in the person of his brother Henry of Blois, Bishop of Winchester. With Henry's support he persuaded the royal treasurer William of Pont de l'Arche, a famous bridge over the Seine above Rouen, to deliver up the treasure and the castle of Winchester. The support of the Archbishop of Canterbury was not so easily gained. William of Corbeil, who had been a clerk of Ranulf Flambard, and whose outward piety and dove-like softness of manner were ill-accompanied by his avarice and miserly habits, recalled the oath that bound the great men of the realm to recognize the Empress Matilda as the dead King's successor, and hesitated to crown one who had also taken part in the oath. But Stephen's supporters argued that Henry on his deathbed had shown repentance for having imposed this choice on his barons. Hugh Bigod, the late King's steward, and the future Earl of Norfolk, even swore that the King in his presence had relieved those who took the oath of the obligation to keep it.

These arguments were supported, at least temporarily, by three of the most powerful men in the country, the King's chancellor Bishop Roger of Salisbury, and his nephews the Bishops of Ely and Lincoln, who between them controlled the administration of England. The Archbishop of Canterbury then yielded. Stephen returned to London and was crowned at Westminster on 22 December 1135. Henry had died on 1 December. Stephen had lost as little time as Rufus in achieving his coronation. Early in the following year the seal was set on this initial success by Pope Innocent II, who confirmed his election as King and thus implicitly absolved the barons of the sin of breaking their oath of allegiance to Matilda. Stephen's position now seemed out of danger.

The new King had found the royal treasury well garnished after the long and peaceful reign of Henry I. At his first court, held at Westminster on 22 March, he restored the pomp which had marked the courts of Henry's predecessors and which the thrifty Henry had gradually abandoned. This first public ceremony provided a test of his strength in the country, and it was remarkably well attended. Nineteen prelates and thirty-two great vassals were present. The son of King David of Scotland came to do him homage. With him were the King's constable, Miles of Gloucester, and Brian FitzCount, the son of Count Alain of Brittany, who afterwards became supporters of the Empress Matilda. Potentially the most dangerous of all, Earl Robert of Gloucester, the favourite natural son of the late King and the half-brother of the Empress, had not

L

yet arrived in England. Stephen adjourned his court to Oxford, and there in April 1136, Earl Robert swore fidelity under certain conditions. Later he made his submission in a dignified treaty signed with Stephen. After Robert's act of allegiance almost the whole of England accepted Stephen as King. At his coronation Stephen, like his predecessor Henry I, had issued a charter of liberties. Before he had reigned a year he had signed a second and far more ample guarantee. He had received the submission of the bishops, conditional on his observance of the rights and liberties of the Church. He had received, as we have seen, a friendly letter from Innocent II in which the Pope noted his election and his consecration, and apparently confirmed his right to the accession. In his charter Stephen used this Papal letter to bolster up his title to the throne. Once again he bound himself to observe good laws and ancient customs. He announced that he would keep the forests held by William I and William II, but that he would renounce possession of the forests reserved in addition by Henry I. The customs, privileges and possessions of the Church were to remain as they had been at the death of his grandfather the Conqueror. He forswore recourse to the feudal seizins against Church property introduced by Ranulf Flambard and the diversion to the royal treasury of the revenues of vacant bishoprics and abbeys. He also promised to end the practice of seizing into his own hands the personal possessions of deceased churchmen, a habit much favoured by his late uncle. In short, Stephen promised everything for which he was asked, and the churchmen who surrounded him were not timid in asking. He had sworn away many of his powers before he had had time to exercise them. The English chronicler, mindful of the harshness of the King's predecessors, described Stephen cruelly but justly as 'soft'.

Nevertheless, in the first year of his reign his authority was not contested, except by the long resistance of the garrison of the castle of Exeter, which was then described as the fourth city in all England. There a local magnate, Baldwin of Redvers, incensed at Stephen's refusal to grant him certain honours, possibly the earldom of Devon which he received some years later, had seized the royal castle and refused to recognize the King's authority. The men of the town appealed to Stephen for aid in quelling the insurrection, and the King himself arrived to lay siege to the castle. The siege lasted for three months. The wells of the castle dried up and the garrison was forced to make bread with flour mixed with wine instead of water. They also had to use wine to extinguish the fires started by the burning torches and arrows launched against the castle by the King's army.

When the supply of wine was exhausted the garrison surrendered. Baldwin of Redvers escaped to another castle in the Isle of Wight, where his ships engaged in piracy between England and Normandy. But Stephen had followed Baldwin from Exeter and the rebellious baron was soon forced to surrender. He asked for the return of his lands, and failing to get satisfaction retired in anger to the court of Geoffrey of Anjou, the husband of the Empress.

Stephen's northern frontiers were for the moment quiet. King David of Scotland, who at one time threatened hostilities, had been bought off with a substantial grant of land. The Englishmen of the North, although they had had no part in Stephen's election, accepted his rule, then and thereafter, without challenge. In the second year of his reign Stephen felt himself strong enough to attempt to checkmate the partial successes realized by the Empress Matilda and her supporters in Normandy. He should in fact have dared that adventure earlier. Many regions in Normandy had been invaded and pillaged by Geoffrey of Anjou and the discontented barons, with at their head those inveterate rebels Roger of Tosny and William Talvas III, who had taken up Geoffrey's cause and no doubt his money. The castles on the borders of Normandy, Alençon, Argentan, Domfront and Séez—those nearest to Geoffrey's dominions in Anjou and Maine—which we find mentioned over and over again in the Norman revolts against the Conqueror, had indeed been seized by or had rallied to Matilda. But in the rest of the duchy the situation was promising in the event of vigorous intervention by Stephen.

Five of the Norman bishops, headed by the Primate Hugh of Rouen, had travelled to England during the previous year to swear allegiance to the King. Louis the Fat, King of France, had acknowledged him as King of England and Duke of Normandy, and his elder brother Count Theobald, a competent and faithful ally, administered the loyal regions of Normandy on his behalf. In March 1137, when Stephen landed at La Hogue, he was within an ace of winning over the malcontents of the duchy. But the same Norman exclusiveness and jealousy of foreigners which had momentarily prevailed against the invasion of the Angevins under Geoffrey and Matilda were now turned against Stephen.

Like his Uncle Henry, he depended largely upon his Flemish mercenaries, and their presence among the royal troops led to disputes and desertions by the Normans. This was the prime cause of the failure of Stephen's expedition against Geoffrey Plantagenet at Argentan. In July Stephen signed a truce with Geoffrey. Six months later he left Normandy in disgust, never to return. With him travelled to England William of

Ypres, the son of the Count of Flanders, and the leader of the Flemish mercenaries, whose presence in England also provoked irritation and jealousy. During the King's absence a large number of barons had fortified themselves in castles of all sizes and descriptions, in defiance of the Conqueror's decree against unlicensed castle-building. Some of them were immense structures of stone, erected on natural eminences, rocks or mounds. Many others were small and hastily constructed defence works of earth and timber, erected on a man-made mound and protected by a palisade and a ditch. One of them at least was so small that it rose on a church-tower. During the civil war which followed the rebels against the King's authority used these local bastions as headquarters from which to plunder and prey upon their neighbours.

In the summer of 1138 the Empress Matilda and her party launched two attacks against Stephen. The first was diplomatic. Matilda appealed to the Pope to re-establish her right to the throne of England. After the normal delays at the Papal court, especially since the case was delicate and embarrassing, arguments were heard from representatives of both parties at the Lateran Council held in the spring of 1139. Finally Pope Innocent II confirmed his recognition of Stephen. The Empress then decided to resort to arms. Her half-brother Robert of Gloucester, who had sworn allegiance to the King, formally renounced his oath of fealty and prepared for war.

Meanwhile in 1139, four years after his accession, Stephen had himself dealt his cause its most deadly blow. By an intemperate act he lost the support of the English Church. For long a situation of great tension had existed between the powerful family of Bishop Roger of Salisbury, his son Roger le Poer, the royal chancellor, and his two nephews Alexander, Bishop of Lincoln, and Richard Nigel, Bishop of Ely, on the one hand, and on the other Count Waléran of Meulan, and his twin brother Robert Earl of Leicester, the sons of Henry I's great minister Robert of Meulan, Waléran had once been arrested and imprisoned by Henry I for rebellion, but now, with his brother, he was an active supporter of Stephen, who had given him his infant daughter in betrothal. Both barons, like many members of the lay nobility, bitterly resented the wealth and ostentation of the three bishops, who lived more like secular princes than ecclesiastics, with large and well-armed retinues of knights and men-at-arms. The chief of the clan, Roger of Salisbury, had built three enormous castles at Sherborne, Malmesbury and Devizes, the last named of which was said to be surpassed by no other fortress in Europe.

A trifling incident sparked off the inevitable quarrel. During a meeting of the Great Council of the realm at Oxford at the midsummer of 1139, a street brawl broke out between the men of the Bishop of Salisbury and the followers of Count Alain of Richmond. This incident, insignificant in itself, was seized by the adversaries of the bishops as a pretext for action. Count Waléran of Meulan and his brother Robert of Leicester, and other members of the great family of Beaumont, urged the King to curb the arrogance of the three bishops. They poured into Stephen's ears stories of the bishops' secret support of the Empress, and of the great hoard of arms and treasure stored in their castles.

Stephen yielded to the pressure. He ordered the arrest of Roger of Salisbury, his son, the Chancellor Roger le Poer, and the two Bishops of Ely and Lincoln. The keys of their castles were demanded of the arrested men and when they refused they were thrown into prison. Bishop Richard Nigel of Lincoln succeeded in escaping and took refuge in his uncle's great fortress at Devizes. King Stephen followed the fugitive to Devizes, taking with him the two Rogers, father and son, and the Bishop of Lincoln.

For once the mild-mannered affable young King seems to have shown the aggressive spirit of his uncles Rufus and Henry. He treated the two captive bishops, but lately the all-powerful leaders of the government of England, with harshness and even with indignity. Bishop Roger of Salisbury was at one time lodged in a cowshed. When Stephen arrived at Devizes he found the great castle defended with vigour by Bishop Roger's mistress Matilda of Ramsbury. But when she learned that the King threatened to hang her son Roger le Poer and his father the Bishop in front of the castle gates, and that the Bishop was deprived of meat and drink, her defiance melted. She surrendered the castle after a siege of three days. Great stores of gold, silver and arms, the evidence of the wealth and power of the Salisbury clan, were found by the King's men in the castle of Devizes and in the other castles which were surrendered into the King's hands at Malmesbury, Salisbury, Sherborne, Newark and Sleaford. The bishops were then released and dismissed to their dioceses.

But Stephen's triumph was of brief duration. By this ill-conceived and ill-managed action he had lost the support of the Church without endangering the prestige of Roger of Salisbury, his son and nephews. He also lost the support of his brother Henry of Blois, Bishop of Winchester. Since the preceding month of March Henry had been vested by the Pope with the powers of Legate. He now summoned a church synod at Winchester on August 29 at which Theobald of Bec, the new

Archbishop of Canterbury was present, and there he denounced the King's action in laying violent hands on the bishops.

The King had been summoned before the synod, but he did not think it dignified to appear in person. He was represented by some of his earls, and sent with them a learned man of law, Aubrey de Vere, who in enumerating the crimes of the bishops made much the same distinction between their secular and their spiritual functions as had been made by Lanfranc in the case of Bishop Odo of Bayeux, Earl of Kent. Roger of Salisbury defended himself in person, and with great vigour. The only ecclesiastic who seems to have supported Stephen was Archbishop Hugh of Rouen, Primate of Normandy, who argued that the King might lawfully seize the bishops' castles because bishops had no right to possess castles. In troubled times, moreover, it was a matter of loyalty to surrender a castle at the King's demand.

The bishops concerned then decided to appeal to Rome, and Stephen, after uttering threats against any who should arraign the King in the Papal court, weakened his case by announcing his own intention to appeal to the authority of the Pope. According to the author of the *Gesta Stephani*, he agreed to submit to some kind of penance, but he refused to return the castles and the arms which he had seized. Roger of Salisbury died on 4 December, three months after the synod. His death was popularly believed to have been hastened by the harsh treatment he had received at the King's hands during his brief captivity. Not all of his immense treasury had been seized by Stephen, for the Bishop left in Salisbury cathedral an immense quantity of money and of gold and silver vessels which the canons of the cathedral promptly offered to the King. To Stephen's credit he returned a part of the treasure to the canons for the needs of their church and he restored to them the lands and other property of the Church which the dead man had appropriated to himself.

It was in this situation of hopeless breach with the higher clergy that Stephen met the first great military crisis of his reign.

XIX

THE EMPRESS GOES TO WAR

THE widow of the Emperor Henry V made her long-threatened invasion of England on 30 September 1139. She landed at Portsmouth with her half-brother Earl Robert of Gloucester, and was received by her young stepmother Adelisa, the second wife and widow of Henry I. After the King's death Adelisa had married William of Albini and in her husband's castle at Arundel she now gave hospitality to the Empress Matilda. Robert of Gloucester had marched directly to his own fortress at Bristol, and it was in Stephen's power to seize Matilda and hold her at his mercy. But the King made one of his frequent but often ill-judged gestures of generosity, and he encouraged his rival's prospects by giving her an armed escort, commanded by his own brother Henry, Bishop of Winchester, now hostile to Stephen, to rejoin her brother in the West.

Robert of Gloucester, a favourite son and leading earl of the late King, is one of the most brilliant and chivalrous characters of the reign of Stephen. In an earlier century, and with more ambition, his courage, talents and intelligence might have recommended him for a disputed succession to the throne. But with rare single-mindedness he devoted himself enthusiastically to the cause of his half-sister, and it is through Robert's loyalty to her, and that of one other man who will soon be named, that a warmer light falls on the forbidding image of Matilda.

In an age of almost general venality and intrigue, Robert of Gloucester was the soul of honour and integrity. He supported Matilda with a disinterested fidelity in spite of her shortcomings, her arrogant and haughty temperament which soon diminished any popularity she may have enjoyed as the daughter of an English queen. William of Malmesbury wrote of Robert that 'alone or almost alone he was never swayed from his loyalty by the hope of gain or the fear of loss'.

From 1139 until his death in 1147 Earl Robert directed the war on behalf of the Empress from his headquarters at Bristol castle.

Two other barons who rallied to the Empress were Miles of Gloucester, the King's Constable, and Brian FitzCount, the son of Alain Fergant of Brittany. Miles of Gloucester was afterwards raised by the Empress to the earldom of Hereford. After seizing a number of castles, among them the great fortress of Wallingford, in the name of Matilda, Miles was killed while hunting, by an arrow despatched, accidentally or not, by an unknown hand. Brian FitzCount defended the eastern limits of the Empress's domain from the isolated castle of Wallingford. He is described as having been the inseparable companion of the Empress during the civil war. He had formed part of Matilda's escort, together with Robert of Gloucester and their knights, when the Empress crossed the Channel for her second marriage. He had been led to join her cause by the arguments of Henry, Bishop of Winchester.

Two years afterwards, when the Bishop reverted to the party of his brother King Stephen, Brian FitzCount wrote to Henry a letter which admirably revealed the character of one of the nobler barons of his time. Cultivated and intelligent, Brian was imbued with higher motives than the majority of his class. He justified his conduct to the fluctuating Bishop as inspired not by hope of reward, nor by expectation of profit, but merely by personal loyalty to the late King who had befriended him (he had married one of Henry's natural daughters). In Matilda's cause he had lost every acre he possessed, and for that reason, he explained candidly in self-defence, he was obliged to live by plundering his neighbours.

Soon after the Empress's arrival in England in the autumn of 1139, events took place in Worcester which bore a curious resemblance to those which Henry I had witnessed at Carentan in Normandy at the Easter feast of 1105. The inhabitants of Worcester had taken alarm at the presence of the Empress and her supporters in Earl Robert's castle at Bristol, fearing rightly that this boded no good for themselves. At dawn on 7 November the army of Bristol marched in order of battle, and apparently comprising innumerable horse- and foot-soldiers, against the city of Worcester with the intent to attack, plunder and burn it to the ground. The citizens of Worcester had prepared, like the inhabitants of the Norman town of Carentan, to resist manfully. They had carried their goods and chattels into the cathedral, which as a result 'looked like a furniture store'. It became a resort and place of gossip for the citizens, in which there was barely room for the servants of God, so many were there with sacks and chests. While the clerk intoned within, the child screamed outside; mingled with the sound of the psalms was the voice of mothers nursing and weeping over their children. Similar scenes might have been witnessed within the Conqueror's great abbey church in Caen during the Allied bombardments eight centuries later.

The first attack of the Empress's troops on Worcester was beaten off, but on the north side of the city no defences stood in the path of the enemy, and infuriated and unresisted a vast mob poured in and set fire to buildings in different parts of the city. The town as a whole did not suffer much from fire, but there was much plundering within and without the walls, and the population were leashed together like dogs and dragged away for ransom, whether they had the means to pay or not. Eleven years later the town of Worcester was again plundered and burned.

The whole of the West of England soon rose in the cause of Matilda. Robert of Gloucester alone raised a levy of 10,000 Welshmen. He was joined by Miles the Constable, by Brian FitzCount and by a natural son of Henry I, Reginald of Dunstanville. Support for the Empress now came from one of the bishops arrested by Stephen. On the death of Roger of Salisbury his nephew Richard Nigel, Bishop of Ely, raised a body of knights and retired into the Isle of Ely in the heart of the fenland. A castle surrounded by water defended the only approach to the island.

King Stephen in person immediately led an attack on the Bishop. He ordered a bridge of boats to be built where the water which surrounded the island was at its narrowest, and a monk named Daniel showed the King a narrow passage through the marshes which denied access to the island at this place. The monk was rewarded for his services by being made Abbot of Ramsey, but was afterwards displaced on appeal to the Pope. The King now had the key to the island's defences. He attacked the castle from the rear and captured it. The Bishop of Ely, humbled and defeated, fled to join the Empress in the West.

In the month of May 1140 Stephen wore his crown at the Whitsuntide Council in London. It was held, not in the palace of Westminster, as had been the custom since the reign of Rufus, its builder, but for greater security in the Tower of the Conqueror. It is significant that only one of the King's bishops, either in England or in Normandy, responded to the royal summons. This was John, Bishop of Séez. After this council, at which the Church had so plainly showed its hostility to Stephen, an attempt was made to conciliate the two rival parties. Stephen's brother Henry, Bishop of Winchester, met Earl Robert of Gloucester at Bath, where Stephen was also represented by Theobald, the new Archbishop of Canterbury. Theobald had succeeded William of Corbeil, and like his famous predecessors Lanfranc and Anselm, was an ornament of the great Norman abbey of Bec. But Stephen's most eloquent advocate at Bath was his wife, named Matilda, like his adversary the Empress. This young and courageous woman now entered a scene on which she was to play a heroic part to the end.

Matilda was the daughter of Eustace III, Count of Boulogne, and the niece of his more famous brother Godfrey Bouillon, the first Christian King of Jerusalem. On her marriage to Stephen she had brought him her great estates in Boulogne and England, and in the war with her imperial namesake she matched Stephen in courage and often outdid him in diplomacy.

The conference in Bath was held in vain. The delegates of the Empress offered to submit her case to an ecclesiastical judgment, but this Stephen, or his wife in his name, indignantly refused. The dice were too evidently loaded against him. The delegates then dispersed, and Bishop Henry of Winchester went to France to seek the mediation of King Louis VII, who had recently betrothed his sister Constance to Stephen's son and heir Eustace.

A desultory warfare of sieges and skirmishes followed the breakdown of the attempt at reconciliation, and Stephen's Queen distinguished herself by organizing the siege of Dover, which had been seized in the name of the Empress by a vassal of Earl Robert of Gloucester, Walkelein Maminot. Queen Matilda besieged the town from the land, and ordered her subjects in Boulogne to cross the Channel and attack the castle from the sea. The reduction of the town was eventually obtained, however, by negotiation. Robert of Ferrières, the father-in-law of the captor of Dover, had recently been created Earl of Derby by Stephen, and he now persuaded his son-in-law to deliver up the town and its castle to the King.

In September 1140 Robert of Gloucester carried the war into the Midlands by capturing and burning Nottingham. In December, when Stephen was in Lincolnshire, a sudden revolt of two earls in whom he trusted, William of Roumare and his half-brother Ranulf, Earl of Chester, placed the castle of Lincoln in their hands while the rest of the city and the shire remained loyal to the King. Ranulf of Chester was one of the greatest magnates of the realm. Besides the important palatinate of Chester on the Welsh marches he had inherited rich estates in Lincolnshire and he hoped to link them to his earldom by a series of intermediate strong-holds. With other members of his family he controlled nearly one-third of all England. He had a grievance against the King in that Stephen, instead of restoring to him the honour of Carlisle, which had belonged to his father until Henry I seized it, had granted it to the son of King David of Scotland.

Ranulf's half-brother William of Roumare was also a great baron in Lincolnshire and had but lately been created Earl. Ranulf's wife, the Countess of Chester, was a daughter of Robert of Gloucester. The wives of both rebellious earls played a vital role in the plot to seize the castle of Lincoln. The two countesses entered the castle first, as if on a friendly visit to the lady of the royal castellan. Then the two earls followed, ostensibly unarmed, and each carrying his wife's cloak on his sword-arm. The knights followed their lords and wore the same peaceful demeanour. Once inside the castle keep all pretence of a courtesy visit was thrown aside. The small force of castle guards was overpowered. The gates of the tower were closed and the earls were in possession.

The odd thing about the incident is that Stephen himself seems at first to have condoned the action of the earls in seizing Lincoln castle. He even rewarded them with titles and honours. It was only when the men of the city and shire of Lincoln, and even the Bishop of Lincoln, although a nephew of Roger of Salisbury and himself once a prisoner of the King, sent messengers to Stephen to protest against the arrogance of the earls, that Stephen changed his attitude. He hastened to the city and besieged the usurpers and their wives in the great castle on the hill. Earl Ranulf of Chester succeeded in escaping from a tower of the castle and in joining his father-in-law Robert of Gloucester. That great leader did not dally. With his 10,000 Welshmen, and their two chieftains Meredith and Cadwalader, now reinforced by Ranulf of Chester and the men of his palatinate, he marched to challenge the King at Lincoln.

The battle which followed is one of the most curious in English history. It showed a King in arms, at his most chivalrous, risking his crown and his life upon a stroke of the sword, against an enemy by far the more powerful; basely deserted by his own followers, and fighting a battle in the open plain with a castle strongly held by his enemy threatening him from behind.

The King had had premonitions of disaster. At dawn on 2 February 1141 he had attended Mass in Lincoln cathedral on the Feast of the Purification. He was carrying a lighted candle, when the light suddenly went out. The candle broke in his hand, but after a moment of darkness it was mended and re-lighted. Afterwards men saw in this incident a strange foreshadowing of the events which followed. Once more Stephen's chivalrous impulses betrayed him. His counsellors urged him to wait for reinforcements before giving battle, and in any case not to abandon his favoured position on the hill. But Stephen refused to take any strategical advantage over the adversary.

The army of Robert of Gloucester had succeeded in making its way through the marshes on the southern and western boundaries of Lincoln, and in crossing the Fossdyke, in spite of its flooded state. He now advanced towards the King on the plain below the city. Refusing to listen to his advisers of prudence, Stephen descended from the heights, dismounted and ordered a number of his knights to dismount, and met his enemy on foot in the plain. His troops were largely Flemish mercenaries, commanded by William of Ypres. The battle was unequal from the outset. On the one side was a host of savage and desperate men who had set out from the West in search of plunder. On the other a band of mercenaries hired in a cause not their own.

The five barons who commanded the knights on Stephen's right wing —the Earls of Richmond, Norfolk, Northampton, Surrey and Worcester —had acquired in France the currently held notion that a battle must begin with ceremonious tilting between individual knights as in a tournament. But the wild adventurers in the cause of the Empress disdained such courtly tactics. They charged in a shouting, disorderly mass, and the five earls and their followers turned and fled from the field.

On the King's left Count Alain of Brittany and William of Ypres had succeeded in scattering a part of the ill-armed Welsh levies, but were themselves routed in their turn by the better-armed knights of Robert of Gloucester. William of Ypres and Alain of Brittany were among the first to make their retreat. The King was thus left with a reserve of dismounted troops to bear the full weight of the enemy's attack, horse and foot. Stephen bore himself in the battle like one of the greatest heroes in English or Norman history. He fought like a lion at bay. When his sword broke under his desperate blows he seized a Danish axe (he was fighting under the walls of a city once conquered by the Danes and still largely peopled by men of Danish blood) and laid about him like one of Harold's house-carles at Hastings. He is said to have dealt a blow of his axe at the helmet of the rebel Earl Ranulf of Chester, and to have brought him to his knees. But the axe then broke in his hands, and Ranulf escaped with his life.

Stephen was at last struck down by a stone thrown at him, and a knight called William of Rains seizing him by the helmet, cried out in a loud voice that he held the King at his mercy. Stephen yielded at last to Robert of Gloucester. Only three men were at Stephen's side when he fell. One of them, fighting to the last, was Baldwin, the son of Gilbert of Clare, an eloquent man who had harangued the King's host before the battle. Another was Richard, the son of Urse, a kinsman perhaps of Urse of Abetot, one of the Conqueror's fiercest followers.

The captive King was led by Earl Robert in triumph to his half-sister the Empress at Gloucester. She received him haughtily and in scorn. Stephen was then transferred to the castle of Bristol, where he was closely confined. The city of Lincoln was sacked and its inhabitants were mercilessly slaughtered by the men of Ranulf of Chester. Five hundred notables of the town were drowned as they attempted to escape by the river.

It was the hour of triumph for the Empress Matilda. She had received news of the victory at Lincoln on 9 February 1141, and while the royal prisoner was held in Bristol she rode through Gloucestershire and Wiltshire to Winchester, where the Bishop and Papal Legate, Henry of Blois, held the royal city in strength. The King's brother only opened the gates to Matilda on his own terms. She was invited to leave all ecclesiastical questions in his hands. This was a bitter pill for the proud Empress to swallow. She had inherited from Henry I a stubborn independence in relations with the Church. Nevertheless, she agreed to the Legate's terms, was welcomed into the city, and was received at a solemn Mass in the cathedral on 3 March 1141. On April 8, at the Legate's direction, Matilda was formally elected to replace his brother Stephen.

But Matilda was not, now or ever, crowned Queen. The title given to her, *Domina Anglorum*, or Lady of the English, was that customarily used between election and coronation. It had been borne by the old English queens, and with it Matilda, who had been Queen and Empress in Germany, Countess in Anjou, and claimed to be Duchess in Normandy, had perforce to be content until she could be crowned at Westminster. But her coronation was not to take place. A delegation of citizens of London had come to Winchester, ostensibly to take part in the election of the new Queen. In fact they made a demonstration, although at the time ineffectual, of their loyalty to Stephen. Not until two months had passed, and the summer of 1141 had arrived, did the men of London agree to receive the Empress within their walls. And then their welcome was short-lived.

After her victory, seemingly decisive, over Stephen at Lincoln, and his capture and imprisonment, the new Lady of the English set out to impress all England with her authority. Accompanied by her uncle King David of Scotland, by the Bishop of Winchester and by her brother

Robert of Gloucester, all of whom she insisted on keeping near her as a permanent retinue, she went from town to town, from castle to castle, receiving the homage of the King's former vassals, and conferring honours and lands on her supporters. Everywhere she gave bitter offence by her arrogant and ungracious manners. And even that accomplished diplomat Bishop Henry of Winchester was secretly dismayed at the conduct of the woman for whose cause he had abandoned his brother Stephen. It may well be that during this apparently triumphal progress of the Empress Henry had already determined that Matilda should never be Queen of England. But the decisive action which lost Matilda the crown was taken by the citizens of London.

All England, save only the men of Kent, was at her feet when the Empress came to London with a large force of followers. She was at first acclaimed on her arrival, but the attitude of the citizens, and especially that of the great merchants, soon changed towards her. Instead of following the example set by Stephen on his coronation and making concession to the proud spirit of the Londoners, the Empress behaved with all the haughty reserve she had acquired in Germany. She claimed the allegiance of the people of London without first promising justice and good law, and provoked their indignation by demanding large sums of money.

The face of the city changed overnight. The bells of the churches rang the tocsin. The citizens flew to arms, unbarred the gates and came swarming out of the city like bees from a hive. The army of the Empress, encamped without the walls, melted visibly. Many of her noble supporters mounted their horses and rode off to the shelter of their castles. Of all her principal followers only the faithful and undaunted Robert of Gloucester and her uncle King David of Scotland accompanied the fugitive Lady of the English to Oxford. There she celebrated her escape by ordering that her captive cousin Stephen should henceforth be confined in chains.

XX

THE WAR OF THE TWO MATILDAS

THE next phase of the anarchy of Stephen's reign saw a struggle for supremacy between the two Matildas. The niece of Godfrey Bouillon, King of Jerusalem, had done much to win back for her husband King Stephen the esteem of the Londoners, if not that of the entire nation. Many of the barons, who had followed the example of Geoffrey of Mandeville, Constable of the Tower of London, in rallying to the Empress, now found it expedient to transfer their allegiance back to the King's party. Stephen's gallant Queen, whose courage had already contributed towards the recapture of Dover, now brought her followers from Kent, with the mercenaries of William of Ypres, into the city of London, after plundering the southern quarters of the city. More successful than her imperial namesake, the Queen obtained a loan from the Justiciar of London, Gervase of Cornhill, after pledging as security for it her own lands in Cambridgeshire. Finally she went to meet her brother-in-law Henry of Blois at Guildford. That astute ecclesiastic had carefully watched the incidents in London, and had possibly even helped to inspire them. He was now ready to abandon the cause of the Empress for that of Stephen. After his conversation with the Queen Henry returned from Guildford to Winchester, once more as an ally of his imprisoned brother.

But the Empress had not yet done with the Bishop. Fully aware of the fluctuating character of his loyalty, she hoped by a display of force to win him back. With a large following she left Oxford on 31 July 1141, and before the citizens of Winchester were apprised of her approach she rode into the city by one gate, only to learn that the Papal Legate on a swift horse had left it by another. The Empress, nothing loth, gave orders to her troops to lay siege to the Legate's magnificent new palace at Wolvesey, fortified like a castle. Henry of Blois, true to the Norman strain in him, retaliated by setting fire to his own city.

His supporters threw flaming torches from the walls of the palace, and the fires they started burned a large part of Winchester to the ground, including a great palace built by William the Conqueror.

Meanwhile an army loyal to Stephen had been mustered outside Winchester by his indefatigable Queen, and now two rival forces confronted each other. The war of the two Matildas began in earnest. The struggle lasted six weeks. Then the royal army, reinforced by nearly a thousand troops sent to aid Stephen by the city of London, forced a decision. The Empress Matilda's followers were weakened by sickness and famine. Discouraged by the defection of the Papal Legate and by the hostility of his flock, the enemies of the King broke and ran. The famous rout of Winchester had begun. The barons and knights in the Empress's following fled in panic, stripping from their bodies their armour and the signs of their rank and wealth, and even, according to the author of the *Gesta Stephani*, giving false names to the peasants who challenged them suspiciously. Archbishop Theobald of Canterbury, narrowly escaped with his life.

The Empress herself fared scarcely better than the humblest of her supporters. Still escorted by her faithful squire Brian FitzCount, she succeeded in gaining the protection of her brother Robert's followers at Gloucester. But Earl Robert himself, who had fought a rearguard action during the retreat to protect his sister's flight, had not the good fortune of the Empress. He was surrounded at Stockbridge and taken prisoner. Each of the rival armies now had a leader in captivity. The obvious course was the release of Stephen in exchange for the liberation of Robert, a King for an Earl. But the negotiations for this exchange proved long and difficult. Henry of Blois, Bishop of Winchester, seized the opportunity to use his talents as a mediator, and his brother Stephen was finally released in 1 November 1141, after a captivity of nine months.

On 7 December a Council met under the presidency of the Legate Henry to confirm Stephen's restoration to the throne. The followers of the Empress were threatened with excommunication if they remained loyal to her. Stephen celebrated his liberation at the Christmas feast, which was held that year at Canterbury instead of at Westminster as had been the custom since Edward the Confessor. There the King wore his crown, and according to one report received a second coronation, although this may merely have meant that the Pope's Legate placed the crown on his head in the presence of the assembled bishops and earls.

Meanwhile the Empress, if defeated, was not discouraged. By 29 September 1141 she had returned to her headquarters at Oxford. Delayed by the long accumulations of affairs of state, and temporarily incapacitated by an illness which gave rise to the rumour that he was dying, Stephen allowed his rival to remain in security until June 1142, when he was again ready to take the field. In the absence of Robert of Gloucester, who had crossed to Normandy to beg assistance from Matilda's husband Geoffrey of Anjou, and was delayed there until the autumn by Geoffrey's own difficulties in mastering the hostile Normans, Stephen reopened the war against the Empress.

This time his strategy was sound. He began by capturing the castle and harbour of Wareham, which was the vital bridge-head of the Empress's communications with Normandy. And he continued by disrupting the communications between her headquarters in Oxford and her supporters in the West of England. To effect this Stephen seized Earl Robert's outposts at Cirencester, Bampton and Badcot. Then, on 26 September 1142, he attacked Oxford itself.

Oxford and its castle, under the command of Robert of Oilly, had become one of the strongest places in the kingdom. Surrounded by water and a stout palisade, defended by steep walls, a supposedly impregnable castle and a high tower, Oxford was the last important town to acknowledge the authority of the Empress. Stephen himself led the assault. He had arrived on the opposite bank of the river with his men. After an exchange of the customary challenges and insults and the discharge of deadly flights of arrows by the defenders of the city, the King ordered an immediate attack. An old and not very shallow ford provided a precarious passage across the river. The King gave courage to his men by plunging first into the water. Swimming rather than wading, he crossed to the other bank successfully and was followed by a few stalwarts. Once across, he attacked the men of the Empress so vigorously that they fled into the city. Stephen followed the fugitives through the open gates and his men threw flaming torches into the houses, setting the town on fire, pillaging it and slaying a number of the inhabitants.

The Empress was forced to retire into the castle, and there Stephen besieged her for nearly three months. At the end of the autumn Earl Robert returned to England, and recaptured the port and castle of Wareham from the King's forces. But he found that his sister had fled. Threatened by famine in Oxford castle, she escaped at night, and after a hazardous and uncomfortable journey in the darkness over icy roads and snow, she found safety among her supporters in the castle of Wallingford.

After the departure of the Empress the garrison of Oxford castle

M

surrendered immediately, and Wallingford alone remained intact as a lonely and isolated outpost of the Empress Matilda's cause in the Thames valley. A year later Stephen incurred a reverse and narrowly escaped capture in a skirmish with the troops of Robert of Gloucester at Wilton. Afterwards he lost the castle of Sherborne to the Empress. But his rival's cause made no further progress, and her brief authority was henceforth confined to the West of England, in which the prestige of her brother Robert remained unchallenged. 'A shadow of peace' was now said by a contemporary chronicler to reign over the West.

An incident characteristic of the lawlessness of Stephen's troubled reign developed from a quarrel between Henry, Bishop of Winchester, and the custodian of the King's treasury at Winchester, William of Pont de l'Arche. William had remained loyal to the Empress, and when he found himself threatened by the troops of the Bishop, now in one of his periods of loyalty to Stephen, he appealed to the Empress for aid. Matilda sent him a body of knights led by Robert FitzHildebrand, who is described as a fine soldier but of low birth, drunken and lascivious. Robert was welcomed enthusiastically by William of Pont de l'Arche and given the freedom of his castle. Afterwards Robert seduced the treasurer's wife and with her complicity laid hands on his host and imprisoned him in chains in the dungeons of his own castle. Then, in possession at once of William's fortress, his treasure and his wife, the seducer betrayed the cause of the Empress and submitted to the King. Robert FitzHildebrand did not long survive his double treachery. He had already incurred the displeasure of the Church by setting fire to a nunnery. He is said to have died of a mysterious and incurable disease.

Meanwhile in Eastern England Geoffrey of Mandeville had become the central figure of scenes of savagery as cruel as any in mediaeval history. With the concessions in privilege, lands and wealth offered him by Stephen's Queen and ratified by Stephen himself on his liberation, Geoffrey had become not only the Constable of the Tower of London but Sheriff and Justiciar of Middlesex, Essex and Hertfordshire, posts which gave him enormous pecuniary advantages as well as judicial powers.

It is characteristic of the insolence and audacity of this great English *condottiere* that probably in 1140 he had abducted Constance, the sister of Louis VII of France. Constance had been married to Stephen's son and heir Eustace, in consideration of the payment to the French King of a large sum of money taken from the treasure of the dead Roger of Salisbury. The French Princess was at the time the guest of Queen Matilda.

Geoffrey seems at first to have kidnapped both the Queen and her guest. He later released the Queen, but kept Constance as his prisoner in the Tower of London. In the end, under pressure and possibly after a gift of money from Stephen, he set Constance at liberty. The reaction of the abducted bride's husband to this strange incident is not on record.

In the summer of 1142 Geoffrey of Mandeville reverted to his support of the Empress in a secret treaty in which the Empress agreed not to make peace with the burghers of London without Geoffrey's consent 'because they are his mortal foes'. Still outwardly a vassal of the King, who had created him Earl of Essex at the outset of his reign, and still attending the royal court, Geoffrey was known to be conspiring in the interests of the Empress. His feud with the Londoners loyal to Stephen, his arrogance, cruelty and suspected treachery, finally induced the King to order his arrest. Geoffrey was taken by surprise at St. Alban's in 1143 and charged with treason. Too generously offered a choice between death by hanging and the surrender of the Tower of London and his castles in Essex, the prisoner chose the latter alternative.

Geoffrey celebrated his release by seizing by violence a great new fief in Cambridgeshire. At the head of a horde of adventurers hardly less savage than himself he marched into Ely, in the heart of the fen country, fortified the island and converted it into an impregnable fortress. During the year which followed the defiant Earl ruled unchallenged over his little kingdom of marsh and swamp, and ravaged and plundered his neighbours at will. He seized the abbey of Ramsey, drove out the monks and transformed the monastery into a military barrack for his army of ruffians. From Ramsey he marched through the fens to Cambridge, plundered and burned it. Churches and monasteries were stripped of their gold and silver ornaments. Men and women were tortured to reveal the secret of their treasure, or to provide an exorbitant ransom. Cattle and crops were seized or destroyed. The inhabitants of the region fled in fear, or were cut down where they stood.

All attempts by Stephen to penetrate the trackless fens and come to grips with the berserk Earl were in vain. Geoffrey of Mandeville in his one year of unbridled savagery possibly caused more deaths by violence or starvation than all the battles of Matilda and Stephen.

But at last retribution fell. In August 1144 he was wounded by an arrow during an attack on a royal outpost at Burwell in Cambridgeshire. The day was hot and he had removed his helmet. The arrow struck him in the head. The wound was slight, but it became infected. He died on 16 September. Geoffrey had been excommunicated by the Church for his destruction of Ramsey abbey and forbidden Christian burial. His body was sealed up in a box and thrown into a pit outside the churchyard of the Old Temple in London. It remained there for twenty years. According to another version, the corpse, wrapped in sheets of lead, hung on a tree in the orchard of the Temple. At last Geoffrey's son offered the monks of Ramsey land in atonement for his father's crime. An appeal was made to Pope Alexander III, who finally consented to Christian burial.

Two years after Geoffrey's death another undisciplined baron, Ranulf, Earl of Chester, who had already played a leading role in the defeat and capture of the King at Lincoln, emulated the example of the terrible Constable of the Tower. He had already made his peace with Stephen and for a time fought for him loyally. But he had always refused to restore the castles he had seized. He was arrested and charged with treason at Northampton in 1146, but was released on the surrender of his castles. The Earl then avenged himself on the King by breaking out into an orgy of plunder, cruelty and destruction. Other lesser magnates imitated these two great nobles. Taking advantage of the war between Stephen and the Empress and the absence of a central authority to slay and plunder, destroy and rob, a large number of petty barons made armed excursions from their castles, marauding and harrying their neighbours.

There was nothing new in this outburst of baronial lawlessness except that it took place in England and not in France or Normandy. The same absence of royal or ducal authority had produced similar conditions on the mainland of Europe for long years past—in Germany and France on the collapse of the Empire of Charlemagne, in Normandy during the minority of the future William the Conqueror, and during the brief reign of his son Robert, and now during the absence of Stephen and the invasion of Geoffrey of Anjou. But in England for more than half a century peace and order had reigned under the firm rule of the Conqueror and his sons. The anarchy of the reign of Stephen was all the more impressive to men who could remember the justice, harsh but equal, of Henry I and his predecessors.

Both the army of Stephen and that of his rival the Empress had their traitors and their deserters. Early in the civil war Robert FitzHubert, a Fleming by race, was a captain of mercenaries in the Empress's service under Robert of Gloucester. Leaving Earl Robert's army secretly with his followers, the Fleming made a successful night attack on the powerful castle of Devizes, which in the previous year the King had seized from Bishop Roger of Salisbury. His method of attack was unusual. He flung over the parapet of the high walls of the castle a series of long scaling ladders strongly and skilfully made of leather, and therefore almost silent. With their aid he and his men crept up the castle walls and surprised the sleeping garrison. Most of the royal troops were overcome before they had realized the situation, but a few of the King's soldiers, awakened by an indiscreet shout of triumph which went up from the invaders, barricaded themselves in a high tower. But a few days later, short of food and water, they were forced to surrender.

When Earl Robert of Gloucester learned of the capture of the great castle of Devizes, in some doubt as to the real intentions of the Flemish captain, he sent his son with a large force as if to reinforce the garrison of Robert FitzHubert. But the Fleming drove Robert's son with insults from the gates of the castle, saying that he had captured the fortress to occupy it himself, not to hand it over to a stronger force than his own.

Such was the disorder of the period that Robert FitzHubert seems to have believed that by force or cunning he could carve out for himself a small independent domain in an England disrupted by internal disputes, as other adventurers had done elsewhere. FitzHubert met his match, however, in another man of equal cunning and treachery, John the Marshal, who commanded the neighbouring castle of Marlborough, ostensibly in the interests of the Empress. When Robert FitzHubert sent messengers to John the Marshal offering a pact of peace and friend-ship, and followed them himself on a visit to Marlborough castle, John welcomed him affably into his fortress, but shut the gates behind him and some of his followers.

Hearing that the Flemish deserter was now a prisoner at Marlborough, Earl Robert arrived on the scene with a large body of knights, took the prisoner in chains to his lately captured castle at Devizes and hanged him on high under the eyes of his own men—the first, but not the last, case of hanging a military prisoner noted in England during the civil war. Before setting out from Devizes the Fleming had instructed his garrison not to deliver up the castle on any condition, even if he were hanged. The followers of the Fleming obeyed his orders. They refused to sur-render to the brother of the Empress, rightly fearing to share the fate of their leaders, but they handed the castle over to King Stephen for a large sum of money.

The King now placed the castle under the command of his son-in-law, Hervey the Breton. Earl Hervey was a good soldier and a man of some distinction. He was subsequently besieged by the soldiers of the Empress and finally by a mob of ill-armed peasants, doubtless irate at the foreigner whom the King had placed over them. Eventually Hervey surrendered the great fortress built by Roger of Salisbury to the Empress and for his disloyalty was banished by Stephen from the kingdom.

The turning-point of the war came in 1145, when Stephen by his capture of the strong castle of Faringdon succeeded in definitely cutting the Empress's communications between the Thames valley and her strongholds in the West. An attempt was now made, but in vain, to reconcile the belligerents. But both maintained their rival claims to the throne. The war dragged on for some years, with minor successes on both sides. The spirit, however, had gone out of the supporters of the Empress. Miles of Hereford, the Constable of Gloucester, had been killed while hunting in 1143. Earl Robert's son Philip proved to be a villainous youth unworthy of his great father, and he deserted his father's cause in disgust. He even joined the King and fought against his father and the Empress. And on 31 October 1147, at Bristol, Robert of Gloucester died.

Three years before Earl Robert's death the Turkish ruler of Aleppo involuntarily came to Stephen's aid in attacking and capturing the Christian city of Edessa on 25 December 1144. This severe blow to the Christians in the East provoked fears for the security of Jerusalem, and the Pope, Eugenius III, aided by the fiery eloquence of St. Bernard of Clairvaux, proclaimed a second Crusade. A great council was held at Vézelay in 1146, at which Louis VII of France and his Queen Eleanor both assumed the cross. The response to the Papal appeal by the Normans, both in England and in Normandy, was hardly less enthusiastic than that which met the call for the first Crusade half a century earlier. With Louis VII and the Emperor Conrad III, a large number of the nobility of Western Europe, eager for battle, for plunder and granted Papal absolution for their past offences, set out from the West on a great adventure which was to prove fatal and disastrous to many who took part in it.

The absence of these trained warriors, many of whom were among the most rebellious as well as the most valorous of their generation, was promptly felt both in England and in Normandy. Among the English earls who took the cross were William of Warenne and Waléran of Meulan. William of Dover, one of the Empress's supporters at the battle of Cricklade, abandoned her to join the Crusade. And even that other deserter, Philip the son of Earl Robert, took the Cross.

The only western success recorded during this disastrous second Crusade fell to a humble force recruited among seafaring folk in Flanders,

Germany, Normandy and England in 1147. Without any princely or noble leaders these sailors from the shores of the North Sea, of whom the English contingent comprised men from London, Bristol, Southampton, Hastings, Kent and Suffolk, sailed from Dartmouth in 164 vessels on 23 May 1147. During their voyage the men of this expedition, no less and no more adventurous than the barons and knights who also had joined the Crusade, landed at Oporto. There they were engaged by King Alfonso, the first ruler of the newly founded kingdom of Portugal, to help him to expel the Moors. The sailors accepted his terms, sailed to the mouth of the Tagus and laid siege to Lisbon. After seventeen weeks the city was captured on 24 October 1147. To celebrate their victory, the King gave the new see of Lisbon to an Englishman, Gilbert of Hastings. Bishop Gilbert organized further attacks against the Moors in 1151 and again in 1189, when the third Crusade was launched. A number of the Englishmen engaged in these operations lingered in Portugal and established the beginnings of Anglo-Portuguese trade.

In the meantime a new belligerent had appeared on the national scene in England. This was young Henry Plantagenet, the eldest son of the Empress and of Geoffrey of Anjou. Henry had been raised by his parents as the rightful heir both of Normandy and of England. Early in 1147 he visited England with a few followers. His men were easily dispersed by the King's troops at Cricklade and at Bourton, and Henry was soon in dire straits. He had brought no money with him from Normandy, depending upon the support of his following in England, and sustaining his knights on promises. Henry was forced to appeal to Stephen for aid, and the King, with characteristic generosity, paid for his rival's return to Normandy. This was the end of the war as far as the Empress was concerned. After eight years of futile struggle, in February 1148 the Lady of the English followed her son Henry and departed from England.

XXI

HENRY PLANTAGENET

DURING the five years which followed the opening of the second Crusade, from 1148 to 1153, Stephen reigned without any serious challenge and without serious disorders. The war had never ranged over the entire kingdom. Apart from the sporadic affrays provoked by individual barons in their own interests, and the sanguinary battle at Lincoln which resulted in Stephen's capture and imprisonment, the dynastic struggle between the King and the Empress Matilda had been largely confined to the Western shires and the Thames valley. The death of Robert of Gloucester and the departure of the Empress had partially restored the King's authority in this region. In the Midlands, between Chester and Lincoln, the challenge of Earl Ranulf of Chester had been curbed by the enforced surrender of his castles. But he was still powerful enough to conclude, on equal terms, with a rival earl, Robert of Leicester, a curious treaty for the government of their mutual relations, and 'the sharing of spheres of interest and zones of neutrality'. In this private agreement two bishops held the stakes, and the King was ignored almost entirely. The feud between the two earls had not been eliminated, but it was controlled and regulated. No better evidence of the ordered eccentricity of the barons of the feudal period could be desired.

Geoffrey of Anjou had ruled in effect over Normandy since the spring of 1144. He had taken three years to subdue the independent Norman barons. Beginning with the gradual reduction of the towns in the West of the duchy, he had entered Rouen in January 1144 and three months later its castle surrendered. Geoffrey then took the title of Duke of Normandy. His nominal suzerain, Louis VII of France, agreed to grant him recognition, and even rode to Rouen to receive his homage. Geoffrey ruled over Normandy for over five years, part of the time in association with his eldest son.

Henry's first visit to England had been made in 1142 at the age of nine. He had stayed for two years under the protection of his uncle Earl Robert at Bristol, where he continued his studies under the learned Adelard of Bath. As 'the rightful heir of England and Normandy' he confirmed a charter issued by his mother the Empress in favour of Aubrey de Vere. His second visit to England in 1147, as we have seen, ended in defeat and an ignominious return to Normandy with the financial aid of his rival Stephen. When he crossed the Channel for the third time in 1149, Henry was sixteen years old, virtually an adult in those precocious times. He travelled to the North to join his great-uncle King David of Scotland. David knighted him at Carlisle on 22 May in the presence of Earl Ranulf of Chester. The young Prince Henry, with the aid of the Scottish King, and probably at the instigation of the ever-turbulent Earl Ranulf, then prepared to launch an attack on York.

But Stephen was now fully alert to the danger. He hastened north-wards with a large force. His son Eustace, who accompanied the King, was knighted at York, ostensibly as a retort to the honour done to his cousin Henry. Faced with an imminent attack by the King's forces, the coalition of Henry dispersed, and the young hope of the Angevin cause then took shelter in successive towns in Gloucestershire and Wiltshire, where the memory of his uncle Robert of Gloucester was still powerful. There he was ceaselessly attacked during the autumn of 1149 by his cousin Eustace. Retiring before these attacks Henry gradually moved southwards into Devon, where he succeeded in capturing Bridport. In the beginning of 1150 he returned to Normandy, and in this year his father Geoffrey Plantagenet wholly transferred the duchy to him. He remained there until 1153.

But Eustace had followed him across the Channel, and in league with his brother-in-law Louis VII (whose sister Constance he had married) pursued his harassing campaign against Henry. After a few months of intermittent warfare Henry became reconciled with the French King by agreeing to render homage for Normandy as his father had done, and to surrender the town and castle of Gisors. With this stronghold, coveted equally by the French and the Normans, Henry also agreed to concede to Louis VII the Norman Vexin, that land between the rivers Epte and Andelle which had been in Norman hands since the memorable tenth-century encounter between Charles the Simple and Rolf the Ganger, the first Duke of Normandy.

But this surrender, so shameful in Norman eyes, was more than com-pensated in Henry's view by his imminent territorial acquisitions. As he was planning a fresh expedition against King Stephen in England, his father Geoffrey of Anjou suddenly died on 7 September 1151, and Henry thus became Count of Anjou as well as Duke of Normandy. Nine months later his new continental domains, rich and considerable in themselves, were more than doubled by his marriage with Eleanor of Aquitaine. Henry was then nearly nineteen years old.

The youth, beauty and independence of Eleanor had long been the talk of Western Europe. Her father, William Duke of Aquitaine, after making war on his neighbours and plundering their lands, had suddenly been overtaken by remorse and had decided to go in pilgrimage to the shrine of St. James of Compostella, where he died, with the Pope's promise of absolution for his many crimes. Before his departure Duke William had offered his heiress in marriage, together with the duchy of Aquitaine, to Louis VII.

Eleanor's marriage with the French King had lasted fourteen years, but it failed to provide a male heir for the French throne, and the piety and asceticism of the French King had repelled his young and vivacious wife. 'The man she had married,' declared Eleanor, 'was more like a monk than a monarch.' The royal couple had both assumed the Cross after St. Bernard's great appeal at Vézelay, and had travelled to the East together. But at Antioch Eleanor had been unduly intimate with the reigning Prince, her uncle Raymond of Poitiers. The King discovered the intrigue, as he admitted after his return to France to his minister and biographer, Abbot Suger of St. Denis, and he left Antioch abruptly. He accomplished his vow in the Church of the Holy Sepulchre at Jerusalem, and during the return journey to France spoke to Eleanor of a separation. Pope Eugenius III, with whom the royal couple stayed during the journey, attempted to mend the shattered union. He made the estranged King and Queen sleep in the same bed, and refused to hear any talk of divorce on the usual ground of consanguinity. But in spite of this temporary reconciliation, and the pregnancy of Eleanor which resulted, a separation became inevitable. Eleanor gave birth to a daughter instead of the long-desired son. And at Beaugency on 21 March 1152 a divorce on the ground of their parentage within the prohibited degrees was pronounced by the Church.

Eleanor was now the most attractive party in Europe, and her suitors were numerous. To avoid any embarrassment, if for no other reason, the divorced queen lost no time in offering her hand and her immense inheritance to the youngest of the neighbouring princes. Six weeks after her divorce she married Henry Plantagenet. Her husband, already Lord of Anjou and Normandy, pretender to the throne of England, was now by the acquisition of the rich lands of Poitou and Aquitaine, the strongest Prince in France and one of the greatest in Western Europe.

Louis VII, the divorced husband of Eleanor, now became, and remained throughout his life, the bitterest enemy of the man who had supplanted him in his wife's affections. The French King, supported by his ally Eustace the son of Stephen, again attacked the Norman territories of Henry. Not until January 1153 was the new Lord of Anjou, Normandy and Aquitaine free to cross the Channel and enforce his claim to the English throne. On this, his third visit to England, Henry met with a success as conspicuous as his previous expeditions had been futile.

In the interval Stephen had been materially strengthened by the successive surrender of all the Angevin castles in England except that of Wallingford, and had been politically weakened by his quarrel with the Church and his loss of the support of the Pope. In 1152 the Pontiff had forbidden Archbishop Theobald of Canterbury to crown Eustace as his father desired, on the ground that 'Stephen appeared to have seized the kingdom contrary to his oath'. A few days after Henry's arrival in England the two rivals, the King and the Duke, faced each other at Malmesbury, separated only by the waters of the Avon, a stream then rendered impassable by the winter rains. The army of Stephen, daunted by a rainstorm of unusual violence, showed no desire to do battle, and the war was virtually over.

Many of the principal actors in this tragic but desultory drama were already dead, or were to die during its last year. Queen Matilda, the brilliant and indefatigable fighter in her husband's cause, daughter and niece of two famous Crusaders and a descendant at once of Charlemagne and of the old English Kings, lay dead and buried in the abbey of Faversham built by Stephen. King David of Scotland and the Earls of Warwick, Northampton and Chester were not to survive the civil war, or by little. The King's son and heir Eustace, a soldier who did little to show himself worthy of his parents' qualities, and who 'whatever he was, did more evil than good', died in August 1153. He had been discontented by the collapse of the war at Wallingford and had marched into the Eastern shires on an expedition of rapine and plunder. He was engaged in pillaging the lands of the abbey of Bury St. Edmunds when he was taken suddenly ill and died.

Stephen was now prematurely aged and fatigued. The brilliant young knight at the court of Henry I, the mild and simple-mannered King who had gained the affection of the citizens of London, the all-too-trusting brother of Henry of Blois, Bishop of Winchester, the generous adversary of the Empress and her son Henry, was worn out by the disillusionments of the long war, the incessant disputes of his barons, the increasing pretensions of the Church. He was a good soldier, an indifferent diplomatist, a poor statesman. He had tried in vain to secure the succession for his son. After Eustace's death, he had no more dynastic pretensions to the throne. His second son William had taken no active part in the struggle of his father, and was well endowed with the lands and revenues of his wife, the heiress of William Earl of Warenne, who had died in 1148 during the second Crusade.

Eustace had been dead but three months when his father decided to make his peace with the Empress's son and acknowledge him as his successor. Archbishop Theobald of Canterbury and Bishop Henry of Winchester had been working in unusual harmony for some time in the hope of promoting a settlement of the long-drawn-out dispute. At last the two adversaries were in agreement. Henry Plantagenet was received at Winchester on 6 November 1153 and there the treaty was drafted. It was afterwards ratified in a charter signed just before Christmas at Westminster by the King and the Duke.

The charter was witnessed by, among others, no fewer than eleven earls and fourteen bishops. Stephen acknowledged Henry as his successor by hereditary right, promised to regard him as his son and heir, and to admit him immediately to a share in the government of the kingdom. The Duke agreed to do homage to the King. The earls and barons of either party agreed to do homage to the other. The bishops promised to enforce the treaty by punishing by excommunication anyone who violated it. Finally the treaty secured to Stephen's surviving son William not only his inheritance of the earldom and lands of his father-in-law William of Warenne, but also the lands which had been in Stephen's possession before he ascended the throne. William was thus endowed with the honours of Lancaster, Eye and Boulogne and the Norman county of Mortain, in addition to considerable lands in Sussex.

Early in 1154 the barons assembled at Oxford and did homage to Duke Henry, now the acknowledged heir to the throne of England. The King and the Duke subsequently met at Dunstable, where Henry complained that the verbal agreement between them on the destruction of the 'adulterine' castles, the unlicensed and irregular strongholds which had arisen in many places during the nineteen years of anarchy, had not been carried out as completely as either party wished.

Henry did not remain long enough in England during the brief remainder of Stephen's reign to enjoy his new role as co-regent. He may have found England insecure. There is an unconfirmed story in the chronicle of Gervase of Canterbury that when Henry accompanied the King to Dover to welcome the Count of Flanders, an attempt was made on his life. In any event, before Easter had come he returned to France, where his now considerable domains claimed his attention. There he remained until the news reached him of Stephen's death. The King died at Dover on 25 October 1154, and was buried in Faversham Abbey beside his faithful and gallant wife Matilda of Boulogne, whom he had married thirty years earlier. Stephen was about sixty years old. His unhappy reign had lasted nineteen years.

The death of this man of many qualities but poor judgment, gallant, brave and merciful, brought to an end the great line of the strictly Norman kings, who had ruled for eighty-eight years over England. William the Conqueror had been dead sixty-seven years when a young Plantagenet, in whose veins ran the blood of his old adversary Geoffrey the Hammer, Count of Maine, came to sit on the throne of Edward the Confessor.

Henry of Anjou, surnamed Plantagenet like his father Geoffrey, was born in Le Mans in 1133. He was only twenty-one years old when he succeeded to Stephen's crown as Henry II of England. Norman by his maternal grandfather Henry I, English and Scottish by his maternal grandmother Matilda of Scotland, he was one-half Angevin and Manceaux by blood. His birthplace Le Mans, the capital of the once independent county of Maine under Count Herbert, nicknamed Wake-Dog, had for many years been the scene of long and bloody disputes between Normans, English and Angevins. Under Henry II, King of England, Duke of Normandy and Count of Anjou and Aquitaine, Le Mans once more came under the authority of an English monarch. The city shared the varying fortunes of the other French dominions of the Plantagenet kings, who were to spend more time in defending their lands in France than in maintaining their English throne.

XXII

STEPHEN AND THE CHURCH

THE nineteen years of the anarchy saw a notable increase in Papal pretensions in regard to the English monarchy. Stephen had gained his crown chiefly by the influence of the Church and especially that of his brother Henry of Blois, Bishop of Winchester. His charter of liberties, issued at Oxford in 1136, confirmed but more explicitly the liberties which his predecessor Henry I had sworn to protect soon after his accession to a throne still insecure. The Church was to be free from secular interference, elections were to be canonical and unsimoniacal; vacant sees were to be guarded by the clergy or by honourable laymen; jurisdiction over churchmen and their estates was to be in the hands of bishops; the possessions which had been taken from the churches since William the Conqueror were to be restored; and finally the clergy could dispose of their effects by will, and they could no longer be seized by the King as legitimate spoil, as under William Rufus and even under Henry I.

At first Stephen observed the promises of his charter in the matter of elections. He sided with the Legate Alberic of Ostia against the interests of his own brother Henry of Blois in the appointment of Theobald, the third great product of the abbey of Bec, to the see of Canterbury. But as the exigencies of the civil war grew more pressing, he became less scrupulous. He often demanded a large sum of money before he would grant freedom in an ecclesiastical election. On some occasions, with or without the agreement of his brother, he attempted to impose a near relative as bishop or abbot. Thus in 1140 he had ordered his nephew, William FitzHerbert, Treasurer of York, to be nominated to the see of York. William was indolent, but did not prove to be a bad archbishop, in spite of the charges of simony and chastity preferred against him, and the fact that he had been introduced to his archiepiscopal office by the interference of the King. When the case was brought before the Pope,

William was supported by the majority of the chapter of York and of the cardinals at Rome, but he was vigorously opposed by the great but impassioned and partisan St. Bernard of Clairvaux, backed by a group of rigid and zealous Cistercians.

The case of William of York was argued before four Popes in succession during the first seven years of the newcomer's archiepiscopate, until finally the Cistercian Pope Eugenius III deposed him in 1147, and appointed Henry Murdac, Abbot of Fountains, in his stead. This arbitrary decision aroused Stephen's anger and brought out in him all his latent obstinacy. For three years the King refused to grant the new Archbishop of York the temporalities of his see. In 1153 the three leading opponents of Stephen's protégé, Pope Eugenius, St. Bernard and Archbishop Murdac, all died, and William was reinstated without further opposition. He lived for one year in full enjoyment of his see. On 8 June 1154 he died, possibly by poisoning. In spite of his alleged simony and inchastity he was canonized seventy-two years later by Pope Honorius III.

On Stephen's accession, as has been noted, he had asked Pope Innocent II for his confirmation, and it was granted without difficulty in view of the overwhelming support the King had received from the English people and the recommendation of the Pope's ally, Louis VII of France. Innocent was at that time also fully engaged in refuting the claims of a rival, the Anti-Pope Anacletus II, who actually held Rome. It was only on this rival's death in 1138 that Innocent II could turn his attention to English affairs. To do him justice, during the few years which remained to him (he died in 1143), Innocent stuck to his previous decision to support Stephen, in spite of the arguments in favour of the Empress Matilda presented to the Lateran Council of 1139. In March of this year the Pope appointed Henry of Blois as his Legate in England, and until the Pope's death, when his mandate ended, Henry dominated public affairs in England.

The Legate was a pompous and picturesque figure in his brother's kingdom. In spite of his political ambitions, and his ostentation in dress and speech, Henry was not without certain solid qualities. He was both brave and intelligent. He was a soldier who loved to ride at the head of his armed followers and at the same time a bishop who efficiently governed his churches. Besides his see of Winchester Henry held the abbey of Glastonbury, the richest in the country. He built at least six castles in addition to several fine churches. Henry had hoped to be appointed to the see of Canterbury in the place of Theobald of Bec, but as long as he was Legate he enjoyed higher rank than the Archbishop.

It was only on the death of Innocent II, and the end of his authority as Legate, that Henry's relations with Theobald deteriorated. No doubt he supported his royal brother in 1148 when Stephen, following the precedent set by his predecessors, forbade the departure of the Archbishop from the kingdom and that of several other prelates summoned to the Papal Council at Reims. Only three bishops were permitted to leave England on this occasion, and Theobald was not among them. The Archbishop, however, was determined to go, and he set sail clandestinely in a small fishing-boat. On his return Stephen deprived him of his temporalities and ordered him to leave the country. Pope Eugenius was incensed at the King's action and threatened excommunication and interdict. But the English bishops refused to carry out the Pope's orders, and Stephen, showing a very uncharacteristic pertinacity, still refused to grant the Archbishop his temporalities.

The dispute lasted nearly a year. The Pope suspended the refractory English bishops, and Henry of Winchester was forced to make the journey to Rome to effect a reconciliation and arrange for the return of Theobald to England. Nevertheless, the relations between the King and Eugenius III, who with his friend St. Bernard had declared his opposition to Stephen, did not improve. In 1150, two years after the dispute over the Council of Reims, Stephen refused to grant a safe-conduct to the new Papal Legate who desired to travel through England to Ireland. In 1151 the Pope granted Theobald, now definitely a supporter of the Empress Matilda against Stephen, a commission as Legate. In the following year he forbade the Archbishop to crown Stephen's heir, Eustace.

But the majority of the English bishops still supported the King against the Pope, although Stephen was obviously weakening politically. In England as in Rome, the Church stood ready to profit by this weakness, and to impose ecclesiastical authority on every occasion when it was challenged. A brilliant band of Englishmen worked in the Roman Curia at this time. Robert Pullen, who taught at Oxford before it became a university, and wrote a learned volume of *Sentences* before the appearance of the standard work of Peter the Lombard, was Cardinal and Chancellor of the Roman Church from 1144 to 1146. Hilary, who afterwards became Bishop of Chichester, worked in the Roman Chancery in 1146, and was soon followed there by Boso, later a Cardinal and Chamberlain. Pope Adrian IV, the Englishman Nicolas Breakspear, who was elected to the Apostolic throne in the last year of Stephen's reign, was a Cardinal in 1149. Finally the future historian of the Pontiffs, John of Salisbury, who entered the service of Pope Eugenius III probably in

Paris in 1147, remained during these years at the Curia and wrote an interesting record of the events which took place there. In England several notable personalities were active in the service of Archbishop Theobald of Canterbury. Among them was Thomas Becket, the future Chancellor, Archbishop and martyr.

The monastic revival which had begun in England under Henry I was rapidly developed under Stephen. The anarchy seems to have profited the reformers. The turbulent barons who during the wars of Stephen and Matilda had wrought such destruction in the country hoped to atone for their ill-doing by the building of churches and monasteries. Thus Henry I's abbey at Reading, which had been damaged by Roger of Hereford during his outbursts of homicidal fury, received a manor from the baron in compensation. The priory of Pontefract was pledged an annual subsidy by Earl Gilbert of Lincoln to repay the monks for the damage done in the course of his private feud with Henry of Lacy. In 1143, in the midst of the civil war, William of Ypres, the commander of Stephen's Flemish mercenaries, founded the Cistercian monastery at Boxley in Kent. William of Newburgh hazarded a statement that during Stephen's reign of nineteen years the number of new monasteries created greatly exceeded those built during the previous century. Actually the respective figures were 247 before Stephen and 115 during his reign.

The abbeys of these rude warriors, who often built churches alongside their castles, have sometimes survived, at least in ruins, all trace of their military neighbours. Thus Ralph of Worcester, who frequently carried out raids into the county of Gloucester, fortified a castle in the hamlet of Hailes near Winchcombe and built a church nearby. The castle has disappeared long since, but the little parish church still stands today alongside the ruins of the abbey founded a century later by Richard, Earl of Cornwall. During Stephen's reign was also continued the building of hospitals and leper-houses, of which twenty-four had been established under Henry I.

Stephen's wife Matilda, who had a personal interest in Jerusalem, gave to the Knights Templars their earliest possessions in England. She granted to the Knights in 1137 the manor of Cressing in Essex and that of Cowley near Oxford two years later. The Templars flourished in England and soon had large estates throughout the country. Another and earlier military order, the Knights of the Hospital of St. John of Jerusalem, had founded their first house in Clerkenwell in the beginning of the reign of Henry I. They continued to prosper under Stephen.

N

XXIII

THE BATTLE OF THE STANDARD

At the death of the Conqueror in 1087 Malcolm Canmore (or Big Head), who had won the throne from Macbeth thirty years earlier, was still reigning over Scotland. He had married Margaret, the sister of Edgar the Ætheling and granddaughter of Edmund Ironside, a marriage which had led to the almost complete anglicization of the lowland Scots and provided the Scottish King with a pretext for frequent forays into England ostensibly to avenge the wrongs of his brother-in-law.

When William Rufus was absent in Normandy in 1091 Malcolm made a border raid which provoked Rufus on his return to retaliate by an invasion of Scotland by land and sea. The English ships were, however, dispersed in a storm, and the army of Rufus was diverted to deal with another enemy, the Welsh. It was not until late in November that Rufus and his two brothers, Robert and Henry, came to the Forth. With more prudence than he commonly showed Rufus permitted his brother Robert, with the aid of Edgar the Ætheling, to negotiate with King Malcolm. They signed a treaty which followed the lines of the agreement made with Malcolm by the Conqueror at Abernethy eight years previously. Malcolm agreed to become the man of Rufus 'with such obedience as he had rendered to his father'. In return he was confirmed in possession of his twelve English vills and was promised an annual payment of twelve gold marks.

But Rufus had no intention of keeping the treaty. A year later, in 1092, he marched on Carlisle and captured it. Then he rebuilt the city and the castle, drove out Dolfin, son of Earl Gospatrick of Northumberland, and planted in the new city a colony of settlers imported from Southern England. Rufus thus advanced his frontier to the Tweed-Cheviot line. In indignation at this breach of the 1092 Treaty, Malcolm rode southwards to the court of Rufus at Gloucester to protest, but the King refused to see him. He sent a message to the Scottish King telling him coldly that he could bring his complaint before the royal court of England like any other vassal. Malcolm's only reply was to return to Scotland, collect another army and prepare for his fifth invasion of England. But he had hardly reached his own frontier before he and his son Edward were treacherously attacked and killed near Alnwick by his intimate friend Morel of Bamborough, in complicity with Robert Mowbray, Earl of Northumberland. Malcolm's wife Margaret, later to be canonized, survived him by but a few days.

Malcolm Bighead was a rough and half-savage King who allowed his much admired wife to take remarkable liberties with his food, his habits and his treasure. He acted as her interpreter with the Gaelic-speaking Scots, indulged her caprices, submitted to her domineering temperament, her love of silks and finery, French wines and the cooking of her native England, and did not protest when she spent his money-hoard on pious works. With the aid of three monks of Canterbury, sent by Lanfranc at her request, Margaret undertook to reform the sadly backward Scottish Church with its married clergy and hereditary benefices. But this complex woman, in whom sincere piety was mingled with a love of ostentation, found the Scottish priests a tough problem. One is not surprised to learn that the deaths of Malcolm and Margaret were followed by a Celtic reaction against innovations from England.

The English followers of Margaret were driven from the court when Donald Bane, the brother of Malcolm, succeeded him on the throne. Donald was opposed by his nephew Duncan, a son of Malcolm by a first marriage, who had been handed over to the Conqueror as a hostage in 1072. But Duncan was killed in 1094, and for three years thereafter Donald Bane governed Scotland in association with Edmund, one of Margaret's sons who did not share her pro-English preferences. But in 1097 Edgar the Ætheling, acting on the advice of William Rufus, marched into Scotland, defeated Donald Bane, and set the eldest of his surviving nephews, Edgar, on the throne. Edgar and his two brothers governed Scotland in succession for more than fifty years. They continued the English innovations introduced by their mother Margaret. Edgar and his brothers had visited England and were familiar with English life. Two of them were married to Englishwomen. Their sisters Edith and Mary had been educated in England by their aunt Christina, the Abbess of Romsey. Edith (afterwards called Matilda) was to marry Henry I, and Mary Count Eustace III of Boulogne, the father of the future King

Stephen. With a court so intimately associated with the Anglo-Norman nation, the anglicization and the English speech of the Scottish lowlands developed naturally.

King Edgar of Scotland, whom a contemporary likened in all things to his kinsman Edward the Confessor, was a mild, peaceful ruler whose reign was only violently interrupted by the Norwegian invasion and conquest of the Western Isles. He left the country north of the Firth of Forth largely to his brother Alexander and abandoned the more anglicized regions of Lothian and Cumbria to his brother David. Alexander ruled over the recalcitrant Highlanders, who were deeply hostile to the English innovations in the south of Scotland. He had a strong streak of his brother Edgar's piety, and he temporarily succeeded in overcoming the rebellious instincts of his Highland clansmen by founding the monastery of Scone, in which he planted Austin canons from Nostell in Yorkshire.

Scotland was still prosperous under the mild rule of Edgar and his brothers Alexander and David when Henry I came to the English throne. David did not succeed his brother Edgar as King of all Scotland until 1124, when he was a mature man and experienced in government. It was afterwards said of David I that at no period of its history had Scotland stood so high in the scale of nations as during his reign. David had lived much in England, where, according to William of Malmesbury, he had 'rubbed off all the tarnish of Scottish barbarism'. He moved familiarly among the Anglo-Norman barons at the court of Henry I. He had married a daughter of the great English Earl Waltheof and had acquired with her the possession of her father's earldom of Huntingdon, and with her too a claim on the great earldom of Northumberland of which her grandfather Siward was the last of the Danish earls.

David I of Scotland was first on the list of the earls and barons of England who swore on 1 January 1127 to recognize his niece the Empress Matilda as Henry I's successor. During the nineteen years of the anarchy he remained more or less consistently on the side of the Empress, in opposition to his other niece, Matilda of Boulogne, who was married to King Stephen. He had made the decision for reasons of personal aggrandisement, and not for dynastic reasons. When Henry I died and Stephen succeeded him it was not long before David crossed the Tweed and laid hands on all the border castles in the coveted earldom of Northumberland except Bamborough. He would not and could not, however, risk a pitched battle, and when Stephen advanced northwards to Durham he withdrew his forces and negotiated a very advantageous treaty.

His son Henry was granted Carlisle, Doncaster and the honour of Huntingdon. For these Henry did homage to Stephen and even lived at his court until a trifling dispute gave King David a pretext for renewing hostilities with Stephen. Henry was recalled from the English court. Stephen was absent at the time in Normandy and the moment seemed to David favourable for a new invasion of England. But a powerful English force had assembled at Newcastle and Henry deferred hostilities. On Stephen's return from Normandy King David issued a solemn challenge. Unless the earldom of Northumberland was granted to his son he would break the truce. Stephen refused the demand, and in 1138, not long before the arrival of the Empress Matilda in England, David marched southwards.

The events which followed the Scottish King's invasion of the northern English counties rank among the most sanguinary of all the barbarities perpetrated during the reign of Stephen. Even the atrocities committed by Geoffrey of Mandeville and his men in the fen country in 1144 were not to outvie the horrors of the invasion of David I. The Scottish King had assembled a wild and barbaric host of Scots and English, of Norwegians from the Orkneys and the Western Isles, of Normans, Germans and Danes, and finally, the most savage of all, of Picts from Galloway. The Picts were 'those bestial men' described in horror by Richard of Hexham, from the walls of whose monastery some of the worst incidents in the campaign were visible. Women and children were ruthlessly slain at the point of the spear; others were roped together nude, and driven off into slavery.

In February 1138 Stephen advanced northwards against the invaders, but David merely retreated before the oncoming tide, and when Stephen retired to meet his other enemies in the South, David advanced again. He now reached as far South as Lancashire, where David's nephew William FitzDuncan defeated English troops at Clitheroe. In the East the main body of the invaders, under David himself, had reached the river Tees.

At last, against this army of vandals, 'more barbarous than any race of pagans', in the words of Richard of Hexham, Archbishop Thurstan of York, together with some northern barons, organized an English resistance. Their soldiers were prepared as for a crusade. Fasts and prayers, crosses and sacred banners preceded them to the battlefield. The famous battle of the Standard was fought near Northallerton. The struggle owes its name to the extraordinary banner which the English army set up in its ranks. A tall ship's mast was fixed on a heavy farm-waggon, and to it were attached a pyx containing the consecrated host, and the banners of St. Peter of York, St. John of Beverley and St. Wilfred of Ripon. The friends and vassals of King David, the Norman barons Robert Bruce and Bernard of Balliol, had attempted to mediate between the two adversaries but their efforts were in vain. David of Scotland was now determined to fight. The battle began at six o'clock on the morning of 22 August 1138. The two armies met in the mist on Cowton Moor, just north of Northallerton.

The half-naked Picts of Galloway, armed with swords or pikes and a leather shield and wearing the shortest of kilts, insisted on fighting in the front line. There, in spite of their desperate courage, they were at a terrible disadvantage against the knights in steel armour, dismounted and interspersed with the archers, who fought in the English van. The superior arms of the Anglo-Normans, the iron hail of their arrows, caused the fiercest of the Picts to fight unavailingly, but for long they did not quail. Ailred of Rievaulx, the friend and admirer of King David I, who wrote the account of the battle, says that 'like a hedgehog with its quills, so might you see a Galwegian bristling with arrows yet still brandishing his sword'.

At last, however, even the Picts broke and fled. The Scottish King, faced with the collapse of his front line, tried gallantly to save the situation but in vain. Three hours after the battle began the remains of the Scottish army were fleeing after the Picts. King David escaped to Carlisle. He continued to plunder and lay waste Northumberland for a month longer until his niece, Stephen's Queen Matilda, and the Papal Legate Alberic of Ostia, prevailed upon him to make peace. Stephen was at that time in no position to impose harsh terms, even if it had been his nature to do so. On the contrary he granted to David the earldom of Northumberland and to his son Henry the strongholds of Bamborough and Newcastle. The King of Scotland and his son gave hostages for their good conduct and swore to live at peace with Stephen.

David I did not altogether keep his pledge of peace. During the Empress's period of ascendancy in England in 1141, after the capture of Stephen at Lincoln, the Scottish King attended her in London and accompanied his niece in her later flight before the royal forces at Winchester, from which he only with difficulty made his escape. In 1149 the son of the Empress, Henry Plantagenet, visited King David at Carlisle and was knighted by him. The campaign they planned together against Stephen, in association with Earl Ranulf of Chester, was not, however, carried out. Stephen gained knowledge of their intentions and hastened to York with a large force, and the expedition against him was abandoned.

David I had succeeded in creating in Southern Scotland an Anglo-Norman community which owed little or nothing to the English influence of Queen Margaret and her brother Edgar the Ætheling. Norman customs and traditions were now introduced into the Scottish lowlands. The Celtic system of land tenure gave way to a feudal system under which the King became the source of all property in land. The titles of earl and thane were substituted for the old Celtic titles of *mormaer* and *toisech*, and the sheriff appeared for the first time as the King's representative in fiscal and judicial matters.

David died in 1153, a year before Stephen. The large territories he had seized or acquired in England during Stephen's reign did not long remain in the hands of his successors during the reign of Henry II.

XXIV

WALES AND IRELAND UNDER THE NORMANS

FOR geographical reasons Wales is a far more difficult country to subdue than Scotland. Nearly all the Norman kings made expeditions against the Welsh, but they accomplished little beyond containing them behind their barrier of mountains. William the Conqueror had set up three earls palatine, one against each of the three old divisions of Wales, Gwynedd, Powys and Deheubarth. He gave them almost complete liberty of action not only in defence of the new Norman kingdom but also in carrying out active measures to curb Welsh independence. Fortresses were built as the Norman knights drove forward. The fertile lowlands of South Wales were first occupied. Castles were set up to protect the new colonists, and in some cases boroughs and markets accompanied the castles.

When the Conqueror died many of the native Welsh princes, even in the more mountainous north, had been partly subdued. Hugh of Avranches, Earl of Chester, nicknamed 'The Wolf' from the device painted on his shield, and also from his ferocity, had pushed his dominions forward to comprise the county of Flint and part of Denbigh. Hugh's cousin, the gallant warrior Robert of Rhuddlan, had built strongholds on the river Clwyd at Rhuddlan and on the river Conway at Degannwy, and had succeeded in establishing Norman rule over Gwynedd, as the region of Snowdon was called. He had captured the local prince, Gruffydd, and taken his prisoner to the castle of Chester in the hands of Earl Hugh the Wolf. This, the most difficult region of all Wales, was for a brief period under Norman domination, and the Conqueror had recognized Robert of Rhuddlan as lord of 'north Wales' in return for an annual payment of forty pounds.

Before Rufus had reigned a year, Robert of Rhuddlan was killed, in 1088, by Welsh pirates at the Great Orme's Head, but his cousin Hugh followed up his successes and even established himself in Anglesey. In the seventh year of the reign of Rufus North Wales seemed to have been permanently conquered by the Normans. This situation was however illusory. Snowdonia was in fact to become for long years the centre of Welsh resistance to invasion. When Rufus was absent on the Continent in 1094 a Welsh leader named Cadogan, of the house of Powys, for all his weak and unstable character headed a movement of revolt, considerably aided no doubt by Gruffydd, the now liberated prince of Gwynedd. The Normans were pushed back east of the Conway and between the Conway and the Dee, into the land called the 'Four Cantreds', which later saw, throughout the twelfth century, almost continual warfare.

William Rufus, in alarm at this Welsh advance, ordered repressive measures against its leaders, but his campaign of 1095 was begun too late in the year. The Welsh had fled into the mountains, or across the Straits to Anglesey. The knights and men-at-arms of Rufus were harassed by the approach of winter, by famine and by enemy ambushes in the bleak valleys around Snowdon. The Normans were forced to retire, and when they came back in the spring of 1097 they met with scarcely greater success.

In the following year Earls Hugh of Chester and Hugh of Shrewsbury made a joint attempt to recover the lost territory. They followed the Welsh leaders Cadogan and Gruffydd across the Menai Straits into Anglesey, and even beyond the sea to Ireland, in which Welsh chiefs in flight from the Normans were in the habit of seeking refuge and arms. But disaster descended upon the victors from an unexpected quarter. The King of Norway, Magnus Barefoot, who had been cruising around the north of Scotland and along the western coast of England, suddenly landed with his pirate crews on the isle of Anglesey and attacked the Normans there. Among those killed was Earl Hugh of Shrewsbury.

The Earl's followers abandoned the attempt to hold the Gwynedd region. Without a fleet the venture was extremely hazardous. The Normans could only communicate with their base at Chester by a narrow strip of land, between the mountains and the coast, which could be easily cut off, leaving them at the mercy of the Welsh. For the next century the regions of Snowdon and Anglesey were left severely undisturbed, except for rare and generally unsuccessful expeditions by the English kings.

The borders of South Wales, at the end of the Conqueror's reign, were still substantially as William FitzOsborn had left them on his premature death in 1071. They were aggressively marked by a chain of Norman castles at Ewias Harold, Wigmore and Clifford. West of Monmouth and Chepstow, however, in the land between the Wye and the Usk, the Normans had succeeded in gaining ground. Nevertheless it was not a Norman but a Welshman, Rhys ap Tudor, who was recognized in Domesday Book as the Lord of South Wales, the ancient kingdom of Deheubarth, in return for a yearly rent of forty pounds.

When Rhys died in 1093 the feuds which followed between his heirs and successors gave the Normans a chance to press forward in Central and southern Wales. Robert FitzHamon, already a great territorial magnate in Gloucestershire, occupied Glamorgan and built a castle at Cardiff. Bernard of Newmarket overran Brecknock, and the family of Braose established itself at Radnor. Earl Roger of Shrewsbury, who had already built a castle in Powys which he christened Montgomery, after the name of the family seat in Normandy, now pushed on westwards. He overcame Cardigan and even reached Pembroke in South-west Wales, which he gave to his youngest son Arnulf.

In 1094 these Norman successes in South Wales were temporarily compromised by a Welsh revolt in the North. The new castles were attacked and demolished. Earl Roger's fortress at Montgomery was captured. Only Pembroke remained in the hands of the Normans. At its origin only a rough stockade on a rock overlooking the sea, but now a strong fortress, Pembroke castle was stoutly defended by its commander Gerald of Windsor, the founder of the great house of FitzGerald. When the besiegers were beaten off Gerald of Windsor set out to reconquer the surrounding country. On the border of South Wales, in Brecknock, Gwent and Glamorgan, the Norman lords had held their own, but between Pembroke and the East lay lands which remained in Welsh hands. This was the situation when Rufus died.

In 1114 his successor Henry I made a concerted attempt to impose his overlordship on North Wales. He sent three armies against Gwynedd, each starting from a different base. Earl Richard and King Alexander I of Scotland led one army along the coastal road. Another was led by the barons of the Southern Welsh marches. Henry himself commanded a third army which took the middle course across the Berwyn mountains. Diplomatically, Gruffydd, now the strongest of the Welsh princes, decided not to risk a battle. He did homage to King Henry, agreed to pay a fine, and was left undisturbed. Gruffydd survived until the end of Henry's reign. He died in 1137, old and blind, having succeeded in extending his border far beyond the Conway.

In South Wales events had happened otherwise. On the death of Rhys ap Tudor in 1093 the incessant Welsh feuds which followed enabled the Normans to establish themselves over a wide region in southern and central Wales. Robert FitzHamon's castle at Cardiff became the administrative centre of an English shire. Under Henry I the most important event in the history of Wales was the fall of the great house of Montgomery, which had been influential since the Conquest of England. When Hugh of Shrewsbury was killed in Anglesey in 1098 he was succeeded by his brother Robert of Bellême. Robert was brilliant as well as unscrupulous and cruel. He had already built many fine castles in Normandy. He was later to build the remarkable fortress at Gisors. And now on the Welsh borders he strongly fortified Shrewsbury itself and built an almost impregnable castle at Bridgnorth on the Severn. Robert of Bellême and other members of the Montgomery clan, including his brother Arnulf in Pembroke, were banished by Henry I in 1102, and the earldom of Shrewsbury remained vacant. Eventually the place of Robert among the lords of the Welsh marches was taken by the family of Mortimer, centred originally at Wigmore. And in the meantime the princes of Powys and their sanguinary feuds fill the pages of Welsh history.

The Welsh chieftain Cadogan, who had led the great revolt in the reign of Rufus, profited by the fall of Robert of Bellême to strengthen his position in Cardigan and in part of Powys. His prestige was compromised, however, by a romantic episode in which his son Owen and a beautiful former mistress of Henry I played the principal roles. The woman concerned was Nest, the daughter of the famous Rhys ap Tudor, the last great prince of Deheubarth. After Nest's liaison with Henry I, during which she had borne him a son, she had married Gerald of Windsor, and the son she bore to her husband, Maurice Fitzgerald, became one of the earliest English conquerors of Ireland. Enamoured of the beauty of Nest, Owen abducted her from Gerald of Windsor's castle, as a result of which King Henry, incensed by this act of defiance, ordered the banishment of both Owen and his father Cadogan. Cadogan went into exile and on his return in 1111 was murdered by one of his nephews. Owen, after some years spent in exile in Ireland, returned to Wales on his father's death and was permitted to establish himself on a part of his father's lands in Powys. In 1114 King Henry pardoned him and received him favourably at his court. Owen followed the King to Normandy and was even knighted by him. But two years later, in 1116, his kidnapping of the beautiful Nest was avenged. He was still in the King's service when a body of Flemings, under Gerald of Windsor, set on him and killed him.

In South Wales the reign of Henry I saw an almost continuous extension of Anglo-Norman power. After his banishment of Robert of Bellême and Arnulf of Montgomery, Henry decided upon the then novel experiment of colonizing the southern part of Pembroke by Flemish settlers. In 1108 a group of Flemings, possibly hitherto employed by the King as mercenary troops, was planted in Pembrokeshire as farmers and traders. The Flemings were courageous and industrious. They so completely displaced the native population that Flemish, and later English, became the spoken language, and the Welsh place-names were replaced by the family names of the new colonists. Pembroke became, like Glamorgan, an English county with a sheriff who paid fines and taxes into the Anglo-Norman exchequer. The county became known as 'little England beyond Wales'.

In 1110 the Welsh chieftain Cadogan was replaced in Cardigan by Gilbert of Clare, son of the founder of the house of Clare in Suffolk. His brother Walter of Clare, who founded Tintern Abbey, dominated the lands between the Wye and the Usk from his great rock fortress at Chepstow. A second generation of Norman barons consolidated the power built up by the first. On the death of Bernard of Newmarket his daughter brought Brecknock in her heritage when she married Miles of Gloucester, the future Earl of Hereford. Similarly Glamorgan, the lordship of Robert FitzHamon, eventually passed with his daughter Mabel to the natural son of Henry I, Earl Robert of Gloucester, for long the faithful champion of his sister the Empress Matilda. By the end of the reign of Henry I South Wales seemed to have become an Anglo-Norman province. Yet revolt was fermenting under the surface.

Hardly more than a week after Stephen's coronation the discontent which had long been smouldering in South Wales burst into flame. The insurrection began on 1 January 1136. In a battle near Swansea the Welsh killed about 500 of the Anglo-Norman settlers. Richard Fitz-Gilbert was ambushed and slain while riding through the forest in Gwent, and the death of this leader resulted in the loss of Cardigan. The castle alone held out for several years as an isolated outpost of the King's authority.

The Welsh war of independence was encouraged by the weakness of King Stephen and the corresponding strength of his adversaries among the Norman barons on the Welsh border. When civil war broke out in England in 1139 the King was clearly incapable of restoring his authority in South Wales. By the end of Stephen's reign the whole of the South, save for the Flemish colony in Pembroke, had liberated itself from the Anglo-Norman power.

Two outstanding Welsh leaders, Owen Gwynedd in the North and Rhys ap Gruffydd in the South, were thus enabled to profit by the years of anarchy in England. Owen, who was gifted with extraordinary capacity, captured the castles of Mold and Rhuddlan, and when Henry Plantagenet succeeded Stephen in 1154 the city of Chepstow itself was almost within his power. Rhys ap Gruffydd, a man of restless energy and caprice, was to dominate the affairs of South Wales until almost the end of the twelfth century.

Although during their reigns Ireland lay an easy prey for resolute Norman military technique and stern Norman government, neither William Rufus nor Henry I nor Stephen made any attempt to conquer the island. There is a story that William Rufus stood one clear day on the shore of Pembroke and sighting Ireland, or what he took to be Ireland, on the western horizon, he boasted that one day he would build a bridge of boats to span the sea and so invade the country. During the reign of his successor Henry, the Irish, under the despotic King Brian Boru, had routed the Scandinavian invaders at the battle of Clontarf in 1014. The Ostmen, as the Norse warriors were called, sustained a decisive defeat and were driven back to the cities they had built on the coast: Dublin, Wexford, Cork, Waterford and Limerick. But in this historic battle Brian Boru himself had been killed, and the unity which he had created under his own harsh authority was destroyed. During the years which followed Ireland fell into an anarchy of lawlessness, battles and feuds which rendered possible the projects of conquest of Henry II.

The Irish Church was already permeated with Norman influence. In the reign of William the Conqueror Archbishop Lanfranc had claimed authority over the Irish bishops, and his claim had been admitted by the Ostmen and even by some native Irish princes. In 1074 the Ostmen requested Lanfranc to consecrate their bishop Böhmer. The Irish Church had remained unaffected by the advance of civilization in Western Europe during the eleventh and twelfth centuries. The monasteries and the religious centres of the country were uncontrolled. The morals of the clergy were as lax as those of their flock. The see of Armagh in the eleventh and early twelfth centuries was held by hereditary succession and eight of the holders were said to be married men and without orders. The Irish bishops appointed under the influence of Lanfranc had been trained in Norman or English monasteries and carried to Ireland the ideas of the reformers.

Nevertheless the general religious situation in Ireland was still far from the ideas of Pope Adrian IV, and he hailed the Irish projects of Henry II as a means of attaching Ireland more closely to Rome. It is said that he publicly blessed the plan of conquest and gave the planners an emerald ring by which the conquerors might be invested with the right to rule over Ireland. Adrian's bull was subsequently confirmed by Pope Alexander III.

XXV

THE COURT OF THE NORMAN KINGS

I F WILLIAM I conquered England, his sons continued the conquest. The country evolved rapidly during their reigns. The Conqueror was King of the Anglo-Normans. While he lived the two nations were sharply distinguished the one from the other. The small Norman military aristocracy created in 1066, together with the generation which followed it, had little contact, except for the inevitable encounter of victor and vanquished, with the mass of the old English thegns, freemen and serfs which it had overcome at Hastings. Invaders and natives were divided in aspect, attire, customs, language, wealth and character. But when Stephen, the last male representative of the Conqueror, died in 1154 eighty-eight years after the Conquest, the two nations were already beginning to fuse. During the twelfth century the dividing barriers began to break down. Henry I, by marrying Edith the descendant of Edmund Ironside, and by his subsequent concessions to the English, gave a powerful impetus to the process. In the latter part of the twelfth century it was said to be well nigh impossible to tell whether a man among the free population was English or Norman.

Yet for nearly a hundred years the Normans flourished as the dominant class in England. They held the greater part of the land, the wealth and the power of the country. The churches and abbeys, the new towns with their growing commerce, the rivers and forests were theirs and theirs almost alone. A few English landowners, a diminishing number of English bishops and abbots, and a larger number of English monks struggled to keep the traditions of pre-Conquest England alive. But in the main the memories and the customs of Anglo-Saxon England were largely maintained by the peasants, the freemen and villeins who had suffered least by the expropriations of the Conquest.

The aspect of England changed rapidly under the Normans. Impressive stone churches and cathedrals in Norman Romanesque were rising all over the country. The towns, walled against wolves and highway robbers, against raiding barons and sometimes against the King himself, were rapidly growing in size and importance, and their citizens, by paying a single tax to a needy monarch, gained a valuable dispensation from paying the often capricious taxes imposed by the King's sheriffs. Much of the forest land, in which the English had been accustomed to seek provender for their cattle, venison for their larder, and wood for repairing their houses and burning in their fires, had been reserved by William I, William Rufus and Henry I. But the people as a whole benefited by the peace and order enforced by the Norman kings.

The Conqueror and his sons ruled as absolute monarchs. The rites of their coronation, the anointing with the sacred oil, had, they believed with all the contemporary jurists, conferred on them divine authority. The author known as the 'Anonymous of York' wrote in the twelfth century that Henry I, who had been in conflict with Anselm, was on a higher plane than the Archbishop and was justified in interfering in ecclesiastical matters. And John of Salisbury, one of the Church reformers, was convinced that the King derived his authority from God.

Until the Normans came the kings of England had been elective. They were not necessarily members of the royal family, and according to the primitive traditions were raised to the throne as the wisest and bravest of their people. The Normans in southern Italy, possibly influenced by their association with the kings of Eastern Europe, introduced the Byzantine notion of ruler-worship. William the Conqueror encouraged the belief in an aura of divine attributes by wearing his crown on three occasions every year at three different places in England, Westminster, Winchester and Gloucester, on the three great religious festivals. To these assemblies he summoned all the great men of England, archbishops and earls, abbots, bishops, barons and knights, all the men who constituted the fabric of English society in the eleventh century.

Later these great national feasts, which symbolized the central role of the monarchy among a highly religious people, were held wherever the King happened to be. On three separate occasions Henry I wore his crown, and heard the monks chant the litany of *Christus vincit* before him, in a wooden chapel at Brampton in Huntingdonshire, where the

King proposed to build a royal palace. As a kinsman by blood and by marriage of Edward the Confessor, Henry I claimed the Confessor's reputed powers of healing the sick, and exercised them on persons afflicted with various diseases, a royal tradition passed on from monarch to monarch in England down to Queen Anne, who touched Samuel Johnson for the scrofula. And when Henry's grandson Henry II persuaded Pope Alexander III to canonize the Confessor, the English kings rose in prestige above their European contemporaries until the canonization of Louis IX (Saint Louis) of France restored the balance.

The Divine authority of the crowned Norman King was very different from the Divine right later claimed by the Stuarts. The Norman kings derived their authority from the sacred rites of the coronation ceremony, not from the accident of birth. Until he was crowned the King's title was merely Lord, *dominus*. At his crowning he assumed responsibilities towards his people. He swore an oath to give them good law and justice. His subjects took the oath of allegiance. Both parties were bound in a mutual pact.

The monarchy of the Normans was like no monarchy seen in England before or since. There was no permanent royal seat, no fixed centre of government, either at Westminster, Winchester or Gloucester. The King moved about England and Normandy with his enormous retinue of archbishops and earls, bishops and barons, never settling down in any one place more than a few weeks or even days. His court was held sometimes in a royal castle, sometimes in an abbey, and on occasion in a hunting-lodge in a clearing in the forest. It assembled in such places as Bury St. Edmunds, Clarendon and Rockingham, little suspected in modern times of having witnessed the feudal ceremonies of a powerful monarch.

The King was accompanied everywhere by his family. In the case of Henry I, whose habits were notoriously different from those of his brother Rufus, not only the Queen travelled with him but also his mistresses and his numerous progeny, legitimate or illegitimate. In addition to the great earls and barons, the royal retinue was swelled by the administrative staff of the Chancellor, the King's clerks with their parchment rolls, his treasurers with the King's hoard of gold and silver, the officers of the royal household, the falconers and their hawks, the huntsmen and their hounds.

This enormous travelling circus lived on the country through which it rode. Its presence weighed heavily on the barons and their tenants. Under Rufus the excesses, exactions and vicious conduct of his courtiers caused such terror that the people of the region took refuge in the forest until the court had moved on. Under Henry I the members of the court were given subsistence allowances and were restrained by the harsh penalties inflicted by the King from exploiting the inhabitants.

The domestic life of the King was then, as under Louis XIV of France, the centre of the nation's activity. Its intimate observers and participants by an unpredictable process became in course of time the founders of the complicated machinery of the modern state. The most menial officers of the King's household were incongruously linked in close association with the predecessors of the great ministers of government. Their wages and their rations of bread and wine, fuel and candles, were carefully adjusted according to their rank and office. A description of the royal household as it was composed under the Norman kings was written soon after Henry I's death in the *Constitutio Domus Regis*, of which the text is given in the Black Book of the Exchequer. The King's Chancellor, the butler, the steward and the constable, who dominated the King's servants, received each a stipend of five shillings a day, and an allowance of one lord's simnel cake, two salted simnels, a measure of clear and a measure of ordinary wine, one thick wax candle and forty bits of candle. Instead of a stipend, or in addition to it, some officials were rewarded with lands for the performance of their court duties. The lowest renumerations were for the menial servants, the laundresses, the scullions, the hearthboy and for the palace watchmen. These, however, received double rations and $1\frac{1}{2}d$ a day for their men and four candles. They had in addition the right to a couple of loaves every morning, one dish and a gallon of beer.

The King's Steward (*dapifer*) had charge of the royal table, including the hall, the kitchen, pantry and larder, each of which was controlled by a chief dispenser. The Chamberlain (*camerarius*) presided over the King's bedroom and the servants under him included the bearer of the royal bed, the King's tailor and the royal ewerer (*aquarius*) who prepared the royal baths. The hall of the royal palace was a great room always crowded with courtiers, guards and suppliants for royal favours. The King dined in the presence of his ministers and the officers of his household. Occasionally a bishop or an abbot to whom the King desired to show favour was admitted to the royal table. It was in the hall of the palace that the King wore his crown at the great religious feasts of the year.

The duties of the royal Treasurer, like those of his superior, the Chamberlain, were limited curiously enough to the King's bedroom.

Under the early English kings the crown and the royal hoard of gold and silver were kept in a coffer in the King's chamber. As might be expected, the wine and dessert were the province of the chief butler (*pincerna*), who reigned over a large staff of cupbearers, cellarers and fruiterers. A considerably larger number of officials and servants were employed to provide for the external distractions and exercises of the King and his courtiers.

This outdoor staff was under the control of the Constable, and under him of a marshal, both responsible for maintaining order and discipline in the large and sometimes unruly court. Under these two officials, in addition to the archers in the royal bodyguard, were placed all the servants who ministered to the King's sport. They included the keepers of the royal mews, in which hawks were bred in pens, the keepers of the hounds, the stag-hunters and the wolf and cat-hunters. For the wild cat, like the wolf, then haunted the English forests. The Constable and the Marshal also supplied the carters and the packhorses required for the incessant journeys of the court from one palace or hunting-lodge to another. In addition to their extra-mural occupations (the Constable, as his name indicates, had under his charge the King's stables), these two officials were also employed in the clerical duties of the Exchequer. The Constable witnessed the King's writs. The Marshal was charged to supply receipts for gifts and payments made by the staff of the King's treasury and bedchamber.

The often humble tasks which devolved upon members of the royal household did not discourage the large number of people who coveted a place at court. Many fathers paid large sums for the attribution of a post in the household to their son. The King's chapel was especially envied for the prestige and profit which accrued to the royal chaplains. It became by fairly rapid stages a school for the statesmen of the Norman and Angevin period. Ranulf Flambard, Roger of Salisbury and other future bishops rose from the royal chapel to the highest posts in the state. Other and humbler departments of the royal household had their share in the promotion of servants. According to William of Malmesbury at least one man rose to the rank and wealth of a bishop from a lowly place in the royal larder.

The King's bedchamber and wardrobe saw the birth of the higher English bureaucracy. Even after the creation of a separate department of the exchequer at Winchester, the room in which the King slept and kept his gold and silver, his private accounts and the royal seal continued to serve as a household treasury. In later times kings who mistrusted or defied their great ministers of state could exercise control over the government of England from the intimacy of their private apartments.

Absolute in theory, the Norman kings in practice sought the consent of the great magnates of the kingdom, the archbishops and earls, the bishops and barons, the Chancellor, Treasurer and Steward. A strong King like William I or Henry I could in the long run make the barons bow to his will, but he was obliged to ask for their advice. The royal links with all the classes of society were not so strong in reality as in theory. The Conqueror had indeed, in his famous assembly of all the landowners of England, great and small, on Salisbury Plain, extended the oath of allegiance to the under-tenants. But an unruly baron defying the King could overawe his knights and tenants into supporting his rebellion against royal authority. And when in the reign of Stephen the building of adulterine or unauthorized castles monstrously increased, the collective feudal oath to William I, which had not been renewed to his successors, at least so spectacularly, was no more than a historic curiosity.

But under the early Norman kings the counsel and consent of the barons, to which Henry I had deferred in a letter to Anselm, and on which he had insisted in his Charter of Liberties, were largely a matter of form. It was not until Henry II that the Abbot of Battle could argue that a King could not make a permanent change in the laws of the country without the common consent of the barons. The Great Council of the realm, whether attended by all the magnates of the land or by the customary familiars of the King, debated and argued all the questions affecting the nation at large as well as their own private interests, whether judicial, administrative or financial. And since the King could not effectively work his will without the material support of his great barons, he must necessarily heed their opposition when it was voiced.

The very nature of feudal society, in which all land was held by the obligation to provide the military service of a specified number of knights at the King's demand, made the King dependent on a loyal baronage. The greatest and wealthiest barons could and indeed did create a corps of knights and men-at-arms far in excess of their feudal obligations, and often sufficiently imposing to rank as a small private army. By this means they could enforce their will on a weak king. Comparatively obscure barons and even a few bishops had enfeoffed far more knights than were required for the purposes of their military service. Thus under Henry I the Bishop of Lincoln, who was liable to provide sixty knights for the King's wars, had created twice that number of knights' fees. And the Bishop of Exeter, liable for seventeen and a half, had doubled this obviously difficult number.

But the increasing use of foreign mercenaries, paid out of the monies received by the King in scutage (shield money) from barons who preferred to evade their personal service, or from the tribute paid for charters by the new and growing towns, made the kings for a time independent of all save their most powerful subjects.

XXVI

FEUDAL ENGLAND

T HE military aristocracy which William the Conqueror had gradually established after his landing in England lasted almost unchanged for more than a century. It began to disintegrate when the Crusades, and the foreign military adventures of the Plantagenet kings Henry II, Richard and John plunged the monarchy and its baronial vassals alike into debts which the resources of the feudal landowners were unable to bear. The growth of commerce and shipping, the steady rise of a new merchant class in the towns, the inflow of foreign bankers and moneylenders, steadily broke down the gates of the closed feudal society which the Normans had created.

Knight service, which came to be the distinguishing mark of the Anglo-Norman feudal system, varied considerably from shire to shire. It was not necessarily performed in the King's army in the field, whether at home or abroad. Knights were expected to carry out garrison duties in the castles of the King or of one of his great barons. Royal and baronial castles were required to be at all times kept in a state of defence. A lord whose lands were dispersed over half of England might call upon a knight to do his allotted share of guard duty in a distant shire. Knight service was often a complicated and exacting duty, and it is not surprising that barons and knights alike preferred to evade it in exchange for a money rent. The normal wage of a hired knight was between sixpence and eightpence a day in the reign of Henry II, and this figure became the basis of the commuted charge which gradually replaced the obligatory knight service under the Plantagenets. 'Ward money', as this money rent came to be known, continued to be paid by some villages in Berkshire as late as the eighteenth century. It was the sole surviving vestige of an ancient feudal obligation to supply knights for the defence of the royal castle at Windsor.

The realistic nature of many early feudal obligations, equally commuted later in cash payments, may be seen from the duties allotted to
tenants in sergeantry, who held their land by some specified form of
service. Magna Carta describes some tenants whose obligation was to
furnish the King with small knives or arrows. The histories of all
monarchies show that gentlemen of high rank were expected to perform
menial as well as symbolic services at the King's coronation. They held
the King's basin and towel, as well as his Sword of State. One of the
King's sergeants was required to provide the monarch with a dinner of
roast pork when he hunted in Wychwood Forest. Others had the duties
of dispenser, launderer, or preparer of herbs. A naperer was ordered to
provide one tablecloth a year. A revealing light is shed on the morals of
the Norman and early Angevin kings and their followers by the record
of Henry de la Mare, who in the thirteenth century held his fief by serving
as an usher at the King's court, with the duty of guarding the court
strumpets.

Another King's sergeant had the honour of carrying the royal banner
within the four ports of England. Henry de la Wade of Stanton Har-
court was expected to strew fodder for the King's beasts, and mow and
carry a meadow of hay in Henry I's park at Woodstock. The King had
transformed his park into a menagerie in which he kept a collection of
wild animals, some of them having been sent to him from countries in
Asia and Africa. The collection comprised lions, leopards, lynxes and
camels. William of Montpellier had sent the King a porcupine. At a
later date it is recorded that Henry de la Wade's service to the King had
been transformed into one of keeping falcons for his hunting.

Estimates of the population of England under the Norman kings
vary considerably. Domesday Book, completed in 1086, omits altogether
the four northern counties, part of Lancashire, London, Winchester,
Bristol and other towns. It reckons only a fraction of the clergy and hardly
takes women and children into account. Its record of the population
based on these insufficient data comprises only 283,242 persons. J. H.
Russell, in his book *British Mediaeval Population*, assesses the inhabitants
of England at the same period as just over 1,100,000. Maitland in *Domesday
Book and Beyond* raises this figure to 1,375,000. In the following century,
after the period of comparative peace and order initiated by the Norman
Conquest, the population of England has been variously assessed at
between 2 millions and 2½ millions. The vast majority of the nation lived
on the land and was engaged in agriculture or as artisans in dependent
occupations.

The meagreness of the population makes it easy to comprehend the comparative smallness of the feudal armies. William the Conqueror is said to have had but 700 knights besides archers and men-at-arms in his duchy of Normandy, but when the proportion of Normans in the invading army at Hastings is considered this figure would seem to be obviously too low. Yet the Conqueror's feudal host in England after the Conquest had been estimated at not much more than 4,000 knights, and the number of his great vassals who furnished them is considered not to have exceeded 180. Later, under Henry I, by the employment of mercenaries, the royal army increased in size, but its numbers were still inconsiderable. Five thousand or six thousand knights and archers composed the English fighting host until the wars of Richard I.

As a rule the knights were not required to serve more than forty days at a time. If the King was at war outside England the service performed beyond this period was remunerated at the King's expense. Some charters signed by Henry I actually stipulated that the knights should only serve with the feudal hosts if the King were present.

The Charter of Liberties issued by Henry I at his coronation gives an extraordinary picture of feudal society in England. The King was the head and fount of all honour and all wealth. He divided the land among his vassals and could require it of them again if they failed in loyalty and obedience. At the death of a baron or tenant-in-chief he could claim a relief or succession duty of his successor, and if the heir were a minor, he could administer the dead man's lands until the heir came of age. He could also give his vassal's widow, sister or daughter in marriage.

The tenant-in-chief claimed similar rights from his sub-tenants, and naturally extorted from them the sums he had been obliged to pay to the King. A reasonable relief on a barony was considered in the time of Henry I to be a hundred pounds, and it was afterwards fixed at this figure in Magna Carta. But sometimes later kings, following the example set by William Rufus, had to be bribed to accept this sum. Henry I's promise that he would exact no payment for the license to marry, and would only refuse the license if the marriage was planned with one of his enemies, was not honoured by the King. Widows and heiresses were sold by Rufus, and even by Henry I, to the highest bidders, unless the lady paid a substantial fine in order 'that she may remain a widow as long as she pleases', or 'that she may marry herself to whom she pleases'. The sums demanded by the King for wardship and marriage were fixed after inquiry by the King's commissioners, who reported on the age of the widows, the age and number of the children, and the size and value of the estate.

The feudal society gradually established in England after the Norman Conquest was extremely complicated and elaborate. The great barons were comparatively few in number: between 180 and 200 at most. The greatest of all had under-tenants who were themselves described as barons. Their households were modelled on that of the King, with stewards, chamberlains, constables and butlers. Some even boasted of a chancellor who issued his lord's writs. The estates of the great barons were often dispersed over several shires, by a wise dispensation of the Conqueror, who, remembering his early struggles with the barons in Normandy, was determined to set a territorial check on the power of his vassals.

Below the greater or lesser barons in the feudal hierarchy came the knights. In the social sense these constituted a select body distinct from the large number of sub-tenants who occupied a mere fraction, sometimes as low as one-hundredth, of a knight's fee. The knights formed the aristocracy of the shires. The ceremony of conferring knighthood was elaborate. The lord who admitted his man to this honour gave him rich garments and a brilliantly coloured robe, a mantle or rain-cloak, a saddle and a pair of bridles, a mattress and a pair of sheets. The new knight was also given a sword, a lance and a shield, and a coat of mail. In the reign of Henry I the system of heraldic devices was probably introduced from France for the first time in England. The simple armour worn by the Normans at the battle of Hastings, a helmet and a coat of ring-mail, had been developed less than a century later by the addition of a steel breastplate and a helmet and visor which covered the face and rendered the wearer unrecognizable.

With the introduction from France of the tournament, which was at first a rough-and-tumble affair of horse-play and charges by one knight against another in the open field, without rules or limits, it became necessary to identify friend from foe. Challenger and challenged began to wear personal devices painted on the shield, or embroidered on the coat of mail or on the trapping of the horse. Heralds, possibly the successors of the trumpeter who sounded the Norman charge at Hastings, began to play their part in the tournaments, and the complicated art of heraldry came into being. In spite of the opposition of the Popes the tournament grew in popularity, and in 1194 under Richard I, who saw in it a means of bringing money into his always diminishing treasury, it was made legal and regulated.

The chief visible sign of the Norman Conquest in England was the lord's castle built on a mound which dominated a village or a town, or commanding a ford on a river. Castles had been practically unknown in

England before the Normans came. There were ruins of Roman fortresses, as at Pevensey, where the abandoned Roman relic was rebuilt by William after his landing. Edward the Confessor, made familiar with castle building during his boyhood in Normandy, had built a single tower on his western border to defend his kingdom from the Welsh. And in Dover, one of the chief ports of the realm, there was a castle which Duke William is said to have mentioned to Harold during the Saxon earl's mysterious and fateful adventure in Normandy. Both the old English King and their Danish conquerors seem to have neglected, or not to have understood, the value of castles.

Even under William the Conqueror and his sons they were not built except for specific military reasons. Then they were destined to dominate the turbulent Scots and Welsh, or to intimidate, as at Exeter, a city which had been in open rebellion. In the case of the Tower of London and of the two other castles built near London by the Normans, they were the outward and visible signs of the King's authority. The Tower of London was the counterpart, even to the very stone of Caen of which it was built, of the Tower of the King's Norman capital of Rouen.

But as the feudal age developed, as the central authority of the kings diminished, the baronial and military caste built castle after castle in England. At first, as in Normandy in the early years of the Conqueror, the castles were built hastily of trees cut down and dragged from the forests, and erected on a mound of earth surrounded by a ditch and a palisade of stakes. Then, as the Normans settled down on the land they had conquered, and as the art of siege warfare progressed and walls of timber were too vulnerable to fire and battering rams, the castles were built of stone. The square Norman keep or dungeon (a word which originally meant lordship and had at first no sinister connotation) rising on its grassy mound, on the crest of a hill or a rocky eminence overlooking a river, became a familiar feature of the English landscape. As the technique of siege warfare and defence improved, the square keep was abandoned in favour of an octagonal or a cylindrical tower, and later the outer defences of the castle were strengthened by the addition of intermediate walls and stout angle towers.

Feuds between the King and his barons, or between one baron and another, were as a rule settled not in pitched battles in the open field but by the siege of castles. Warfare was rapidly becoming an affair of artificers and archers. The construction of the great catapults and battering rams employed in the reduction of a powerful fortress demanded not only a considerable period of time but also the labour and skill of a large number of artisans. When the walls were battered down or were undermined by fire and frost, the foot-soldiers climbed into the breach. The battles of the English, beginning with Tinchebray, were fought mainly on foot, the King himself dismounting and fighting with his infantry. The use of mounted knights in warfare was less frequent, and the knights, released from personal combat by scutage, or the commutation of their obligation to engage in armed service in a payment known as shield money, were available for other purposes. As knights of the shire they had valuable judicial and administrative duties to perform. They served on juries and as coroners, and they continued the admirable system of local government which the Conqueror had inherited from the old English kings.

Hunting was in the very blood of the Norman rulers of England. The Conqueror and his elder sons had brought with them the memories of the great forests of Normandy which covered the low hills and the broad green valleys in which ran rivers teeming with fish. Although the English kings before Edward the Confessor, and the Confessor himself, had hunted the deer and established rigorous laws against encroachment on their forest privileges, they do not seem to have aroused popular resentment or protest. No single act of William the Conqueror or his successors impressed itself so deeply on public opinion in England as the reservation and depopulation of a wide region in Hampshire to create the New Forest.

Under William's sons and their successors the royal game preserves grew steadily in dimensions until under Henry II, it has been estimated, they embraced almost one-third of the entire kingdom. The county of Essex lay under forest law, as did a great strip of country from Lincolnshire south to the Thames. Only three counties, Norfolk, Suffolk and Kent, contained no land subject to this law. In all other areas which were under the law, the King claimed the exclusive rights of the chase. Whether the land in question belonged to the King to his barons, or to the Church, it was 'the safe mansion of wild beasts'—safe, that is, except from the monarch and his companions.

In spite of the promises made at his coronation, Henry I had afforested lands spared by his father and his brother. In Stephen's second Charter of Liberties he promised to disafforest these lands, and even made an attempt to carry out his promise. During the years of the anarchy some forest land was reclaimed. But Henry II, when he had restored order in the country after the destructions of the civil war, increased the royal forests. Later Kings, especially Richard and John, used their forests as a means of raising money.

The forest gave the Norman Kings their only sport, apart from war. It afforded them a complete relaxation from the cares of state, and from the occasional sense of oppression, if not of actual danger, which they may have felt in the midst of a conquered and alien, but still proud and independent people. Edward the Confessor had built hunting-lodges in Wiltshire and Gloucestershire where he transacted business as well as hunted the deer. His successors followed his example.

The King reserved to himself without exception the right to hunt the red and the fallow deer, the roe and the wild boar, and also the growing timber of the enclosures which gave them shelter. Later the roe was excluded from this reserved list. But the King frequently granted to some of his ecclesiastical tenants the right to keep hounds and to hunt the smaller game within and without the royal coverts. They could take foxes, hares and wild cats. A lucky landowner on his own estates might be permitted to take the same animals, in addition to pheasants and partridges. After the period of the Norman kings the royal hunting monopolies were slightly relaxed. Lords of the manor were frequently granted the privilege of 'free warren', which gave them the exclusive right to the smaller game on their own lands. The meagre remainder of the folk-land, and what small game it maintained, was left to the large category of men below the rank of the manorial lord.

Even the saintly Edward the Confessor had cruelly punished the taking of his deer, and the Norman kings followed his example. The penalties for breaches of the Forest Laws were harsh and inexorable. Mutilation of limbs and even hanging might result from the killing of a deer. The King employed a large force of foresters and verderers, who were often petty tyrants and almost always venal. At intervals of three years the King's justices held the forest eyre to try offenders. If a deer had been slain and no culprit had been captured or traced, there were cases when a whole village was seized into the King's hands. A fishpond, because a hart had been found drowned in it, was similarly sequestered. When a beast was found dead in the forest the four neighbouring villages were held responsible, and their representatives were required to hold an inquest on the carcase.

Under the Angevin or Plantagenet kings the penalties for breaches of the Forest Laws became less cruel. The increasing demands upon the royal treasury inclined the rulers towards the imposition of heavy fines rather than execution or mutilation. But the New Forest continued to be the subject of special vigilance by the King, and the punishments for offences in that royal preserve were heavier than elsewhere, as would seem to be

implied in a charter granted by Henry I after his reconciliation to Ranulf
Flambard, Bishop of Durham. The charter grants Flambard protection
for his hunting rights, and concludes in these significant words:

'I especially forbid you, Guy of Balliol, to hunt in his [Ranulf's]
forests. If anyone presumes upon this, he shall pay me a heavy fine, as if
he were hunting in my New Forest.'

The forest dweller was granted, nevertheless, certain minor privileges.
On payment of a small annual fee he might graze his pigs and cattle in
the woods, except during the midsummer month when the deer were
fawning. He was permitted within limits to collect dead wood for fuel
and for the repair of his house. But he was punished if he cut down a
tree or lopped a branch. He was forbidden to carry a bow. His dog must
be mutilated by 'lawing', that is the cutting off of three claws from the
fore-paw, so that it could not hunt game.

Outside the forest areas the life of the peasants in the villages was
precisely organized. Agriculture was the main, and for the vast majority
the only, occupation. Sheep were regarded as the most valuable product
of the farm and were bred largely for their wool, their milk and cheese.
A hundred sheep would add one pound a year to the profits of the farm.
Their fleeces could be marketed, their skins were valuable for the making
of parchment, then the only writing material. In the regions of rich grass-
land, especially in the marshes of Essex, Lincolnshire and Kent, the sheep's
milk produced an excellent cheese. Some of the flocks maintained were
very large. The nuns of the abbey of the Holy Trinity at Caen, founded
by the Conqueror's wife Matilda, kept in the reign of Henry I a flock of
1,700 on their land on Minchinhampton Common in Gloucestershire.
Nearly 100 years later the Bishop of Winchester kept 1,764 sheep on his
manor at Downton in Wiltshire. About this time, in the Glastonbury
Abbey manor of Damerham in Wiltshire, the 198 villagers kept the
enormous number of 3,760 sheep.

At the end of the Norman era, in a time of agricultural prosperity,
the royal manors were re-stocked and the prices to be paid were regulated
by the King's commissioners: 'The price of an ox shall be four shillings,
and of a cow the same, and of a farm-horse the same; and of a fine-woolled
sheep tenpence, and of a course-woolled sheep sixpence; and of a sow one
shilling, and of a boar one shilling.'

The development of the English towns under the Normans led to the
creation of markets, and to a demand for agricultural produce which had
been hitherto largely consumed in the homes of the producers. The
lords of the manor and the abbots of monasteries sent their excess farm

produce to the towns, often over a distance of thirty or forty miles. The task of carting over rough and difficult roads fell on the lord's tenants. An export trade in agricultural products and even in industrial goods also began at this time. Bacon-pigs and horse-shoes were shipped to the King's armies in Normandy. Ireland, when the English kings or their barons began to cast covetous eyes upon the sister-isle, also absorbed large quantities of English corn. And the important trade with Flanders in English wool began at this time.

In spite of the feudal system the village and not the manor still represented the legal unit of organized life in England, and it continued to shoulder the duties and responsibilities placed upon it by the old English kings. In the hundred and shire courts the village was represented by the reeve, the priest and four responsible men. When a crime had been committed it was the duty of the villagers to raise the hue and cry, to capture the criminal if they could, and to hold him in custody until his trial. If the village failed in this duty, it was fined. It could also be fined for many other offences, real or imaginary; for failing to pursue a criminal, for concealing his crime, for hanging a thief in the absence of the King's officer, for fishing in royal fishponds, for ploughing up the King's highway, for taking illegal toll, for submitting a man to the ordeal of water without a warrant, and for allowing Flemings to carry away their chattels. The village was fined as a whole, as it was assessed for taxation, and the amount was divided as the men of the village decided.

The lord of the manor, with his knights, his court, his feudal relationship to the greater lord whose vassal he was, his domestic and farm servants drawn from the English families of the manor, provided the chief link between the village and the otherwise closed world outside. The priest stood much nearer to the peasants of his flock than to the lord in his manorhouse. He was generally a humble and poorly educated man, who ploughed his strip of land like the other peasants, and depended largely for his sustenance upon his meagre share of the church tithes. Sometimes the priest even worked on weekdays for his lord in payment of rent for his land. It also devolved upon the priest to provide the breeding animals of the little community—the parish bull and parish boar, and sometimes the ram and the stallion.

Around the church, rather than around the alien manorhouse, the social life of the village was centred. Religious festivals were not only occasions of pious celebration in the parish church. Despite the denunciations of the bishops, the church was often the scene of the village's merry-making. Dances and drinking bouts often ended in brawls. The youth of the English village in the twelfth century, as throughout the Middle Ages, engaged in strenuous or barbarous sports. Wrestling, swimming, cockfighting and bull-baiting were practised in summer. In winter the youths amused themselves by sliding or skating on the frozen ponds and rivers. Ale-drinking, with a prize in prestige or in money for the man capable of drinking the other men under the table, had been since the earliest Saxon times a favourite sport of the English, and like the majority of old English customs, it was unaffected by the Norman Conquest.

EPILOGUE

Eighty-eight years separate the death of Stephen from the landing of his grandfather William of Normandy on the English shore at Pevensey, and sixty-seven from the Conqueror's death outside Rouen. William Rufus has been mysteriously killed in the New Forest. Robert Curthose has died in captivity in his brother's castle at Cardiff. Henry, the youngest of the Conqueror's sons, having died like his father in Normandy, lies buried in his own abbey at Reading. The long and bitter dispute between Stephen and the Empress Matilda, the two surviving grandchildren of William of Normandy, has ended. The son of Matilda, Henry II, the first of the Plantagenet kings, has succeeded Stephen on the throne.

Neither the sons of the Conqueror nor his grandchildren inherited his formidable mixture of sober piety, domestic fidelity, political idealism and harsh military pragmatism which in later centuries distinguished the Puritans of Cromwell. Of all his children his eldest son Robert was the least Norman in character and temperament. He has been seen as a gallant and romantic figure in the light of his exploits in the first Crusade, his reputation as a knight whom no other rider, Christian or Saracen, could unhorse. His long years of captivity in his brother's prisons complete the legend with a touch of pathos. Gay and generous, improvident, bestowing his lands and his treasure upon the first-comer, wise in counsel to others, foolish in his own decisions, he remains a complex and attractive character. Robert resembled his father William a little. He carried on the vein of fantasy struck by his grandfather Duke Robert of Normandy, nicknamed the Magnificent. But he probably had more than his share of the Flemish, French and English strain in the blood of his mother Matilda of Flanders, who was half French on her own mother's side, and for whom descent was also claimed from King Alfred.

Of all the Conqueror's sons, excluding the shadowy young Richard, an early victim of the New Forest, Robert Curthose was in modern eyes the most attractive. The inextricable confusion caused by his ineffectual government of Normandy after his father's death was at least spared to England by the Conqueror's decision to grant the English throne to Rufus. Yet his uncle Odo of Bayeux and a number of other powerful Normans would have preferred to see him King of England rather than his brother.

Robert's last years in Cardiff Castle, learning Welsh and writing a pathetic little poem to a tree glimpsed through the bars of his cell, give his death a modern romantic touch denied to any other of the Conqueror's progeny, with the exception perhaps of Robert's own son William Clito. Most of the other figures among the descendants of William are cast in a sterner and harsher mould, more capable and more ruthless. His other grandson, the young Ætheling William, who perished in the foundering of the *White Ship* off Barfleur, gave early signs of the sternness of his father and grandfather.

Rufus has been cast by historians for the most ungrateful role. His vices and his spoliation of the Church treasuries have been censured by the monastic writers of the time to the exclusion possibly of his good qualities. Yet he governed England for nearly thirteen years, and Normandy for four years after the departure of Robert for the first Crusade. And his government of both countries was on the whole wise and firm. We know little or nothing about his activities during the Conqueror's lifetime, yet on his accession he was popular with the English, who presumably knew him well and rallied enthusiastically to his standard against the revolt of Bishop Odo and his companions.

Rufus was the favourite son of the Conqueror. He had been crowned by Lanfranc, who had educated him, and whose many sources of intelligence had probably made him acquainted with the prince's sexual aberrations. But there is no record of any reproof from the great Archbishop. It was left to Lanfranc's successor Anselm to rebuke Rufus for the vices of his court, and to Anselm's biographer, the Englishman Eadmer, to particularize the King's especial addiction.

The devotion of Rufus to the memory of his great father was manifest in many things, among others the costly and elaborate monument he caused to be erected by the goldsmith Otto over the Conqueror's tomb in the abbey church at Caen. Rufus also seems to have been sincerely devoted to the newly established cult of chivalry. He insisted on setting free prisoners of war in whose favour the principles of chivalry could be invoked. On the other hand, once the revolt of Odo and the other barons

P

was crushed, with the aid of the English, he was as ruthless in his enforcement of the forest laws against the native population as against the Normans.

He often combined a sardonic humour with blasphemy. Thus on one occasion fifty Englishmen were accused, in one of the Red King's courts, justly or falsely, of having killed, taken and eaten deer. They denied the charge and the Norman judges imposed on them the ordeal by fire. An eye-witness reported that on the day appointed all the accused courageously endured the ordeal, and that their hands showed no marks of burning. After three days it was reported to the King that the hands of the accused men were unscathed. 'What of that?' said Rufus. 'God is no judge of these things. These things concern me, and it is I who have the right to judge them.' The chronicler Eadmer does not record what sentence was passed on the men whose innocence had been miraculously proven, or if it was executed.

Rufus has sometimes been considered the worst king who ever sat on the throne of England, but this is surely an exaggeration. Later rulers, who apart from their personal morals have been given a far better reputation, also sold ecclesiastical benefices and enjoyed the revenues of bishoprics and abbeys deliberately kept vacant. But their histories were not wholly written by disapproving clerics. An appreciation of the acts of the Norman kings by a lay observer, if it had been available, would assuredly give a different estimate of their characters.

Henry I has had better treatment from the chroniclers, although in the later years of his life he too practised simony and extorted the revenues of vacant sees hardly less vigorously than his brother had done at the instigation of Ranulf Flambard. The chronicler Orderic Vital extols Henry as the Lion of Justice whose reign was foretold by the enchanter Merlin. He was unmistakably the most intelligent of the Conqueror's sons. He alone of them seems to have had the sense of statecraft which was the most admirable feature of William I. Henry owed much of his success as a ruler over England to his English birth and marriage. His apprenticeship in the art of government was served in the confused rebellions of Normandy during the inept government of his brother Robert. Out of the quarrels and mutual jealousies of the three brothers, the negligent generosity of Robert, the self-assertiveness of Rufus, after Henry's own impetuous youth, his impatience and disappointment as the youngest son at the apparently meagre heritage left him by the Conqueror, came the revelation of the real character of Henry. Schooled in adversity, remembering all his life the days when he too, like his brother

Robert, had wandered landless in the countries on the borders of his father's dominions, Henry developed a cool, hard, calculating intelligence which made him a worthy successor of his father.

In many ways Henry I was one of the greatest of the English mediaeval Kings. He left the memory of a long reign of peace and justice, in which laws were imposed fairly and firmly, false moneying, the great scouge of the Middle Ages, was severely dealt with, agriculture prospered and commerce grew. The country was recovering from the ravages committed, especially in the North, in the repression of the English rebellion in the early years of the Conqueror's reign. The monasteries founded under William I and his sons had taken root. Their civilizing influence had begun to be felt in the bleak and desolate valleys of the wasted lands.

Although his promises were not all kept, the Charter of Liberties issued by Henry I on his coronation was a notable concession for the period, and marks a considerable constitutional advance. A short step had now to be taken to the Magna Carta of King John. That Henry had a talent for diplomacy, an energy and a force of character not underestimated in his age, is shown by the fact that after the battle of Tinchebray his long reign was undisturbed by any baronial revolts. Even the formidable Robert of Bellême gradually lost his power and eventually his liberty, when he set himself up in systematic opposition to the subtle and tireless King. The most unruly and unmanageable aristocracy in Europe for years remained docile if not undiscontented under Henry's firmly held sceptre.

A judgment of Henry's character, which might at first glance be mistaken as cold and ruthless, is to some extent corrected and softened by what we know of his private life. Like all his Norman predecessors on both sides of the Channel, with the single exceptions of the continent William I and the homosexual William II, Henry had many mistresses and by them a large number of illegitimate children. There was a strong philoprogenitive streak in his temperament. Save for his high-spirited and rebellious natural daughter Juliana, he displayed his pride in all his numerous sons and daughters, legitimate or not, married them off handsomely and endowed them richly. Alone William and Matilda, the two children of his English queen Edith, seem to have inherited the Norman arrogance. In the last years before his death in the Forest of Lyons, Henry saw two of his grandchildren born—Henry Plantagenet, the future Henry II of England, and his younger brother Geoffrey.

Henry I had ruled as a despot, in spite of his pledge to Anselm to respect the counsels of his barons and prelates. But he was on the whole an intelligent despot. It is doubtful if a King less wise and resolute could have so long restrained the barons from rebelling against a government overcentralized for the age. The reaction set in when a less-arbitrary king, uncertain of his title, over-dependent upon the support of the clergy for his survival, succeeded to the throne of Henry I.

The rich stock of the Conqueror, which had yielded such eccentric products as Robert and Rufus, and which had so justified itself in Henry, became exhausted in the bitter rivalry which developed between William's grandchildren Stephen and the Empress Matilda. Stephen is another of our only partly appreciated English kings. In some histories he sometimes gives the impression of being a continental intruder, as if the Normans, and even the Saxons and Danes, were not all intruders. But on closer inspection he emerges as a true Shakespearian character, less or more than a king, a man of generous loyalties, chivalrous to a fault to his enemies, but nevertheless capable of some queer conduct to his own elder brother Theobald, whom he overtook in the race for the throne.

There may be reasons for Stephen's action in respect of Theobald, and for Theobald's later complete loyalty to Stephen, on which their contemporaries are silent. Stephen was undoubtedly the favourite nephew of Henry I, by whom he was treated as a son during the fifteen years which followed the death of the Ætheling William. But Theobald is described by a contemporary writer as Henry's *comte du palais*, or chief minister, and Henry supported Theobald's claims against Louis VII of France vigorously and occasionally with arms. The Norman barons rallied to Theobald instead of Stephen and were in the midst of electing him Duke of Normandy at Le Neubourg when Stephen's emissary arrived to announce that he had already been crowned King of England. But it may be that this re-enactment of the succession to William I, when the eldest son was chosen as Duke of Normandy, and the second was destined to wear the English crown, seemed logical enough both to Theobald and to Stephen. In any event Stephen won the crown of England and for a time the ducal crown of Normandy.

The third generation of the Norman rulers of England ended with Stephen. When he died Normandy was again united to England, and his successor Henry II was to increase the English dominions on the Continent of Europe. It would be left to Henry's youngest son John to lose the duchy. The great drama of the Conquest did not end even with John. The character and achievement of William I and his sons left a permanent mark on the English monarchy, on English law and custom.

All life in England was sooner or later changed by it. The feudal system introduced by the Norman kings was developed and perfected under their successors. Art and learning, which had reflected German and Scandinavian sources under the old English kings, were now thrown open to influences from Western and Southern Europe. Two tongues, old English and Romance-French, were henceforth in common usage, and one would eventually merge with the other, to its own permanent enrichment.

The island in the North Sea became a market-place for French, Flemish and German traders, with a continual movement of ships and men, of men and ideas, between the English and the European shore. During the hundred years which followed the Norman Conquest England underwent a social and administrative transformation unknown since the Roman age. The land was held by a new people. New faces and a new speech were seen and heard in the towns and villages. Large and handsome stone churches and a new style of architecture arose in England. The village greens and the folk-land still remained in English hands, but the ancient forests of England were reserved for the sport of the new kings. The castles rising on many a rock and mound were the signs of their dominion.

A BRIEF BIBLIOGRAPHY

Dictionary of National Biography
Edward A. Freeman: *The Reign of William Rufus* (2 vols., Oxford, 1882)
C. W. David: *Robert Curthose* (Harvard, 1920)
Orderic Vital: *Historia Ecclesiastica* (Edition of Guizot, Paris, 1826)
Eadmer: *Vita Sancta Anselmi* (Edition M. Rule, 1884)
John of Salisbury: *Historia Pontificalis* (London, 1958)
Guillaume de Tyr: *Histoire des Croisades* (Paris, 1824)
Albert d'Aix: *Histoire des Croisades* (Paris, 1824)
Abbé Suger: *Vie de Louis le Gros* (Paris, 1825)
Gesta Stephani edited by K. R. Potter (London, 1955)
Ailred de Rievaulx edited by F. M. Powicke (London, 1955)
J. H. Round: *Geoffrey de Mandeville* (London, 1892)
A. L. Poole: *From Domesday Book to Magna Carta* (Oxford, 1955)
   (To this invaluable volume of the *Oxford History of England* the
author wishes to express his particular indebtedness.)

INDEX

H